British Women's Cinema

British Women's Cinema examines the place of female-centred films throughout British film history, from silent melodrama and 1940s costume dramas right up to the contemporary British 'chick flick'.

The woman's film has sometimes been regarded as a cuckoo-in-the-nest of a national cinema dominated by ideas of restraint and realism, but this collection of essays by leading scholars in the field sets out to demonstrate the central position in British cinema of films for and about women.

Discussing an impressive variety of films, including *The Tidal Wave*, *Love Story*, *Ladies in Lavender*, *Calendar Girls* and *The Mother*, contributors consider the importance of both female stars and female audiences in understanding the British woman's film and engage in a lively dialogue with key themes such as class, community, domesticity, romance, sexuality, motherhood, friendship, ageing and female creative agency in British cinema.

Contributors: Justine Ashby, Josephine Dolan, Mark Glancy, Sue Harper, Marcia Landy, Brian McFarlane, Claire Monk, Nathalie Morris, Rachel Moseley, Sarah Street and Imelda Whelehan.

Melanie Bell is Lecturer in Film at Newcastle University. She is a member of the Women's Film History project and has published on British cinema and gender in the *Journal of British Cinema and Television* and *Women's History Review*. She is the author of *Femininity in the Frame: Women and 1950s British Popular Cinema* (2009).

Melanie Williams is Lecturer in Film Studies at the University of East Anglia. Her work on British cinema has appeared in various books and journals including *Screen*, *Sight and Sound* and *Cinema Journal* and she is the author of *Prisoners of Gender: Women in the Films of J. Lee Thompson* (2009).

British Popular Cinema

Series Editors: Steve Chibnall and I. Q. Hunter, DeMontfort University, Leicester

At a time when there is a growing popular and scholarly interest in British film, with new sources of funding and notable successes in world markets, this series explores the largely submerged history of the UK's cinema of entertainment.

The series rediscovers and evaluates not only individual films but whole genres, such as science fiction and the crime film, that have been ignored by a past generation of critics. Dismissed for decades as aberrations in the national cinema and anaemic imitations of American originals, these films are now being celebrated in some quarters as important contributions to our cinematic heritage.

The emergence of cult genre movies from the apparently respectable lineage of British film emphasises the gap between traditional academic criticism and a new alliance between revisionist film theorists and extra-mural (but well-informed) cinema enthusiasts who wish to take the study of British film in unexpected directions. This series offers the opportunity for both established cineastes and new writers to examine long-neglected areas of British film production or to develop new approaches to more familiar territory. The books will enhance our understanding of how ideas and representations in films relate to changing gender and class relations in post-war Britain, and their accessible writing style will make these insights available to a much wider readership.

Books in the Series:

British Crime Cinema
Edited by Steve Chibnall and Robert Murphy

British Science Fiction Cinema
Edited by I. Q. Hunter

British Horror Cinema
Edited by Julian Petley and Steve Chibnall

British Historical Cinema
Edited by Claire Monk and Amy Sargeant

British Queer Cinema
Edited by Robin Griffiths

British Women's Cinema
Edited by Melanie Bell and Melanie Williams

British Women's Cinema

Edited by
Melanie Bell and Melanie Williams

Routledge
Taylor & Francis Group

LONDON AND NEW YORK

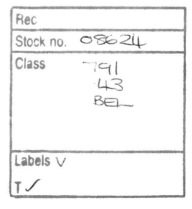

First published 2010
by Routledge
2 Park Square, Milton Park, Abingdon, Oxon OX14 4RN

Simultaneously published in the USA and Canada
by Routledge
270 Madison Ave, New York, NY 10016

Routledge is an imprint of the Taylor & Francis Group, an informa business

Editorial selection and material © 2009 Melanie Bell and Melanie Williams;
Individual chapters © 2009 the Contributors

Typeset in Sabon by
Taylor & Francis Books
Printed and bound in Great Britain by
TJ International Ltd, Padstow, Cornwall

British Library Cataloguing in Publication Data
A catalogue record for this book is available from the British Library

Library of Congress Cataloging in Publication Data
British women's cinema / edited by Melanie Bell and Melanie Williams.
    p. cm. – (British popular cinema)
    Includes bibliographical references.
    1. Women in motion pictures. 2. Motion pictures for women–Great Britain.
    3. Feminist films–Great Britain–History and criticism. 4. Feminism and
    motion pictures–Great Britain. 5. Women motion picture producers and
    directors–Great Britain. I. Bell, Melanie. II. Williams, Melanie.
    PN1995.9.W6B75 2009
791.43'6522–dc22   2009007741

ISBN 978-0-415-46696-7 (hbk)
ISBN 978-0-415-46697-4 (pbk)
ISBN 978-0-203-87200-0 (ebk)

Contents

Illustrations

Contributors

Justine Ashby is Senior Lecturer in Film at the University of Huddersfield. She has published chapters on a number of themes including Albert Finney and stardom, women film-makers, the British woman's film, post-feminism, and has co-edited (with Andrew Higson) *British Cinema, Past and Present* (Routledge, 2000). She is currently working on a book about feminism and post-feminism in the age of New Labour.

Melanie Bell is Lecturer in Film at Newcastle University. She is a member of the Women's Film History project and has published on British cinema and gender in the *Journal of British Cinema and Television* and *Women's History Review*. Her work on the British femme fatale has been published in *The Femme Fatale: Images, Histories, Contexts* (Palgrave, 2009) and she has recently published *Femininity in the Frame: Women and 1950s British Popular Cinema* (I.B. Tauris, 2009).

Josephine Dolan is Senior Lecturer in Film and Cultural Studies at the University of the West of England. Her research encompasses film, popular writing and radio and is organised around questions of British identity such as femininity, respectability, whiteness and childhood. Her work has been published in *Journal of British Cinema and Television*, *Visual Culture in Britain* and the *Historical Journal of Film, Radio and Television*.

Mark Glancy is Senior Lecturer in History at Queen Mary, University of London. He has conducted research in many areas of film history, including the Hollywood studio system, Alfred Hitchcock's films, feature films in wartime, and cinema-going in the United States. Recently he was awarded an AHRC grant for a research project centred on the reception of American films in Britain, and this research forms the basis of his next book, *Hollywood and the Americanization of Britain, from the 1920s to the present* (I.B. Tauris, forthcoming).

Sue Harper is Professor of Film History in the School of Creative Arts, Film and Media at the University of Portsmouth. She has published widely on British Cinema and her books include *Picturing the Past: the Rise and Fall of the British Costume Film* (BFI, 1994) *Women in British Cinema: Mad, Bad and*

Dangerous to Know (Continuum, 2000), *British Cinema in the 1950s: The Decline of Deference* (with Vincent Porter) (OUP, 2003) and *The New Film History* (co-edited with James Chapman and Mark Glancy) (Palgrave, 2007). She is currently leading an AHRC-funded research project on British cinema of the 1970s.

Marcia Landy is Distinguished Professor of English/Film Studies with a secondary appointment in the French and Italian Languages and Literatures Department at the University of Pittsburgh. Her books include *Fascism in Film: The Italian Commercial Cinema, 1931–1943* (1986); *Imitations of Life: A Reader on Film and Television Melodrama* (1991), *British Genres: Cinema and Society, 1930–1960* (1991); *Film, Politics, and Gramsci* (1994); *Queen Christina* (1996 with Amy Villarejo); *Cinematic Uses of the Past* (1996); *The Folklore of Consensus: Theatricality and Spectacle in Italian Cinema 1930–1943* (1998); *Italian Film* (2000); *The Historical Film: History and Memory in Media* (2000); *Stars: The Film Reader* (2004 co-edited with Lucy Fischer); *Monty Python's Flying Circus* (2005); and *Stardom, Italian Style: Screen Performance and Personality in Italian Cinema* (2008).

Brian McFarlane is Honorary Associate Professor in the School of English, Communication and Performance Studies at Monash University, Melbourne, and Visiting Professor in Film Studies at the University of Hull. He is the author of numerous books and articles on British cinema, most recently the third edition of the *Encyclopedia of British Film* (Methuen, 2008).

Claire Monk is Senior Lecturer in Film Studies at De Montfort University. Her research and publications to date have focused on British cinema in its cultural, political and social contexts since the 1970s, most notably her contributions to the debate around heritage cinema as well as her work on post-1990 British cinema in the context of Blairism. She is currently preparing a monograph *Heritage Film Audiences: Period Films and Contemporary Audiences in the UK* for Edinburgh University Press, drawing on her PhD thesis. She is also co-editor with Amy Sargeant of the collection *British Historical Cinema* (Routledge, 2002).

Nathalie Morris is the BFI's Curator of Special Collections. She is a member of the Women's Film History project, co-creator of the Women and Silent Britain website, and contributor to the *Women Film Pioneers Sourcebook* (Volume II, Duke University Press, 2009). Her PhD was on the Stoll Film Companies (1918–28) and she has published on various aspects of British silent cinema in the *Journal of British Cinema and Television* and *The Hitchcock Annual Anthology*. She is currently co-editing (with Andrew Higson, Kristian Moen and Jonathan Stubbs) *The Routledge Encyclopedia of Film History* (forthcoming 2011).

Rachel Moseley is Senior Lecturer in Film and Television Studies at the University of Warwick. She has published widely on questions of gender and representation in popular film and television, television for women and teen television, and is currently working on a long-term project about the representation of Cornwall in film, television, art and literature.

Sarah Street is Professor of Film at the University of Bristol. Her books include *Cinema and State: The Film Industry and the British Government, 1927–84* (co-authored with Margaret Dickinson, British Film Institute, 1985), *British National Cinema* (Routledge, 1997), *British Cinema in Documents* (Routledge, 2000), *Costume and Cinema: Dress Codes in Popular Film* (Wallflower Press, 2001), *Transatlantic Crossings: British Feature Films in the USA* (Continuum, 2002) and *Black Narcissus* (I.B. Tauris, 2005).

Imelda Whelehan is Professor of English and Women's Studies at De Montfort University. Her research is in the fields of women's writing, feminism, popular culture and literary adaptations. She is the author of *Modern Feminist Thought* (1995), *Overloaded* (2000), *Helen Fielding's Bridget Jones's Diary: A Reader's Guide* (2002) and *The Feminist Bestseller* (2005). She is co-author of *Fifty Key Concepts in Gender Studies* (with Jane Pilcher, 2004) and co-edited *Adaptations: From Text to Screen, Screen to Text* (with Deborah Cartmell, 1999) and *The Cambridge Companion to Literature on Screen* (with Deborah Cartmell, 2007).

Melanie Williams is Lecturer in Film Studies at the University of East Anglia. She has written on British cinema for *Screen*, *Cinema Journal*, *Film Quarterly*, *Journal of British Cinema and Television*, *Sight and Sound* and the *Independent* as well as the edited collections *British Cinema of the 1950s* (2003), *24 Frames: The Cinema of Britain and Ireland* (2005), *50 Key British Films* (2008) and the third edition of *The British Cinema Book* (2009). She is the author of *Prisoners of Gender: Women in the Films of J. Lee Thompson* (2009).

Acknowledgements

We would like to thank all the contributors, and the series editors Steve Chibnall and Ian Hunter for their help and encouragement in getting the project off the ground (thanks also to Steve Chibnall for invaluable assistance in providing illustrations), and Natalie Foster, Charlotte Wood and Sarah Hamilton at Routledge for shepherding the book successfully to publication. Their patience, sensitivity and kindness has been much appreciated.

Chapter four contains material that first appeared in '"What would Bette Davis do?": British reactions to Bette Davis in the 1940s: a case study of *Now, Voyager*', *Screen*, 49.1, Spring 2008. Chapter eleven is an extended version of an earlier chapter, 'Crossing thresholds: the contemporary British woman's film', in Andrew Higson (ed.), *Dissolving Views: Key Writings on British Cinema* (London: Cassell, 1996).

Every effort has been made to obtain permissions to reproduce copyright material. If any proper acknowledgement has not been made, we apologise and invite copyright holders to inform us of the oversight.

Melanie Bell would like to thank colleagues at Newcastle University for their support, particularly Bruce Babington, and Sue Harper who gave generously of her time. Special thanks to Chris Curtis and Eris Williams Reed for love, support and shared good times.

Melanie Williams would like to thank her former colleagues at Hull for their support and good advice, especially Neil Sinyard, and Matthew Bailey for everything, as always. Her work on this book is dedicated to the two most important women in her life: her daughter Lara and her much-loved, much-missed mother Mary Jean Williams (1955–2008).

1 The hour of the cuckoo

Reclaiming the British woman's film

Melanie Bell and Melanie Williams

> Yes, but what makes a woman's picture? Is it a fabulous fashion show, decked out in Technicolor – and guaranteed to make any woman view her last year's good tweed with distaste? Is it a highly strung yarn of feminine conflict with *All About Eve*-ish undertones? Is it a dominating female star performance? Or is it a trio of handsome heroes, all amorously inclined and romantically involved? *It Started in Paradise* is all this, but something more. Personally, I'm inclined to think it's that something more that makes this tale of an ambitious woman and a fashion house so successfully yet so simply a woman's picture. Dramatic intensity is the nearest I can get to it in print.
>
> (Hinxman 1952: 12)

In the pages of *Picturegoer* in the early 1950s, the critic Margaret Hinxman considers a new British release *It Started in Paradise* and mulls over the various elements that make it a 'woman's picture', citing the importance of qualities such as visual splendour (and indirect encouragement to go shopping in emulation of said splendour), feminine conflict, female star performance and handsome heroes before finally deciding that 'dramatic intensity' is the distinguishing feature of the species. In its attempt to get to grips with the conventions of this particular genre, Hinxman's article pre-empts a very sizeable body of academic literature engaged in the same task from the 1970s onwards. One of the earliest examples was Molly Haskell's *From Reverence to Rape*, which queried the idea that the pejorative industry category of 'woman's picture' offered nothing more than 'soft-core emotional porn for the frustrated housewife'. Instead she tentatively celebrated a filmic form in which 'the woman – a woman – is at the center of the universe' for a change (1974: 155), drawing attention to powerful performances by actresses such as Bette Davis, Joan Crawford, Olivia de Havilland, Margaret Sullavan, Katharine Hepburn, Barbara Stanwyck and Joan Fontaine in movies dealing with the grand themes of 'sacrifice, affliction, choice, competition' (1974: 163).

Scholarly interest in the woman's picture continued into the 1980s, part of a growing feminist interest in 'gynocentric' cultural forms such as soap opera and romantic fiction (Kuhn 1984; Modleski 1984; Brunsdon 1986; Doane 1987b; Radway 1987). With their unabashed courtship of the female cinema goer, woman's films posed an interesting challenge to psychoanalytic theories of cinema

Figure 1.1 Fabulous fashion, feminine conflict, dramatic intensity: Kay Kendall and Jane
     Hylton in *It Started in Paradise*, directed by Compton Bennett (1952).
Source: The Steve Chibnall Collection.

spectatorship which had hitherto conceptualised the gaze as inflexibly male.
The very nomenclature of the genre, as Mary Ann Doane pointed out, 'stipu-
lates that the films are in some sense the "possession" of women and that their
terms of address are dictated by the anticipated presence of the female spectator' (1987a: 284). However, this is not to say that the woman's film is necessarily a progressive or proto-feminist genre. Unsurprisingly, many critics have
taken issue with the gender ghetto-ism implicit in the generic label 'woman's
film' (pointing out the lack of any masculine equivalent, the 'man's picture')
and have questioned the automatic assumptions about women's cinematic preferences that such categorisation seemed to entail. In 1949, British critic Catherine De La Roche complained that in film marketing 'you will find that
sentimentality, lavish and facile effects, the melodramatic, extravagant, naively
romantic and highly coloured, the flattering, trivial and phoney – these are the
elements in pictures, whatever their overall qualities, that are supposed to draw
women' (De La Roche 1949: 27). A few years later, Eleanor Wintour, occa-
sional critic for *Tribune*, went even further in her angry dismissal of a special
category of films just for women:

If the frustrated female audience is really so important to the film producers, can they not give them special showings as they do of films for small
boys? Screen them on Saturday afternoons at reduced prices, and frankly
call them Ladies' Afternoons. Adults of both sexes could then avoid them
as they avoid the Saturday morning cowboy films.

(Wintour 1955)

Moreover, the pleasures of woman's pictures are often masochistic ones,
delighting in feminine agony, and the films frequently close on a conservative
note, with the heroine safely ensconced in a traditional female role in spite of
what adventures may have gone before. Yet the woman's film is above all else a
Janus-faced genre which is simultaneously complicit with and critical of the
gender status quo. In spite of attempts at narrative closure, woman's films are
frequently riddled with contradictions that cannot be contained, and in fact, as
Laura Mulvey has argued of Douglas Sirk's melodramas, the value of such a
form for feminist critics 'lies in the amount of dust the story raises along the
road, a cloud of over-determined irreconcilables which put up a resistance to
being neatly settled in the last five minutes' (Mulvey 1989: 40).

One of the key issues for scholars of the woman's film has been the question
of where to draw the precise perimeters of a genre variously thought of 'as
escapist entertainment for women, simply as films that men do not like, as
examinations of capable, independent female characters and their empowerment, as emotional "tearjerkers", as tales of female bonding, and as the
antithesis to male-orientated action films' (Hollinger 2008: 225). Often considered alongside or as a sub-section of melodrama (as in the 1987 essay collection *Home is Where the Heart is: Studies in Melodrama and the Woman's
Film*) because of a shared concern with effect and pathos, the woman's film is
defined by Maria LaPlace (in the above collection) as being 'distinguished by its
female protagonist, female point of view and its narrative which most often
revolves around the traditional realms of women's experience: the familial, the
domestic, the romantic – those arenas where love, emotion and relationships
take precedence over action and events' (LaPlace 1987: 139): a useful encapsu-
lation of the standard definition of the genre. However, Janine Basinger has
suggested a more catholic categorisation which can find room for films such as
'Rosalind Russell's career comedies, musical biographies of real-life women,
combat films featuring brave nurses on Bataan, and westerns in which women
drive cattle west' (Basinger 1993: 7) alongside the more familiar romances and
melodramas. Basinger finally settles on a pluralistic working definition of the
woman's film as simply 'a movie that places at the center of its universe a
female who is trying to deal with the emotional, social, and psychological problems that are specifically connected to the fact that she is a woman' (20).

This collection of essays will mobilise Basinger's admirably open definition of
the woman's film, originally formulated in relation to classic Hollywood, but
apply it to the very different national context of British cinema, in the hope of
bringing to light a parallel heritage of British woman's films, perhaps less well

known than their Hollywood counterparts but no less significant. These range from the female-centred dramas of silent British cinema right through to the contemporary British 'chick flick', covering the work of actresses from Mabel Poulton to Keira Knightley, and literary inspirations ranging from Ethel M. Dell to Helen Fielding; films that have performed the same function as their American cousins – 'to articulate female concerns, angers, and desires, to give substance to a woman's dreams and a woman's problems' (Basinger 1993: 36) – but imagined within a British cinematic consciousness. The contributors to the collection deploy various methodologies in their respective chapters but they are linked in their common aim to re-address the question Margaret Hinxman first asked her readers back in 1952 – what makes a woman's picture – and what does it mean when (as with *It Started in Paradise*) the woman's picture is also a British picture?

The woman's film and British cinema

As we have seen, the focus has tended traditionally to fall on Hollywood in critical discussion of the genre, with substantial attention paid to *Stella Dallas* (1937), *Rebecca* (1940), *Now, Voyager* (1942), *Mildred Pierce* (1945), *Letter from an Unknown Woman* (1948) and the work of émigré directors Douglas Sirk and Max Ophuls. In spite of the existence of British films such as the female-centred, fashion-orientated, dramatically intense *It Started in Paradise*, the woman's film has rarely been seen as an inherently British genre. In one of the few pieces of academic writing to examine this phenomenon (updated for this collection), Justine Ashby (writing as Justine King) suggests why 'British' and 'woman's film' seem to have been incompatible terms:

> The conceptualisation of the 'typically English film' constantly seems to attract the ideologically loaded epithet 'restrained' (which reflects not only a middle-class bias but, I would argue, a masculinist bias too) whereby demonstrative displays of 'excessive' emotionality – worst of all, tears – are regarded as inappropriate, both on and off screen. It is, then, an easy enough matter to see why the woman's film might be regarded as something of an unwelcome cuckoo-in-the-nest here. For, despite twenty years or more of sustained critical attention which has repeatedly demonstrated the aesthetic and ideological complexities of the genre, the woman's film still carries the taint of triviality, emotional excessiveness and brash Hollywood populism. In short, it might well be considered as rather 'un-British'.
>
> (King 1996: 218–19)

Back in the 1940s, the association of the woman's film with triviality, excessiveness and brashness stood uncontested, and as a result British films clearly identifiable as woman's pictures, such as the Gainsborough melodramas of the 1940s, suffered extreme critical derision at the time of their release. For instance, the *Sunday Graphic*'s review of *Caravan* (1946) suggested that 'to enjoy it, you need to have a mind that throbs to every sob of the novelette and a heart that throbs to every exposure of Stewart Granger's torso' (quoted in Harper 1987: 168); a damning dismissal that simultaneously aligns lowbrow culture (the novelette), excessive emotion (the sobbing), intellectual vapidity (a throbbing mind), bodily thrills (a throbbing heart) and inappropriate female desire sparked by a bare male chest – a potent stew of misogynist assumptions if there ever was one.[1] Gainsborough films, populated by lively heroines and dashing heroes, usually showed scant regard for the niceties of historical accuracy, preferring instead to use the exoticism of the past to 'usher women into a realm of female pleasure' (Harper 1994: 122). The visual lushness of the films often prompted imitative behaviour, with women apeing the look of their favourite heroines: 'Margaret Lockwood's beauty spot was something new, we all started to add them on with eye pencil'; 'My mother, like many others, bought the fashionable "Wicked Lady" style hat' (quoted in Thumim 1992: 167).[2] Further proof of their psychological influence is provided by their appearance in cinema-goers' dreams, as recorded in J. P. Mayer's 1946 book *Sociology of Film* in which subjects recalled oneiric visions of female instability and male brutality indebted to *Madonna of the Seven Moons* (1944) and *The Man in Grey* (1943) (cited in Harper 1987: 189–90). The threat they posed to rationality was enough to have them relegated to outer darkness in the British critical milieu of the 1940s with its emphasis on realist 'quality' cinema (Ellis 1996), even though it was (ironically) also the source of their later critical rehabilitation from the 1980s onwards (Aspinall and Murphy 1983; Harper 1994; Cook 1996) when they played an important role, along with Hammer horror, in the reconfiguration of British cinema and the rediscovery of significant traditions other than reticent restrained realism in its history.

However, Ashby discerns a further disavowal of a native tradition of British women's cinema. While some woman's pictures are openly disparaged, other potential candidates for woman's film status are not recognised or categorised as such due to 'a peculiarly skewed and selective characterisation which fails to take account of British cinema's sustained investment in melodramatic emotionality', and hence many female-centred films like *Millions Like Us* (1943), *Two Thousand Women* (1944), *A Taste of Honey* (1961), *The L-Shaped Room* (1962), *Jane Eyre* (1970) and *A Room with a View* (1985) find themselves 'swept under the umbrella of other film movements or genres (the wartime morale film, the New Wave film, the "quality" literary adaptation) in order to fit them, however reductively, into a dominant scheme of national cinema' (King 1996: 219). If one returns to British cinema with Ashby's revisionist schema in mind, many other instances of potential woman's pictures spring to mind, often from the heart of the British cinema canon; *Brief Encounter* (1945), for instance, is an example of 'quality' realist cinema but it is also a masterpiece of 'melodramatic emotionality' (Ashby's phrase) and 'dramatic intensity' (Hinxman's phrase) with a very 'un-British' soundtrack of pounding Rachmaninov. It features a woman at the centre of its universe (and in control of its voice-over narration) and focuses on what Janine Basinger deems 'the major action of a woman's film: making a choice' (1993: 19), in this case between untrammelled passion and marital fidelity. The woman's choice also lies at the heart of *The Red Shoes* (1948), a film more frequently discussed in terms of the authorship and aestheticism of Powell and Pressburger (represented on screen by the diabolical impresario Lermontov) than the dilemma of its heroine Vicky, who must choose between fulfilment in her private life or her career; a typical woman's film conflict. It's not that either film has been mistakenly *mis*-categorised as anything other than a woman's film, merely that placing them in a continuum of British woman's films permits another way of interpreting them. In short, such films are not *solely* woman's films but they are *also* woman's films, and to fail to recognise that means ignoring a large part of their substance and their appeal.

It should be noted that in non-academic discussions of cinema, there is no suggestion that the woman's film is somehow 'un-British', and a number of more populist film books happily include many British productions in their discussions of woman's films alongside Hollywood's output. For instance, Samantha Cook's *Rough Guide to Chick Flicks* gives honourable mentions to the 1940s classics *Black Narcissus* (1947), *Brief Encounter*, *The Red Shoes* and *The Wicked Lady* (1945) as well as more recent favourites like *Bend it like Beckham* (2002), *Bhaji on the Beach* (1993) and *Bridget Jones's Diary* (2001) along with Merchant Ivory films and Richard Curtis rom-coms (Cook 2006). In addition, Jo Berry and Angie Errigo's *Chick Flicks: Movies Women Love* name-checks many of these and adds the bio-pics *Dance With a Stranger* (1985), *Elizabeth* (1998), *Iris* (2002), *Mrs Brown* (1997), *Odette* (1950) and *That Hamilton Woman* (1941), the buddy movies *Career Girls* (1997), *Girl's Night* (1998) and *Me Without You* (2001), the weepies *Shadowlands* (1993) and *Truly Madly Deeply* (1990), the wartime dramas *Charlotte Gray* (2001) and *Yanks* (1979) and the literary adaptations *The Heart of Me* (2002), *Hideous Kinky* (1998), *Howards End* (1992), *I Capture the Castle* (2003) and *The Prime of Miss Jean Brodie* (1969), along with many other British films (Berry and Errigo 2004). The sheer abundance of British titles in two books with an international scope suggests the wealth and diversity of woman's picture material that exists in British cinema history for those willing to look with an open mind. Even looking back at Molly Haskell's original analysis of the genre, one finds a remarkable amount of room given over to discuss British films such as *The Seventh Veil* (1945) and *Love Story* (1944) and in fact it is British cinema rather than Hollywood that inspires one of Haskell's most rhapsodic paeans to the form:

> [H]ow is one to explain the degree to which some of them enthral us: the mesmerized absorption, the choking, the welling up of tears over some lugubrious rendition of a famous piano concerto that will haunt us forever afterward with the memory of James Mason rapping Ann Todd's knuckles or Margaret Lockwood banging away in [the] Albert Hall?
>
> (Haskell 1974: 164)

No shortage of dramatic intensity there. Instead, Haskell presents an evocation of overwhelming effect achieved through the synergy of powerful music and striking image that is the very antithesis of British cinema as 'emotionally quite frozen', to use Lindsay Anderson's memorable phrase (quoted in Barr 1998: 119).

The clinching evidence for the centrality of the woman's film to British cinema history is provided by the British Film Institute's 2005 compilation of the top 100 films at the British box office over the past 75 years (Gilbey 2005). All three of the *British* films that make the top ten could be considered woman's pictures: at number five, the spritely Anna Neagle romantic comedy with terpsichorean interludes, *Spring in Park Lane* (1948); at number nine, Gainsborough's highway-robbery bodice-ripper *The Wicked Lady*; at number ten, that delirious confection of psychoanalysis, sadism and symphonies, *The Seventh Veil*.

These films come way ahead of more canonical British cinema, in the shape of *The Third Man* (1949) at number 26, and surpass even the successful Harry Potter and Bond franchises in popularity. Their high position clearly demonstrates that in order to achieve any understanding of British cinema at its most domestically successful, it is imperative to look at the place of female-centred films within the national cinema. Such films are not cuckoos-in-the-nest or exceptional aberrations but rather form the very core of popular national cinema. Similarly, there needs to be an acknowledgement of the 'woman's-picture-ness'

Figure 1.2 British cinema at its most domestically popular: James Mason and Margaret Lockwood in *The Wicked Lady*, directed by Leslie Arliss (1945).
Source: The Steve Chibnall Collection.

of many key British films which are usually siphoned off into other generic categories. As Pam Cook asserts in her work on Gainsborough melodrama, 'the reassessment of femininity is central to any discussion about national identity in and of "British" cinema' (Cook 1996: 7) and with its sustained focus on the British woman's film, this collection of essays aims to play its part in that process of reassessment.

Tracing British women's cinema from the 1920s to now

Even in its earliest decades, British cinema was attuned to the female audience, and Nathalie Morris's chapter demonstrates how well established the woman's film had become by the 1920s. With a focus on literary and theatrical adaptation (Wilde, Dickens), and bio-pics of key female historical figures from Boadicea to Mary Queen of Scots, the woman's film was instrumental in the battle waged by domestic film producers to stake a claim for a distinctively British cinema in opposition to Hollywood's emerging hegemony. Morris explores how the idea of a 'distinctively British product' was central to the activities of the Stoll Film Company, whose film adaptations of Ethel M. Dell's popular romance novels were intended to capitalise on 'feminine interest'. Dell's spirited heroines sought romantic and sexual fulfilment in escapist fantasies that were extremely popular, not least because they responded imaginatively to women's hopes and fears for social mobility and marriage at a time when society was still adjusting to the decimation of the male population caused by the Great War. The critical derision heaped on these films points to the frequent marginalisation of women's literary and cinematic culture, in Britain as elsewhere, and this misogynistic disparagement runs throughout the history of the British woman's film. Stoll's use of Ethel M. Dell as a lure to female cinema-goers is a reminder of the centrality of literary adaptation to the British woman's film. Although the work of writers such as Olive Higgins Prouty and Fannie Hurst often provided source material for Hollywood, the inter-relationship between literature and film seems even more pronounced in the British woman's film, which frequently has a literary bent, perhaps reflecting the high value placed upon literary culture in Britain. Fine films have been made from proto-feminist novels and plays such as Shelagh Delaney's *A Taste of Honey* (1961), Lynne Reid-Banks's *The L-Shaped Room* (1962), Penelope Mortimer's *The Pumpkin Eater* (1964) and Nell Dunn's *Poor Cow* (1967). Gainsborough's celebrated melodramas often took novels by female authors such as Eleanor Smith, Margery Lawrence and Dorothy Whipple as their starting point. More recently, Jane Austen has become a central figure in female-orientated British film and television whether in terms of direct adaptation (*Sense and Sensibility* (1995), *Emma* (1996), *Mansfield Park* (1999), *Pride and Prejudice* (2005) on film in addition to several television adaptations, most notably the BBC's hugely popular 1995 *Pride and Prejudice*) or indirect inspiration, as with Gurinder Chadha's *Bride and Prejudice* (2004), ITV's time-travel drama *Lost in Austen* (2008) and Bridget Jones's fixation on Colin Firth as *Pride and Prejudice*'s Mr Darcy, fuelled by the aforementioned BBC series, intertextually referenced by having Firth also play her love-interest in the film, the serendipitously named Mark Darcy.

With the growth of the 'picture palace' in the 1920s, Morris reminds us, cinema was increasingly imagined as a feminine space graced with decor and amenities designed with female pleasure and comfort in mind. While the films on screen often worked through feminine dilemmas, the exhibition space itself afforded a temporary reprieve from those problems. Winifred Holtby provides a blissful evocation of the delights awaiting female patrons of a provincial 'super-cinema' in her 1936 novel *South Riding*:

> It blazed with lights and rippled with palms; a commissionaire in a gold-and-scarlet uniform paraded the entrance. Up on the first floor Lily could see ladies in green arm-chairs eating muffins behind great sheets of plate glass. The thought of tea and toast suddenly tempted her. She went in and dragged herself up the shallow carpeted staircase.
>
> The tea-room was palatial. Marble pillars swelled into branching archways. Painted cupids billowed across the ceiling. Waitresses in green taffeta tripped between the tables; from some hidden source a fountain of music throbbed and quivered, 'Tum tum tum *tum*, ter-um, ter-um, tum tum tum *tum*, ter-um, ter-um.' The beautiful Blue Danube. ... She lay back in her chair. It was richly padded. The tea was good. The toast was hot, dripping with butter.
>
> (Holtby 1988: 214)

From 1929 to 1939, according to Nicholas Hiley, no fewer than 60 per cent of British cinema-goers were women (Hiley 1999: 47) and at the beginning of the 1930s the woman's picture flourished in the guise of the 'society drama' (Aldgate 1998). Several of the most popular British stars of the 1930s were women, among them the musical stars Gracie Fields and Jessie Matthews, as well as Anna Neagle (the subject of Josephine Dolan and Sarah Street's chapter) who would go on to enjoy even greater success in the 1940s. Indeed, one of the greatest shocks of the BFI's 2005 'ultimate film' research was the unexpectedly high placing of Neagle's films, with *Spring in Park Lane* at number five followed by *The Courtneys of Curzon Street* (1947) at 17, *Piccadilly Incident* (1946) at 42 and *I Live in Grosvenor Square* (1945) at 49. Neagle embodied a version of glamorous yet dignified femininity that was carefully differentiated from more overtly sexualised images of contemporary womanhood aligned in the popular consciousness with brash Americanism. Dolan and Street demonstrate the importance of her voice to her popularity, with its gentle tonal register functioning as the 'physical articulation of feminine ideals' and sustaining 'a glimmer of warmth and hope even within the bleakest scenario' of war-time. They also examine the star's presentation on screen via the new technology of colour photography, used for patriotic pageantry in some of her films such as the regal biopic *Victoria the Great* (1937) but also for female-orientated fashion fantasy in *Maytime in Mayfair* (1949). The popularity of Neagle's 'quintessential English femininity' indicates some of the ways in which the woman's film is simultaneously disavowed while its icons of femininity are pressed into the service of national cinema.

In spite of her remarkable popularity with British audiences, Anna Neagle's films are yet to receive the same kind of critical attention and rehabilitation as the contemporaneous Gainsborough melodramas, perhaps because her more measured and well-behaved output is much less appealing to revisionist scholars of British cinema than the lively vulgarity of Gainsborough which addressed itself primarily to working-class women. Neagle's films belong in the category of the 'middlebrow', offering neither the proletarian vigour of the lowbrow nor the intellectual acerbity of the highbrow, and seldom seen as a happy hunting ground for those seeking cultural treasures. Nonetheless, as Lawrence Napper has demonstrated, it is a significant category in British cinema to which many underrated films worthy of rediscovery belong (Napper 2000), and this is perhaps particularly true of many British woman's films whose more polite pleasures have been eclipsed by the focus on Gainsborough's excessive modes. Undoubtedly the ultimate middlebrow grouping is the heritage film, which often functions as a kind of 'woman's film *manqué*'. Alan Parker's much-quoted comment on Merchant Ivory productions as the 'Laura Ashley school of film-making' damns the most visible exponents of heritage film by association with femininity and consumption through reference to a female-headed retailer of faux-vintage clothes and homeware. Yet the heritage film's attention to decor and costume are a source of considerable spectatorial enjoyment, appealing to what are frequently characterised as feminine reading competences. Furthermore, heritage films continue to offer central roles to women and provide a valuable forum for actresses of all ages to deliver powerful and articulate performances that may not be viable in other more action-orientated genres (Geraghty 2002). Such films may not attract the passionate advocacy of 'Young Turk' film critics (it's difficult to imagine the likes of *Ladies in Lavender* ever gaining a cult following) but their importance to British cinema's cultural formation (not to mention its appeal to audiences both home and overseas) is indisputable.

Given how the woman's picture is generally identified as a Hollywood genre, it seems fitting to spend time examining how an exemplar of the form was greeted on British soil. Mark Glancy's chapter investigates the British reception of the quintessential Hollywood woman's film *Now, Voyager* and its star Bette Davis. At a time when British film critics (and middle-class audiences) prioritised realism and maturity in film production, Davis's well-publicised defiance of Hollywood star conventions and demand for 'serious' film roles contributed significantly to the critical and popular success she enjoyed in Britain. Her hard-working, anti-glamour Yankee persona suited British film critics who were steeped in anti-Hollywood discourses, and had a particular emotional resonance for a nation at war. Drawing from a range of sociological studies of cinema audiences, Glancy demonstrates the importance of class to questions of taste. Middle-class audiences couched their approval of Davis through a focus on her acting ability and an eschewal of the label 'woman's film' while working-class audiences used direct, emotional terms to explain the pleasure they derived from Davis, who also functioned for many as an aspirational figure. Glancy also provides a salutary reminder that many men also enjoy films that are deemed to be 'woman's pictures', putting the brakes on an overly strict categorisation of film according to gender and acknowledging the polymorphous identifications inherent in all film spectatorship.

The transatlantic traffic in woman's films was certainly not all one way, and while British audiences gloried in Bette Davis at her finest, British woman's films such as *The Seventh Veil* enjoyed considerable success in the USA (as implied by its rapturous description in American critic Molly Haskell's book). In addition, Marcia Landy has written warmly of her enjoyment of Gainsborough films in the American Midwest in the 1940s, and notes the prominent position given to an interview with Margaret Lockwood in an Ohio-based newspaper (Landy 2000: 67), suggesting something of the British woman's picture's reach into the American heartland, in spite of the 'serious obstacles' (Street 2002: 1) of protectionism and prejudice facing British films across the Atlantic. Arguably, the British woman's film of the 1940s even influenced the Hollywood genre: the Joan Crawford film *Possessed* (1947) begins with the mentally disturbed heroine being injected with a truth-serum to help her yield her secrets (and the narrative), strongly recalling the opening of *The Seventh Veil*, a film which enjoyed significant success in the USA in the previous year, 1946. In addition, Hollywood woman's films of the period frequently drew inspiration from British women's literature ranging from classics by the Brontës and Jane Austen to contemporary works by Jan Struther (author of *Mrs Miniver*) and Daphne du Maurier.

Back in the context of British studio production, Brian McFarlane's chapter compares the careers of two key actresses of the 1940s, Phyllis Calvert and Googie Withers, and explores the range of cinematic femininities available in wartime and post-war Britain. Calvert, McFarlane argues, was 'the ideal woman of the times', whose gentle, hard-working and determined persona brought a degree of complexity to the paradigm of the good woman. In comparison, the roles played by Withers afforded greater scope to showcase qualities of strength and independence of spirit. Both women, in different ways, dramatised some of the problems of, and responses to, being a woman in Britain in this period. Their critical reception, however, must be understood within wider discourses of British cinema. Withers has received greater critical attention (and approval) than Calvert, whose prolific career as 'good girl' of Gainsborough melodrama ensured her marginalisation. By comparison, Withers was cast in roles that fitted a realist bill and worked for Ealing, a studio ineluctably linked to dramatising the national character. However, one of the advantages of applying Janine Basinger's more open definition of the woman's film genre (any film 'that places at the center of its universe a female who is trying to deal with the emotional, social, and psychological problems that are specifically connected to the fact that she is a woman') is that it encourages us to look beyond the conventional generic placement of films and to connect otherwise disparate texts in terms of their shared evocation of female subjectivity and experience. Calvert's *Madonna of the Seven Moons* with its exotic setting and melodramatic scenario is a woman's picture, but so is Withers's *It Always Rains on Sunday* (1947) despite its deliberate focus on the quotidian world of Bethnal Green and eschewal of flamboyant fantasy. Both films focus on women with a split personality, but while Calvert's Maddelena expresses hers through psychological disorder and the creation of a passionate peasant alter-ego, Withers's Rose suffers in silence, glowering over the trappings of domesticity, only coming to life in flashback and with the reappearance of her criminal ex-lover. Only the former film would normally be classified as a woman's film but the lineaments of the genre are clearly present in both, and as Christine Geraghty suggests, 'although Ealing's drive for realism certainly makes [its] films different from Gainsborough's costume dramas, it does not necessarily mean that they fail to acknowledge the concerns of women in the late 1940s or to deny the emotional cost of the decisions they make' (Geraghty 2000: 86).

While chapters three to five stress the important of stars, Rachel Moseley's chapter shifts the focus to landscape, specifically Cornwall as a recurring romantic setting in the British woman's film. In films ranging from Gainsborough's *Love Story* (1944) to the more contemporary *Ladies in Lavender* (2004), Cornwall functions as a 'passionate periphery' where female desire can be expressed, an idea that Moseley examines through the careful scrutiny of a number of gendered views of the landscape in both films. This is perhaps another distinctive feature of the British woman's film: the relationship of woman and landscape, which has been central to British romance texts from the Brontë sisters onwards. In comparison with the studio-bound or urban settings of the classic Hollywood woman's film, the British woman's film frequently features natural locations, revelling in the beauties of the English countryside (and the well-ordered country house estate in the heritage film) or wilder Celtic topographies as in *I Know Where I'm Going!* (1945), and sometimes placing its women characters in ravishing and transformative foreign landscapes, from the Greek islands of *Shirley Valentine* (1989) and the Italy of *Enchanted April* (1992) to the India of *Heat and Dust* (1983) and *A Passage to India* (1984).

Ensemble playing has always been a feature of British cinema, and this extends to the British woman's film, encompassing wartime productions with predominantly female casts such as *The Gentle Sex* (1943) and *Two Thousand Women* through to comedy-dramas of the 1980s and 1990s such as *She'll Be Wearing Pink Pyjamas* (1985) and *Bhaji on the Beach*. Melanie Bell's chapter focuses on the recurrence of the female group film in British cinema and examines how it extends the demands of the woman's film beyond the heterosexual 'love and emotion' of LaPlace's description, opening up a space where female friendships take precedence and older women play an important and valued role in the proceedings. Through a case study of two popular 1950s films – *A Town Like Alice* (1956) and *The Weak and the Wicked* (1954) – Bell demonstrates how British cinema continued to produce variants of the woman's film in a decade often considered inhospitable to engaging with women's issues.

In common with the status of the woman's film as a Janus-faced genre, Bell illustrates how female agency is offset by strategies that 're-feminise' the women in accordance with gender norms. Despite such limitations these group films offer complex portrayals of femininity and their commercial success suggests that their particular depiction of women's concerns resonated with the social and psychological needs of 1950s audiences.

The 1960s saw seismic changes in the position of women in British society, on the surface at least, and this was reflected in changes to the British woman's film. Marcia Landy's chapter explores a number of films produced in Britain and Italy in the 1960s that share a common concern with the mobile young woman who makes physical and conceptual journeys across borders of nation-hood, class, generation and sexuality. In British films such as *Girl with Green Eyes* (1964), *The Knack and How to Get It* (1965) and *Darling* (1965), the young woman becomes the adventurer in search of an independent existence and sexual fulfilment, loosening the traditional bonds of femininity. In the Italian film *La Ragazza con la Pistola* (1968), the heroine played by Monica Vitti moves from Sicily to Britain where she can ultimately transform herself into the 'trans-national embodiment of newly liberated femininity'. Just as British women in woman's films often 'find themselves' abroad, the reverse is also true in con-tinental films featuring European women drawn to the emancipatory opportu-nities of the then-swinging British metropolis. These kind of cultural exchanges are an important aspect of the British woman's film, with Gainsborough films, for instance, frequently inviting British audiences to 'identity with British stars playing French, Spanish, Italian and ethnically mixed characters, and to journey into a fictionalised "Europe" which called into question many of the prevailing notions of Britishness' (Cook 1996: 6), evoking a 'vagrant spirit' (Cook 1996: 3) reminiscent of Virginia Woolf's famous assertion that as a woman she had no country. In fact, Pam Cook suggests that the transnationality of the British woman's film may have been just as much of a stumbling block to its critical acceptance as its melodramatic excess, with films like *Madonna of the Seven Moons* 'doubly threatening to the criteria of 40s consensus cinema: not only overwhelmingly feminine but also chaotically "foreign"' (Cook 1996: 96). Such films are much less easily mobilised to the patriotic cause of constructing a national cinema, since they openly admit the lure of 'abroad' in comparison with the perceived inadequacies of home (and in an indirect slur on British masculinity, that Britain cannot offer any sight as fair as Ivor Novello gor-geously essaying the role of Parisian thief in *The Rat* (1925) or Stewart Granger kitted out in figure-revealing Spanish bolero and gypsy earrings for *Caravan*).

Sue Harper's chapter opens up for discussion questions of methodology con-cerning the woman's film, distinguishing between films *by* women, necessitating a focus on female agency; films *for* women which address a female audience, a market category that flourished during the 1930s and 1940s but which was lar-gely defunct in British film production in later decades; and films *about* women which shed light on the symbolic function of the female figure at any given historical moment. For Harper, films may be usefully defined as either 'limit-texts' demarcating a boundary between the 'acceptable and unacceptable female libido', those operating as 'comfort-zones' offering the viewer the 'delights of the sexual status quo' or, most radical of all, 'gauntlet-throwers' which challenge established sexual politics. Throughout she emphasises the centrality of industrial organisation in shaping the narrative function of women (or any other group) in film. Her case study of the 1970s demonstrates how the social and sexual advancements of the 1960s were absorbed into the mainstream, and how the erratic funding and organisational structures of the British film industry threw up a 'swirling kaleidoscope of contrasting takes on women'. Through an analysis of the performance style of a number of key actresses of the 1970s, Harper identifies distance and irony as common features, strategically deployed to mediate the effects of feminism and the challenges it brought to bear on patriarchal structures, among them cinema. The decade may not have offered riches in terms of the woman's picture but it gave rise to a number of memorable female performances across a variety of genres in British cinema.

Moving into the 1980s, Claire Monk presents a detailed case study of *Breaking Glass* (1980), a film whose credentials as a woman's film are ambivalent despite its narrative being centred on a protagonist described by Margaret Hinxman (still reviewing nearly 30 years after *It Started in Paradise*) as 'the best female role in British films for years'. It would appear on the surface to be the kind of film ripe for re-categorisation as yet another 'woman's film *manqué*', swept under the umbrella of the punk film. However, this is somewhat problematised by the film's deliberate refusal of gender-consciousness. Monk reads the film in terms of punk's utopian gender-neutral ethos where 'the hurdles of gender difference and acceptable femininity can be overcome just by ignoring them at will' (and to which obvious gender-targeted marketing would be anathema).

However, as the 1980s progressed, the woman's film gathered pace, as documented in Justine Ashby's aforementioned 1996 article 'Crossing Thresholds', which is revisited and updated in chapter eleven. Ashby traces the impact of feminist cultural politics on British cinema, looking at a number of 1980s films including *Educating Rita* (1983), *Letter to Brezhnev* (1985), *Wish You Were Here* (1987) and *Shirley Valentine* which share a 'motif of escape', as each film's heroine crosses a threshold into a new more emancipated identity which challenges, to an extent, formations of class as well as gender. Bringing her assessment of the British woman's film up to date, Ashby finds later examples of the genre such as *The Land Girls* (1998), *Morvern Callar* (2002) and *Bend it like Beckham* more diverse in their 'emotional and thematic complexity', and 'politically opaque' rather than overtly feminist; a reflection perhaps of broader changes in contemporary culture, particularly the shift from feminism to postfeminism. Despite the possible dilution of the genre's radicalism, Ashby concludes, the woman's film's 'formal and political elasticity' stands as evidence of its continuing place in a changing commercial and cultural climate. Her discussion of Gurinder Chadha's *Bend it like Beckham* provides a reminder of the significance of the stories of women from ethnic minorities to the formation of the modern British woman's film, with Chadha's light-hearted work complemented by films tackling British Asian experience in a more art-house mode, such as the accomplished adaptation of Monica Ali's best-selling novel, *Brick Lane* (2007), a film which self-consciously references its indebtedness to a tradition of British women's cinema with intertextual mentions of *Brief Encounter*.

All three of Ashby's recent examples of woman's films devote considerable space to the depiction of friendships between women, and this might be seen as a hallmark of the modern British woman's film which often dwells on the intense pleasures and perils of close female friendships, as in *Women Talking Dirty* (1999), *Crush* (2001), *Me Without You* (2001), *Anita and Me* (2002), *My Summer of Love* (2004), *Notes on a Scandal* (2006), and *The Edge of Love* (2008).

Women's friendship is also pivotal to *Calendar Girls* (2003), one of the films discussed by Imelda Whelehan in the collection's concluding chapter. She considers the importance of older women to recent British cinema and how their visibility calls into question some of the assumptions of youth-driven contemporary culture. Films such as *Calendar Girls* and *The Mother* (2003) challenge long-held ideas about the 'social place and function' of the ageing woman, traditionally located in the role of spinster or mother of grown-up children, and considered beyond sexual desirability. In these films, post-menopausal women become objects of desire, their active sexuality partially destabilising the established social order. Whelehan concludes her chapter (and the book) with an upbeat assertion of hope that more 'nuanced and challenging' representations of the ageing women will gradually emerge as popular culture responds to an ageing demographic.

From the vantage point of 2009, it seems that the maxim that C.A. Lejeune coined back in 1926 – 'the kinema must please women or die' (quoted in Lant

Figure 1.3 The pleasures and perils of close female friendship: Imelda Staunton, Andie MacDowell and Anna Chancellor in *Crush*, directed by John McKay (2001).

2006: 1) – has never seemed truer. The enormous blockbuster success of two unabashed woman's films, *Sex and the City: The Movie* and *Mamma Mia!*, during the summer of 2008 has consolidated the renewed importance of the female viewer to contemporary cinema. This phenomenon spans all age groups, ranging from the young girls characterised as 'strong moviegoers' by Clark Woods, president of theatrical distribution at MGM (in comparison with boys the same age who are 'more interested in Xboxes and cable television' than cinema) to older women who 'hadn't got out of the cinema-going habit, had cash flow and plenty of time on their hands', according to producer Nik Powell (both quoted in Solomons 2007). Of course, many of these female cinema-goers will continue to reject the notion of a separate sub-category of film-making aimed only at women (just as Catherine De La Roche and Eleanor Wintour did) but many others will embrace it and derive satisfaction from its specifically feminine address. While the Hollywood 'chick flick' offers its myriad gratifications, the 'Brit chick flick' is also likely to continue its strong showing, providing a variant of the genre which evokes what it is to be female within the particular context of British society. For instance, Gurinder Chadha's *Angus, Thongs and Perfect Snogging* (2008), although part-funded by Paramount and Nickelodeon, locates its story of the eternal tribulations of being a 15-year-old girl within the defiantly British setting of the genteel seaside town of Eastbourne. Chadha is a film-maker who has demonstrated a recurrent interest in the lives of girls and women but she also emphasises how she 'relish[es] telling culturally specific stories about our nation' (quoted in Clarke 2008: 6), indicating how questions of femininity and nationality can overlap in the British woman's film. Other recent films with female directors at the helm have told women's stories of great 'dramatic intensity' within unmistakably British contexts, among them Andrea Arnold's grim Glaswegian *Red Road* (2006) and Joanna Hogg's *Unrelated* (2007) which uses the typical woman's picture manoeuvre of deploying a foreign setting to throw Anglo-Saxon attitudes into relief. The continuing presence of these films and others like them, running the gamut from tortured to tinselly, demonstrates the ongoing cultural currency of feminine narratives in British cinema. Although the woman's film has often been considered a foreign interloper – an 'un-British' genre – it has constituted a significant proportion of British film production and continues to do so. Its contribution to British film culture is considerable and worthy of attention: the cuckoo-in-the-nest may be viewed suspiciously but it is a native species nonetheless.

Notes

1 Although it should be noted that more highbrow women were far from immune to the charms of Granger, with C. A. Lejeune even pronouncing him 'scrumptious' (quoted in Sargeant 2005: 179).

2 Other important non-Gainsborough woman's films of the period elicited a similar imitative response, with one woman confessing that after seeing Ann Todd in *The Seventh Veil* (1945) she 'learnt to play Beethoven's *Pathetique* Sonata and made myself a dirndl skirt from a cretonne curtain' (quoted in Thumim 1992: 167).

Bibliography

Aldgate, A. (1998) 'Loose ends, hidden gems and the moment of "melodramatic emotionality"', in J. Richards (ed.), *The Unknown 1930s: An Alternative History of the British Cinema, 1929–1939*, London: I.B. Tauris.

Aspinall, S. and Murphy, R. (1983) *Gainsborough Melodrama*, London: BFI.

Barr, C. (1998) *Ealing Studios*, Berkeley: University of California Press.

Basinger, J. (1993) *A Woman's View: How Hollywood Spoke to Women, 1930–1960*, New York: Knopf.

Berry, J. and Errigo, A. (2004) *Chick Flicks: Movies Women Love*, London: Orion.

Brunsdon, C. (ed.) (1986) *Films for Women*, London: BFI.

Clarke, C. (2008) 'Thongs in the key of life', *Guardian* (Films and Music), 11 July: 6.

Cook, P. (1996) *Fashioning the Nation: Costume and Identity in British Cinema*, London: BFI.

Cook, S. (2006) *The Rough Guide to Chick Flicks*, London: Rough Guides.

De La Roche, C. (1949) 'The "feminine angle"', *Penguin Film Review*, 8, Harmondsworth: Penguin.

Doane, M. A. (1987a) 'The woman's film: possession and address', in C. Gledhill (ed.), *Home is Where the Heart is: Studies in Melodrama and the Woman's Film*, London: BFI.

——(1987b) *The Desire to Desire: The Woman's Film of the 1940s*, Basingstoke: Macmillan.

Ellis, J. (1996) 'The quality film adventure: British critics and the cinema, 1942–48', in A. Higson (ed.), *Dissolving Views: Key Writings on British Cinema*, London: Cassell.

Geraghty, C. (2000) *British Cinema in the Fifties: Gender, Genre and the 'New Look'*, London: Routledge.

——(2002) 'Crossing over: performing as a lady and a dame', *Screen*, 43.1: 41–56.

Gilbey, R. (2005) *The Ultimate Film*, London: BFI.

Harper, S. (1987) 'Historical pleasures: Gainsborough costume melodrama', in C. Gledhill (ed.), *Home is Where the Heart is: Studies in Melodrama and the Woman's Film*, London: BFI.

——(1994) *Picturing the Past: The Rise and Fall of the British Costume Film*, London: BFI.

Haskell, M. (1974) *From Reverence to Rape: The Treatment of Women in the Movies*, Chicago, IL: University of Chicago Press.

Hiley, N. (1999) '"Let's go to the pictures": the British cinema audience in the 1920s and 1930s', *Journal of Popular British Cinema*, 2: 39–53.

Hinxman, M. (1952) 'Pinewood makes a woman's film', *Picturegoer*, 1 November: 12–13.

Hollinger, K. (2008) 'Afterword: once I got beyond the name *chick flick*', in S. Ferriss and M. Young (eds), *Chick Flicks: Contemporary Women at the Movies*, London: Routledge.

Holtby, W. (1988) *South Riding*, London: Virago.

King, J. (1996) 'Crossing thresholds: the contemporary British woman's film', in A. Higson (ed.), *Dissolving Views: Key Writings on British Cinema*, London: Cassell.

Kuhn, A. (1984) 'Women's genres: melodrama, soap opera and theory', *Screen*, 25.1: 18–28.

Landy, M. (2000) 'The other side of paradise: British cinema from an American perspective', in J. Ashby and A. Higson (eds), *British Cinema, Past and Present*, London: Routledge.

LaPlace, M. (1987) 'Producing and Consuming the Woman's Film: Discursive Struggle in *Now, Voyager*', in C. Gledhill (ed.), *Home is where the heart is: Studies in Melodrama and the Woman's Film*, London: BFI.

Lant, A. (ed.) (2006) *The Red Velvet Seat: Women's Writing on the First Fifty Years of Cinema*, London: Verso.

Modleski, T. (1984) *Loving with a Vengeance: Mass-produced Fantasies for Women*, New York: Methuen.

Mulvey, L. (1989) *Visual and Other Pleasures*, Basingstoke: Macmillan.

Napper, L. (2000) 'British cinema and the middlebrow', in J. Ashby and A. Higson (eds), *British Cinema, Past and Present*, London: Routledge.

Radway, J. (1987) *Reading the Romance*, London: Verso.

Sargeant, A. (2005) *British Cinema: A Critical History*, London: BFI.

Solomons, J. (2007) 'Hollywood's New First Ladies', *Observer* (Review section), 14 January: 12.

Street, S. (2002) *Transatlantic Crossings: British Feature Films in the U.S.A.*, London: Continuum.

Thumim, J. (1992) *Celluloid Sisters: Women and Popular Cinema*, Basingstoke: Macmillan.

Wintour, E. (1955) 'Do women really want this?', *Tribune*, 7 October: no page number (article taken from BFI microfiche on *Summer Madness*).

2 Pictures, romance and luxury

Women and British cinema in the 1910s and 1920s

Nathalie Morris

In 1926, the film critic Iris Barry urged that the 'one thing never to be lost sight of in considering the cinema is that it exists for the purpose of pleasing women. Three out of every four of all cinema audiences are women' (Barry 1926: 59). The importance of the female patron had, in fact, long been recognized by the industry, and from the earliest days of moving pictures women had been courted as audience members. Their attendance at fairground film shows and penny gaffs was thought to confer an element of family respectability on the new entertainment form (although the presence of unmarried women simultaneously gave rise to moral concerns) (Shapiro Sanders 2002; Stamp 2000) and as the cinema negotiated its move upmarket during the 1910s, women were increasingly targeted through the creation of purpose-built venues, the provision of films deemed to have a 'feminine interest', and the emergence of a wealth of associated print media. The first film fan magazines appeared in Britain in 1911 and, as Jane Bryan has argued, these publications addressed a female readership to such an extent that, by the middle of the decade, they had effectively become a 'sub-genre of the woman's magazine' (Bryan 2006: 191).

By 1916 it was estimated that women made up over half of the British cinema-going public (Hiley 1995: 162). While it is difficult to accurately ascertain audience composition during this period, there is little doubt that women did constitute a substantial, and growing, section of the cinema audience by the mid-1910s. Miriam Hansen has pointed out that after the First World War women became 'the primary target of Hollywood's publicity and products' (1991: 18) and as American films began to occupy an increasing percentage of British screens in the post-war period, it can be safely surmised that these films and their stars made up a generous part of the viewing of British women cinema-goers.[1] At the same time, however, domestic producers also recognized and made determined bids for female audiences, often seeking to entice them with products which could be recognized as distinctively British (through their literary, theatrical and historical sources, their filmmaking style, and their use of well-known British actors and/or British settings and location work, for example). This audience was, of course, by no means homogenous. In 1926, Marjorie Williams, a columnist for the trade paper *Kinematograph Weekly*, attempted to outline what she saw as the main groups of women cinema patrons:

a   Mothers of the non-leisured class who are either employed in industrial centres or in bringing up their families.
b   Mothers of the leisured class, infrequent patrons, but by no means negligible in certain centres.
c   Single women of middle age with mother instincts and home loving tendencies, either living on small incomes or employed in domestic occupation.
d   Office girls and those employed in shops, domestic service and other forms of work. These form a large proportion of kinemagoers.
e   Girls and young married women of the leisure class.

(27 May 1926: 30)

Despite the diversity of these groups, Williams nevertheless asserted that on the whole it had 'been possible to arrive at the type of picture that [was] generally approved by women' and a generous proportion of the films made in Britain during the 1910s and 1920s can be conceptualized in terms of the 'woman's picture'. In this chapter I will focus on one group of these, a series of film romances made in the late 1910s and early 1920s by the Stoll Film Company, one of the largest British studios of the time. Like all films labelled as woman's pictures, they would not have appealed to all female cinema patrons. Nevertheless, while not all women's films are romances, the romance can be seen unquestionably to fulfil the criteria of the woman's film. In *A Woman's View: How Hollywood Spoke to Women 1930–1960*, Jeanine Basinger defines the woman's film as one which puts female characters at the centre of the narrative, puts women's problems centre stage and provides a temporary escape from everyday life (1993: 13–14). Likewise, Pamela Regis associates the romance with female liberation and suggests that 'for most of the history of the romance novel … restrictions were placed upon the heroine simply because she was female. The romance novel's focus on the heroine, then, is a focus on women's problems' (2003: 29).

As was the case with a number of British studios of the time, Stoll was a distributor as well as film producer. Furthermore, through the business interests of its founder and chairman, the variety theatre impresario Sir Oswald Stoll, the company was also connected to a small chain of cinemas. Like other exhibitors of the period, Stoll saw the value in attracting female patronage and his London flagship venue, the Stoll Picture Theatre, was regularly promoted as 'Britain's most luxurious cinema' (*Kinematograph Weekly* 5 November 1925: 18). The company also recognized and attempted to exploit the vast readership of film fan magazines such as *The Picturegoer* and *Picture Show*. Throughout the 1920s, it offered supporting parts to aspiring readers, and in 1925, ran a major talent competition with the prize being a leading role in a forthcoming production, *Sahara Love* (1926). The publicity generated by the contest promoted both the new film and the studio's activities more widely, and a film recording the hopeful entrants' auditions, *Starlings of the Screen* (1925), was screened at the Stoll Picture Theatre as a further means of publicity. As one of the earliest British film concerns to move towards vertical integration, the activities and interactions of the Stoll companies offer a particularly interesting insight into the way in which the female audience was conceptualized at all stages of film production, marketing and consumption.

This chapter begins with an overview of some of the films, genres and modes of production from the silent period which can be categorized as women's pictures.[2] This survey is necessarily brief and full of omissions (a study of women and British cinema covering the years to 1930 merits a book in itself) but hopefully conveys something of the richness and variety of production from this period.[3] Stoll's films are then placed within the context of the company's policy of adaptation and the romantic fiction market of the 1910s and 1920s. Some of the pleasures on offer in the texts themselves are considered before I go on to discuss the extra-textual enjoyments offered by post-war cinema-going experience, with particular reference to the London Stoll Picture Theatre.

The British woman's film before 1930

Like their Hollywood counterparts, British feature film producers hoped to interest women cinema-goers with female-centred narratives; the deployment of subjects, genres and themes which were deemed of interest to women; and, to a lesser extent, the use of stars. These included British film and/or theatre stars such as Alma Taylor, Constance Collier, Betty Balfour, Violet Hopson and Madeleine Carroll, but also European and American film stars, such as Pola Negri, Mae Marsh, Dorothy Gish and Anna May Wong. An early example of a narrative with a strong (albeit criminal) female protagonist is the series *The Exploits of Three-Fingered Kate* (1909–12). The eponymous heroine was played by intrepid ex-circus performer Ivy Martinek, and can be seen as a forerunner of the 'serial queens' of popular American titles such as *The Perils of Pauline* (1914) (Marlow Mann 2002; Bryan 2000). Independent and more legitimately employed female characters populated a range of other titles throughout the period, from Squibs (Betty Balfour), the Cockney flower-seller-turned-MP, whose adventures form the basis of a series of four films produced between 1921 and 1923, to Lancashire mill girl Fanny Hawthorn in two versions of *Hindle Wakes* (played by Colette O' Neill in 1918 and Estelle Brody in 1927). The silent film industry supported a large female workforce of writers, editors, actors and, to a lesser extent, producers and directors, and these women commanded varying degrees of agency in determining the on-screen representation of women. At the end of the 1910s, for instance, Violet Hopson set up her own company and produced and starred in a number of dramas including *The Gentleman Rider* (1919) and *When Greek Meets Greek* (1922) in which the heroines prove themselves capable and determined in the workplace (Gledhill 2007).

Traditionally 'feminine' issues regarding love, marriage and the family formed the central basis for innumerable films of the 1910s and 1920s. *Tansy* (1921) and *The Likeness of the Night* (1921) depict love-triangle relationships, while marital and child-bearing problems drive Stoll's *The Fruitful Vine* (1921) as well as *Tesha* (1928) and *The First Born* (1928). *The Woman Who Did* (1915), based on Grant Allen's controversial 1895 novel, tells the story of a 'New Woman' who defies social conventions, and the 'woman with a past', often adapted from literary and/or theatrical sources, featured in a number of films such as *The Second Mrs Tanqueray* (1915); *Lady Windermere's Fan* (1916); *Lady Audley's Secret* (1920); *The Skin Game* (1920); *Easy Virtue* (1928); and the 1920 version of Charles Dickens' *Bleak House*, which was reworked by screenwriter William J. Elliott to focus solely on the story of Lady Deadlock (Constance Collier). Many of these films, as Amy Sargeant has suggested, explore the 'moral judgements of one generation upon another and [the] different moral code prevailing between men and women' (2005: 33). The pleasures of the transformation or makeover narrative feature in films such as *The Vagabond Queen* (1929), in which Betty Balfour plays both a Princess and her Cockney double, and several of the 'heritage' films and biopics of the period can additionally qualify as women's pictures. Cecil Hepworth's 1923 version of *Comin' Thro' the Rye* (based on Helen Mathers' 1875 novel), for instance, is a romantic Victorian-set period drama; while a number of costume films focus on well-known historical figures, including *Sixty Years a Queen* (Queen Victoria) (1913), *The Loves of Mary Queen of Scots* (1923), *Nell Gwynne* (1926), *Madame Pompadour* (1927) and Stoll's *Boadicea* (1926).

As a final coda, it is also worth noting that pictures for women were not limited to fiction films. There was also an important strand of non-fiction entertainment for women in cine-magazines such as *Eve's Film Review* (1921– 33) which were screened as part of mixed programmes throughout the 1910s and 1920s. As the name of *Eve's Film Review* suggests, many of these short, weekly productions were largely directed towards female audiences. They regularly featured the obligatory fashion and beauty items and practical household advice, but also, as Jenny Hammerton has shown, a range of stories and reports which focused on women's lives and work, 'document[ing] them … with a didactic seriousness' (2002: 169).

While I have limited my examples to the years preceding 1930, this is not to suggest that the silent and sound eras should necessarily be considered as two separate periods. There is a great deal of continuity between the filmmaking practices established during the 1910s and 1920s and those that followed in the 1930s, 1940s and beyond. *The Skin Game* (1931), *Hindle Wakes* (1931) and *Squibs* (1935) were all re-made (or re-adapted from their original sources) in later years, while the historical biopic formed the basis of several Herbert Wilcox/Anna Neagle collaborations in the 1930s, including *Nell Gwyn* (1934), *Victoria the Great* (1937) and *Sixty Glorious Years* (1938), and has remained a significant genre up to the present day with *Elizabeth: The Golden Age* (2007) serving as a recent cinematic example.

Stoll, adaptation and the 'feminine interest'

As many of the titles cited above demonstrate, literary and theatrical adaptations made up an important part of British film production, and of British films which hoped to appeal to women. It was felt by many producers that the adaptation of proven successes was the most effective way of guaranteeing audiences and the Stoll Film Company was the most radical proponent of this belief: the company produced well over 100 features between 1918 and its demise in 1928 and virtually all of these are literary adaptations. In 1920 Stoll launched its 'Eminent British Authors' series, an ongoing programme of films based on the works of contemporary (or near contemporary) bestselling writers including H. G. Wells, Sir Arthur Conan Doyle, Edgar Wallace – and, more significantly for the purpose of this chapter, Ethel M. Dell. Although Stoll occasionally attempted to promote its actors as stars, during the early 1920s it was generally the Eminent Authors who served as the company's stars (Burrows 2001: 22; Gifford 1997: 117). As the title of the series indicates, Stoll also sought to promote these films as a distinctively British product, believing that the deployment of indigenous writers and stories, as well as British settings, would assist its attempts to compete with the steadily increasing volume of Hollywood imports.

British cinema's reliance on literary adaptation has often been viewed negatively. A range of contemporary voices including critics and screenwriters championed the concept of the original film story in the post-war years, and since then, the influential historian Rachael Low has forcefully conveyed a sense of Stoll's strategy being a woefully misguided one. She sees its adaptations as unimaginative and uninspiring, and criticizes the company for assuming that 'the size of a popular novel's public … would ensure the success of a film' (Low 1971: 124). However, as Lawrence Napper (2008) and Alexis Weedon (1999) have demonstrated, there was undoubtedly a large crossover between the novel-reading and cinema-going populations before and during the interwar years. As the contemporary bestselling novel became an increasingly important commodity for filmmakers, popular fiction aimed at women – and in particular the romance novel – made up a significant part of this. The British author E. M. Hull's controversial desert romance of 1919, *The Sheik*, for example, was a phenomenal success, spawning the 1921 Hollywood film with Rudolph Valentino in the title role (Mellman 1988: 46). Later in the decade, the biggest British film of 1928 was Gainsborough's *The Constant Nymph*, adapted from Margaret Kennedy's bestselling novel (1924) and successful stage-play (1926) and starring Mabel Poulton and matinee idol Ivor Novello.

The genealogy of the English romance novel can be traced back via the Brontës and Jane Austen to Samuel Richardson's *Pamela* (1740) (Regis 2003: xiii and *passim*) but by the beginning of the 1910s changes in society and developments in the publishing industry had opened up a new and large market for the mass-produced popular romance. Upon its publication in 1907, Elinor Glyn's *Three Weeks* was a massive, albeit scandalous, success, and in its tale of an illicit and passionate love affair, set the tone for much romantic fiction published during and after the First World War. Regis suggests that a new type of romantic heroine, with a greater level of autonomy, became the norm at this time and that a greater emphasis was placed on the emotional, rather than societal, dimensions of courtship (2003: 109–11). Another feature of much of the romantic fiction of the period was a greater eroticism and concern with female desire (Light 1991: 175) and by 1920, as the sales of Glyn's and Hull's novels testify, there was an enormous market for literature of this type.

Ethel M. Dell: queen of romance

Stoll anticipated that the adaptation of similarly popular authors would enable it to tap into the vast, and growing, population of British romance readers. In an article entitled 'The Feminine Interest', Stoll's publicist, Pearkes Withers, argued for the commercial benefits of producing 'the sort of film story that appeals to women and girls by the thousand', suggesting that it 'is exactly the sort of film the exhibitor likes and wants ... it is the sort that fills his [sic] picture-palace and his cash-box' (1920: 15). As an example of this type of story Withers cited the works of the novelist Ethel M. Dell. In her survey of the interwar women's novel, Nicola Beauman describes Dell as 'a pleasure giver pure and simple', and although Dell is largely forgotten now, she was one of the most popular British writers of the 1910s and 20s (Beauman 1983: 183). Her first novel was published in 1911 and by the end of the First World War she had written enough bestselling books to become one of the wealthiest writers in Britain (Bloom 2002: 134). These sold in their tens and even hundreds of thousands, and far from declining, her popularity continued to grow in the post-war period.[4] Dell was to become Stoll's most regularly adapted author: between 1919 and 1924, 18 films based on her works were made. The company's writers and directors were careful to discuss each of these with her and nothing was done without her agreement (Gifford: 1997: 119).

Dell's works are characterized by their spirited and petulant heroines, alpha male heroes, love-triangle plotlines, exotic settings and streaks of sado-masochistic violence. Given the wide critical disparagement of the romance genre, both then and now, it is perhaps unsurprising that Dell's popularity with readers was not matched by critical acclaim. If popular culture has historically been criticized as harmful, popular texts aimed at women (whether they be novels, films or television programmes) have generally been further consigned to the bottom of this cultural hierarchy (Stacey 1994: 90; Modleski 1982: 13). As romantic fiction boomed in the post-war period, it increasingly became the focus of negative cultural discourse. Alison Light has highlighted the way in which 'for many critics of the new forms of mass entertainment, it was romance which provided the model of all that was meretricious about the popular cultural forms of modernity' (1991: 160). It was thought to insidiously infuse its passive readers with dangerous and transgressive desires,[5] and the attention that writers such as Dell, Glyn and Hull paid to female sexuality, and their depictions of sexual violence, led to them being widely described as pornographers (Mellman 1988: 45). Theatre critic St John Ervine felt that Dell's books were 'bad for people's minds' (the *Observer* 28 May 1922: 15) while for Rebecca West, it was literary rather than moral sensibilities that were piqued (1928: 323). George Orwell too was critical of Dell and her readers, and later expressed a rather misogynistic surprise that her readership was made up of 'women of all kinds and ages' and not, 'as one might expect, merely … wistful spinsters and the fat wives of tobacconists' ([1936] 1968: 244).

The inclusion of Dell within Stoll's pantheon of 'Eminent Authors' has led film historian Kenton Bamford to 'question [the company's] interpretation of eminence', describing her work as 'devastatingly silly' and characterized by 'a wearisome litany of middle-class prejudices' (1999: 74). Bamford takes his cue from contemporary reviews, which display a similar hostility towards popular romantic fiction and its (female) readers. Reviewing the Ruritanian tale of revolution and romance, *A Question of Trust* (1920), *Kinematograph Weekly* expressed an aversion towards 'authors who write for the cheapest public', and saw the film as one of a 'fairly common type … which serve[s] chiefly to demonstrate the utter unreality and impossibility of much modern fiction' (26 August 1920: 106). The paper complained that *The Woman of His Dream* (1921), which tells the story of a woman who fakes her death to escape a brutal and drunken husband, was 'rather back-boneless and insipid, and the only people to whom it will make an appeal is to those to whom Ethel M. Dell is the literary master of the century – there are apparently many such' (28 July 1921: 31).

Hostility towards women's pictures, combined with a long-standing (although now changing) disparagement of much commercial British feature production of the 1910s and 1920s, led to a widespread dismissal of these films. More recently, while the woman's film remains a highly contested genre, much has been done to re-evaluate certain forms of popular culture aimed at women. In her work on the British costume film, Sue Harper has suggested that Gainsborough's 1940s historical dramas attracted critical hostility precisely because they sought to attract working-class women (Harper 1994: 122). Like a number of other studies which have explored the role of romance, fantasy and escapism, and which have challenged the notion of the passive consumer (Radway 1991; Pearce and Stacey 1995; Regis 2003), Harper argues that popular fictions frequently demand active and creative engagement on the part of audiences. She demonstrates that the fantasy world created in Gainsborough's bodice-rippers could address female desires and offer viewers a powerful 'means of imaginative liberation' (145, 188). The escapist impulse of the romance novel too has long been recognized as an important part of its appeal. For Tania Modleski, although these fictions may 'reinforce conservative notions of women's place', they can still have a use-value for readers and speak 'meaningfully to women's fears, desires and hopes' (1998: 56). The traditional happy ending of the romance (the heterosexual union) has often been seen as rendering the genre inherently conservative. However, it has also been argued that the action of the narrative and the agency of the heroine are the most important and memorable aspects of these stories. As Regis suggests, the romance is read (or watched) as much for its process, as for its conclusion (2003: 13).

The new breed of twentieth-century heroines portrayed by Dell's novels and Stoll's films have control over their lives and actively seek adventure, romance and personal fulfilment. In Stoll's version of *The Tidal Wave* (1920), for instance, Columbine (Poppy Wyndham), escapes from an impoverished life in the urban slums and goes to live with her aunt and uncle in a Cornish fishing village. She initially resists their wish that she will marry her fisherman cousin Rufus (Sydney Seaward) and, like Alice (Anny Ondra) in Hitchcock's *Blackmail* (1929), seeks a more exciting bohemian alternative in the shape of the aristocratic painter Knight (Pardoe Woodman), who has come to Cornwall in search of inspiration. Knight finds this in Columbine and it is only after he has been revealed as a serial womanizer and has endangered her life in his pursuit of his artistic vision (to paint her standing on the rocks by a tumultuous sea), that Rufus' heroism and powerful masculinity (in contrast to the dandified artist) finally win Columbine over. The notion that Columbine strives to control her own future is further played up by one of Stoll's suggested taglines for the film: '[h]er quest carried her from the slums to the ocean's rim' (*Stoll's Editorial News* 25 August 1921: ii). For Kathleen Mason, writer of 'Through a Woman's Eyes', a regular *Kinematograph Weekly* column throughout 1921, female agency was an essential part of a film's appeal for women cinema-goers. Mason felt that female viewers would enjoy the characterization of Naomi Coningsby (Mary Dibley), heroine of *The Woman of His Dream*, who was 'the prototype of all high-spirited, freedom-loving women' (28 July 1921: 28) but not Dinah Bathurst (Madge Stuart), the put-upon lead of *Greatheart* (1921): 'men might be attracted by her timid shrinking, women never' (16 July 1921: 38).

Further, and more intrepid, questing heroines feature in *The Prey of the Dragon* and *The Lamp in the Desert* (both 1921). In both films, the protagonists journey overseas to marry or to find a partner. This was a familiar trope of the post-war romance and can be linked to discourses regarding the emigration of single women to the colonies or Dominions where, it was (erroneously) suggested, marriageable males were more plentiful than in Britain (so plentiful, in fact, that *The Lamp in the Desert*'s Stella ends up committing bigamy). Britain's male population had been seriously affected by the First World War, and the question of 'surplus' or 'superfluous' women pervaded the popular press throughout the decade. One *Daily Mail* headline announced: 'A Million Women Too Many, 1920 Husband Hunt' (5 February 1920: np) and after the census of 1921, which revealed that within England and Wales there were 19,803,222 females compared to 18,082,220 males (Nicholson 2007: 22) the issue inspired even greater coverage. While the hysterical press response reveals a strongly misogynistic strain underlying post-war society, a large part of the female population did nevertheless find that the expectations of love and marriage that they had been brought up with were now seriously undermined.[6]

Billie Mellman suggests that the post-war 'romance solved this problem by reversing the balance between the sexes' (1988: 21). Virtually all of Stoll's Dell adaptations feature two or more men in competition for the heroine, who is then forced to choose between them. While Columbine of *The Tidal Wave* has to decide between Knight and Rufus, Maud (Mary Glynne) in *The Hundredth Chance* (book 1917; film 1920) must choose between the dissolute Lord Saltash and honest horse-trainer Jack (Sydney Seaward); and in *The Experiment* (1922),

Figure 2.1 Selling Cornish romance: advertising images for Stoll's *The Tidal Wave*,
      directed by Sinclair Hill (1920).
Source: Author's private collection.

Doris (Evelyn Brent) is engaged to Vivian (Clive Brook) but plans an elopement
with the louche Major Brandon (Templer Powell). Such stories indulge in a fantasy
world in which men are abundant, women are scarce and desirable, and the female
protagonist actively and successfully acquires a suitable romantic partner.

   It is not only women's perceived romantic desires which are addressed by Stoll's
films. Although Kenton Bamford complains of the films' 'weary litany of middle-
class prejudices' and suggests this alienated working-class (and presumably
lower middle-class) audiences, the social settings of Stoll's films can also be seen
to address other needs and provide other pleasures. Nicola Beauman argues that

romantic heroines were often 'one rung up the social ladder' from their readers and posits that this was not for reasons of snobbery but 'part of a pattern of wish fulfilment, the assumption being that [readers] would prefer to be a little better off, a little better connected than they in fact [were]' (1983: 195). Stoll's films enable similar escapist pleasures. Like many other British films of this period and beyond, they display a fascination with the aristocracy (albeit one often characterized by ambivalence) and rather than discourage audiences, I would suggest that the settings and characters of these stories provided some of their appeal. This is supported by the results of a survey conducted by the exhibitor Sidney Bernstein in 1927, which revealed that of the women questioned, the most popular type of film was the society drama (*The Bioscope* 4 August 1927: 20).

The settings of the films additionally provide visual pleasure through their location work and mise-en-scène. In her column, Kathleen Mason argued that romance in its widest sense provided much of the appeal of the cinema:

> The greatest craving in the heart of a woman is for Romance, for the glamour and tinsel of life, with shaded lights, jewels and beautiful clothes. The drab, uninteresting life which most women are forced to lead … has not killed this emotion: it has merely dammed it up.
>
> (*Kinematograph Weekly* 24 February 1921: 94)

The social standing of many of Stoll's heroines allowed for an impressive array of fashionable attire to be put on display, while the upper-class social milieu of films such as *The Experiment* and *The Knight Errant* (both 1922) gave the company's art directors the opportunity to create lavishly furnished interiors. A number of the films were shot on location in beautiful country houses, giving scope for both extravagant garden parties and secluded romantic encounters, as in *The Rocks of Valpré* (1919). *The Tidal Wave* is an exception to this, but the picturesque Cornish/Devonshire coastal setting renders it suitably magical and desirable (see Rachel Moseley's chapter for more on the imaginative properties of the West Country). Foreign settings also provide exotic spectacle and often play an important part in creating the fantasy world of the romance. While Stoll's budgets precluded the company from funding filmmaking trips to far-flung locations such as India, Africa or Australia, Dell stories set in continental Europe often enabled imaginative and very beautiful locations to be used. For *Greatheart* (1921), director George Ridgwell took his cast and crew to the French Alps; while much of *A Question of Trust* and *The Hundredth Chance* (both 1920) were filmed on location in the south of France.

'I never thought it was possible for a picture theatre to be so luxurious and comfortable': women patrons and the Stoll Picture Theatre

The pleasures offered to female spectators were not limited to the films themselves. Janice Radway (1991) emphasizes the importance of the act of romance reading and suggests that, for some readers, this can be just as (if not more) important than the texts themselves. The same can be said for cinema-going, perhaps particularly during this period of mixed programmes when the main feature was less of a central focus than in later years. Although, as I have shown, many films were made with a female audience in mind, it is also necessary to consider the ways in which the cinema-going experience was about more than just the film on the screen. A trip to the cinema was often seen as an institutionalized afternoon or evening out, independent of the artistic merits of the entertainment (Low 1948: 107–8) and during the 1920s, as Robert C. Allen argues, 'many viewers were not particularly interested in what feature film was playing, they were attracted to the theatre by the theatre itself' (1990: 352).[7] In an environment in which women made up the majority of audiences (and would additionally bring along their boyfriends, husbands and families) it was to women that these venues predominantly sought to appeal.

Jeanne Allen suggests that this appeal was established through interior decoration and lighting 'designed to appeal to women's tastes and to their desire for comfort and relaxation' (1980: 486). For the critic C. A. Lejeune, 'the small cushioned seats' of the cinema were 'women's seats' and '[t]he warmth in the winter, the coolness in summer, the darkness, the sleepy music, the chance to relax unseen [were] all women's pleasures which no man, however tired he may be, [could] ever quite appreciate or understand' (*Manchester Guardian* 16 January 1926: 9). A large number of theatres also sought to provide amenities for women patrons, such as tearooms, cloakrooms for coats, hats, parcels and shopping bags, crèches and even powder-rooms with complimentary beauty products (*Kinematograph Weekly* 26 July 1928: 44–3; Hammerton 2001: 12).[8] The Stoll Picture Theatre, for instance, prided itself on the fact that the facilities it provided meant that a woman could pleasantly spend a whole day there (*Kinematograph Weekly* 17 September 1925: 108). Furthermore, the venue itself was elegant (as can be seen in Figure. 2.2) and beautifully decorated. One article in the *Kinematograph Weekly* rapturously described the delicate colour scheme of its tearooms (pale cream, deep rose and gold), its flattering lighting and attractive Wedgwood tea service, all of which 'stir[red] the mind into new bypaths of beauty' (3 September 1925: 85). It was thought that the comforts and luxuries of the theatre could go some way towards addressing some of the deficiencies of everyday reality. As publicity for the cinema stated: 'The desire for beauty exists in every human mind although, through the economic conditions of modern life, it is often impossible to satisfy it at home [and it] must, therefore, be sought elsewhere' (*Kinematograph Weekly* 3 September 1925: 85). A letter from a patron suggests that the venue was successful in this respect: 'I cannot explain how delighted I was', the visitor wrote. 'I never thought it was possible for a picture theatre to be so luxurious and comfortable' (*Stoll Herald* 15 January 1923: 7).[9]

Like most cinemas, the Stoll Picture Theatre appears to have targeted the sort of cross-class customer base described by Marjorie Williams earlier in this chapter. Cinema seats and refreshments were available at a range of prices, and

Figure 2.2 New bypaths of beauty: The Stoll Picture Theatre, June 1925
Source: Reproduced by permission of English Heritage, National Monuments Record.

its location in Holborn had the potential to attract both working women and urban shoppers.[10] The association of the cinema with (female) consumerism has often been noted. Then, as now, cinemas were built in shopping areas, and, as Shelley Stamp has highlighted, attempts were made to 'integrat[e] cinema into women's daytime patterns of shopping and visiting' (2000: 17). Cinema managers promoted the restorative qualities of a trip to their theatres, offering teas and luncheons alongside matinee screenings in bids to tempt female shoppers. The Stoll Picture Theatre also directed publicity towards these women, suggesting that 'after shopping a lady can have lunch', go to the pictures and then 'have the 1s 6d theatre tea, or meet her husband and have ... dinner' in the cinema restaurant (*Kinematograph Weekly* 17 September 1925: 108). Its success in tapping into a market of weary female shoppers is revealed in a letter from another cinema-goer who simply signed herself 'Feminine':

> I saw a note in your *Stoll Herald* which indicated that I could get a lunch at the theatre as soon as the programme begins. I was tired out with shopping, disinclined to go home but hungry. I tried the experiment and chose a table where it was possible to see the screen. I enjoyed my meal and saw the commencement of the programme at the same time. You have certainly gained one constant matinee patron through this policy.
>
> (*Stoll Herald* 3 September 1923: 7)

Conclusion

During the 1910s and 1920s, women became established as the most important section of the cinema-going public. As my case study of the Stoll Film Company and Picture Theatre shows, the necessity of appealing to female patrons was recognized by producers and exhibitors alike. While the romance film was only one of the ways in which filmmakers attempted to attract women, and would not necessarily appeal to all, it nevertheless contains several of the characteristics that would come to define the woman's film, most notably a focus on an active female protagonist and a temporary escape from, or reworking of, some of the problems of women's everyday lives. Furthermore, Stoll's romance films can be viewed as part of a determined attempt to appeal to female audiences with productions that were distinctively British. Made and promoted as part of the Eminent *British* Authors series, the films not only drew on the long lineage of the English romance novel but also often utilized aspects of British heritage thought to contain popular appeal, most notably country house settings and picturesque rural and coastal landscapes.

The actual success of Stoll's production programme is difficult to gauge but its long-standing pursuit of literary adaptation, and in particular of Ethel M. Dell romance novels, suggests that the company continued to believe in the value of this policy. Stoll produced films with a strong female interest until its demise in 1928. It was by no means alone in targeting female audiences and although the woman's picture is more traditionally associated with both Hollywood, and a later time period (the 1930s to the 1960s), it is clear that the concept of the woman's film was one which was already well established in Britain by the 1920s.

Notes

1 Eighty-seven out of 118 films shown in Britain in 1918 were American (73.1 per cent) (Thompson 1985: 215). The predominance of Hollywood films and stars within the British market is backed up by a survey of film fan magazines at this time, although, it should be noted, this was not to the exclusion of British ones.
2 For further examples see K. Newey (2000: 151).
3 For an excellent and wide-ranging survey of British production of the 1910s and 1920s see the relevant chapters of A. Sargeant (2005).

4 Dell's novels were published in increasingly large print runs. Her 1916 novel, *Bars of Iron* had a 6s first edition of 40,000 copies, for example, and *The Lamp in the Desert* (1919), a 6s 9d first edition of 60,000. *The Times*, 29 February 1916: 4; and 27 June 1919: 15.

5 In 1932 Q. D. Leavis posited that 'a habit of fantasising will lead to maladjustment in actual life' ([1932] 1965: 54).

6 See the numerous post-war discourses reprinted, and personal testimonies recorded by Nicholson (2007).

7 Indeed, many visitors to cinemas did not see the films at all and merely availed themselves of their tearoom facilities. *Kinematograph Weekly* 17 September 1925: 108; Nicholson 2007: 115.

8 For the American context see also Stamp (2000: 17).

9 The *Herald* was the Stoll Picture Theatre's magazine-style house organ.

10 It should be acknowledged that the Stoll Picture Theatre also appears to have attracted a sizeable male audience, a fact attributed to the cinema's location amid the offices of central London. 'Mr and Mrs Picturegoer at the Stoll Opera House', *The Picturegoer*, reprinted in *Stoll's Editorial News*, 29 December 1921: 3–4.

Bibliography

Allen, J. (1980) 'The film viewer as consumer', *Quarterly Review of Film Studies*, 5.4: 481–99.

Allen, R. C. (1990) 'From exhibition to reception: reflections on the audience in film history', *Screen*, 31.4, Winter: 347–56.

Bamford, K. (1999) *Distorted Images: British National Identity and Film in the 1920s*, London: I. B. Tauris.

Barry, I. (1926) *Let's Go to the Pictures*, London: Chatto and Windus.

Basinger, J. (1993) *A Woman's View: How Hollywood Spoke to Women 1930–1960*, Hanover, PA: Wesleyan University Press.

Beauman, N. (1983) *A Very Great Profession: The Woman's Novel 1914–1939*, London: Virago.

Bloom, C. (2002) *Bestsellers: Popular Fiction Since 1900*, Basingstoke: Palgrave Macmillan.

Bryan, J. (2000) 'The Exploitation of Elaine: the serial queen melodrama and the American girl', unpublished MA thesis, University of East Anglia.

——(2006) 'The cinema looking glass: the film fan magazine 1911–18', unpublished thesis, University of East Anglia.

Burrows, J. (2001) 'Big studio production in the pre-quota years', in R. Murphy (ed.), *The British Cinema Book*, 2nd edn, London: BFI.

Gifford, D. (1997) 'The early memories of Maurice Elvey', *Griffithiana*, 60/61: 76–125.

Gledhill, C. (2007) 'Reframing women in 1920s British cinema: the case of Violet Hopson and Dinah Shurey', *The Journal of British Cinema and Television* 4.1: 1–17.

Hammerton, J. (2001) *For Ladies Only? Eve's Film Review: Pathe Cinemagazine 1921–33*, Hastings: The Projection Box.

——(2002) 'The spice of the perfect programme: the weekly magazine film during the silent period', in A. Higson (ed.), *Young and Innocent? The Cinema in Britain 1896–1930*, Exeter: University of Exeter Press.

Hansen, M. (1991) *Babel and Babylon: Spectatorship in American Silent Film*, Cambridge, MA: Harvard University Press.

Harper, S. (1994) *Picturing the Past: The Rise and Fall of the British Costume Film*, London: BFI.

Hiley, N. (1995) 'The British cinema auditorium', in K. Dibbet and B. Hogenkamp (eds), *Film and the First World War*, Amsterdam: University of Amsterdam Press.

Leavis, Q. D. [1932] (1965) *Fiction and the Reading Public*, London: Chatto and Windus.

Light, A. (1991) *Forever England: Femininity, Literature and Conservatism Between the Wars*, London: Routledge.

Low, R. (1948) 'The implications behind the social survey', in R. Manvell (ed.), *The Penguin Film Review 7*, London: Penguin.

——(1971) *The History of the British Film 1918–1929*, London: Allen and Unwin.

Marlow Mann, A. (2002) 'British series and serials in the silent era', in A. Higson (ed.), *Young and Innocent? The Cinema in Britain 1896–1930*, Exeter: University of Exeter Press.

Mellman, B. (1988) *Women and the Popular Imagination in the Nineteen Twenties: Flapper and Nymphs*, Basingstoke: Macmillan.

Modleski, T. (1982) *Loving with a Vengeance: Mass Produced Fantasies for Women*, London: Routledge.

——(1998) 'My Life as a Romance Reader', *Old Wives Tales: Feminist Revisions of Film and Other Fictions*, London: I. B. Tauris.

Napper, L. (2008) *British Cinema and the Middlebrow in the Interwar Years*, Exeter: University of Exeter Press.

Newey, K. (2000) 'Women and early British film: finding a screen of her own', in L. Fitzsimmons and S. Street (eds), *Moving Performance: British Stage and Screen 1890s–1920s*, Trowbridge: Flicks Books.

Nicholson, V. (2007) *Singled Out: How Two Million Women Survived Without Men after the First World War*, London: Viking.

Orwell, G. [1936] (1968) 'Book shop memories', *The Collected Essays, Journalism and Letters Vol. I*, London: Secker & Warburg.

Pearce, L. and Stacey, J. (eds) (1995) *Romance Revisited*, London: Lawrence and Wishart.

Radway, J. (1991) *Reading the Romance*, 2nd edn, London: University of North Carolina Press.

Regis, P. (2003) *A Natural History of the Romance Novel*, Philadelphia: University of Pennsylvania Press.

Sargeant, A. (2005) *British Cinema: A Critical History*, London: BFI.

Shapiro Sanders, L. (2002) 'Indecent incentives to vice: regulating films and audience behaviour from the 1890s to the 1910s', in A. Higson (ed.), *Young and Innocent? The Cinema in Britain 1896–1930*, Exeter: University of Exeter Press.

Stacey, J. (1994) *Stargazing: Hollywood Cinema and Female Spectatorship*, London: Routledge.

Stamp, S. (2000) *Movie Struck Girls: Women and Motion Picture Culture after the Nickelodeon*, Princeton, NJ: Princeton University Press.

Thompson, K. (1985) *Exporting Entertainment: America in the World Film Market 1907–1934*, London: BFI.

Weedon, A. (1999) 'From three-deckers to film rights: a turn in British publishing strategies, 1870–1930', *Book History*, 2.1: 188–206.

West, R. (1928) 'The Tosh Horse', *The Strange Necessity: Essays and Reviews*, London: Jonathan Cape.

Withers, P. (1920) 'The Feminine Interest', *Stoll's Editorial News*, 16 September: 15–16.

3 'Twenty million people can't be wrong'
Anna Neagle and popular British stardom

Josephine Dolan and Sarah Street

On 22 July 1969, British film star Anna Neagle was invested as Dame Commander of the British Empire. This occasion marks an institutionalised recognition of the outstanding commercial success and popular acclaim that she enjoyed from the 1930s through to the mid-1950s. Her box-office appeal is registered in the BFI Ultimate Chart in which four Neagle productions appear in the top fifty: *Spring in Park Lane* (1948; 20.5 million admissions) at no. 5, *The Courtneys of Curzon Street* (1947; 15.9 million) at no. 17; *Piccadilly Incident* (1946; 11.5 million) at no. 42 and *I Live in Grosvenor Square* (1945; 10.3 million) at no. 49. This prominent chart position translates into numerous awards received by Neagle, the most notable being the Gold Cup at the Venice Film Festival for *Victoria the Great* (1937). Between the years 1948 and 1951 the exhibitors' journal, *Motion Picture Herald*, acclaimed her as top International Box Office Star and best British Box-Office Star in 1941, 1947 and 1952. In 1938, 1947, 1948, 1949 and 1951, a poll of *Picturegoer* readers awarded the Gold Medal for best picture respectively to *Victoria the Great*, *Piccadilly Incident*, *The Courtneys of Curzon Street*, *Spring in Park Lane* and *Odette* (1950).[1] The latter two films also won the *Daily Mail* National Film Awards while *Odette* was also singled out for the *Kinematograph Weekly*'s Josh Billings Award for individual acting. Neagle's final 'trade' accolade arrived in 1966 in the guise of a Variety Club Special Award. Loved by millions Neagle is now recognised as 'possibly the most successful cinema actress in British film history'.[2]

It is not coincidental to Neagle's unrivalled popular appeal that she deftly moved across a blend of genres that fully exploited British audience constituencies at key junctures in the turbulent decades of pre to post World War Two. Direct appeal was made to women audiences through musical and romantic comedies whose distinctly British formulations of costume and mise en scène offered feminine plenitudinal pleasures in the specific deprivations of inter to post-war contexts. These British variants of the woman's film were punctuated by biopics of national heroines as diverse as Queen Victoria and Odette Churchill and ensured that Neagle's acclaim was broadly inclusive in its gender appeal.

Throughout her career, Neagle's box office success was generally matched by widespread critical acclaim for her performances, even when the films themselves were considered to leave much to be desired. For instance, a review of

Piccadilly Incident in *The Times* suggests that 'not even some pretty acting by Miss Anna Neagle and Mr. Michael Wilding can make *Piccadilly Incident* anything but a disappointing British Film' (26 September 1946: np). Similarly, *Yellow Canary* (1943) spurred the reviewer of the trade journal *Kinematograph Weekly* to praise Neagle's dignified acting while describing the film as 'hearty, nay thrilling, hokum' (21 October 1943: 29). Despite this outstanding commercial and critical reputation, Neagle had, until recently, largely slipped from public memory.

Generally, this decline is attributed to changing audience tastes (Street 1997: 134), but clearly, this should not be taken at face value. Account must be taken of cinematic technologies at an intersection with Hollywood hegemony and the production of film canons. Prior to the introduction of video and DVD technologies that now underpin popular cinematic memory, film screenings were reliant on the provision of public spaces and technologies. In Britain, US controlled screening circuits have privileged Hollywood products to the detriment of indigenous material and have effectively elided market dominance with aesthetic superiority. And with the advent of home entertainment technologies and the related availability and distribution of back catalogues, Hollywood hegemony has largely prevailed. Hollywood films are positioned as the 'classics' in want of recuperation from technology-bound obscurity, while British films are frequently neglected as having no aesthetic or popular value. Consequently, it is only relatively recently that British films from back catalogues have been inserted into the home entertainment market in any significant numbers. This has impacted on the public memory of great British stars such as Neagle who have largely been forgotten, except by specialist academics and fans. Consequently Neagle's prominent position in the BFI charts came as something of a shock to many cinephiles. However, following the 'surprise' revelation of Neagle's prominence, the release of a DVD box set by Studio Canal in 2008 indicates that the public recuperation of Neagle is finally underway.

But it is highly unlikely that Neagle will generate the kind of popular appeal with current audiences that she enjoyed with her contemporaries since she was schooled in a style of acting that is nowadays perceived to be risibly wooden. Sue Harper observes that:

> We cannot ascribe the variety of Neagle's roles to her acting ability, since on the technical level they are all the same. The same mannerisms inhabit them all: the infrequent blink rate, the measured inflected tones. Neagle's movements are curiously uncoordinated: they are like building blocks wedged together without cement.
>
> (2000: 149)

Harper attributes this curious consistency to the domineering control of Herbert Wilcox, who directed her in twenty-nine starring roles and who she married in 1943. The singularity of this direction undoubtedly impacted on Neagle's performance regardless of fashions in acting style. Despite the catalogue of accolades noted above, as early as 1951 cracks were appearing in critical assessments of Neagle. Yet, equally, there was a perplexed recognition that millions of people can't be wrong. Leonard Wallace of *Picturegoer* encapsulates this tension: 'There are better actresses than she; there are more devastating personalities; but there is no one else who can touch the hearts of the ordinary cinemagoer as she can' (quoted in Coulson 1967: 149). So what is it about Neagle? How did she touch the hearts of millions? This chapter will probe deeper into the creation of Neagle's popular image, with particular focus on how the technological changes introduced by sound cinema and the introduction of colour helped to bolster her reputation for representing quintessential English femininity.

Establishing the Neagle image

A former chorus girl with W. B. Cochrane's 'Young Ladies', Neagle made the transition into film with a minor role in Maurice Elvey's *The School for Scandal* (1930). By 1932, following bit parts in two other productions, Neagle had been taken up by Wilcox, an independent director/producer whose consistent direction established Neagle's reputation as an actress who could rise to the challenges presented by dramatic bio-pics such as *Victoria the Great* and *Odette* as much as fluffy, romantic comedies exemplified by the 'Mayfair' cycle. Certainly, this rise to fame exemplifies the ordinary/extraordinary paradox that Dyer (1979: 50) suggests underpins stardom. At one and the same time, stars are typical – just like you and me – and therefore we can all aspire to success. Yet, stars have some special quality that sets them apart. There is little doubt that this paradox was fully exploited by Wilcox, who was the driving force behind the production of Neagle's star image: an image which eventually coalesced as quintessential English femininity (Dolan 1996: 72–86; Harper 2000: 54–56; Street 1997: 124–34).

    Yet, during the earlier stages of Neagle's rise to stardom there were few indications that she would eventually take on the mantle of English respectability. Indeed, an almost transparent dress designed by Dorothy Zinkeisen for *The Little Damozel* (1933) that was subsequently employed in highly sexualised publicity stills and public appearances had quite the opposite effect (Neagle 1974: 72). A year later, similar exploitation of the sexualised female body and performance shaped Neagle's first major success as the eponymous *Nell Gwyn* (1934) (Harper 2000: 17). Despite generating a huge controversy on its American release that damaged the economic return of the film (Street 2002: 71–4), the bawdy bio-pic formula was repeated a year later in *Peg of Old Drury* (1935). Thus the emergent star image was infused with an explicit sexual allure. This allure resonated with residual Victorian ideologies that linked the figure of the actress with that of the prostitute. While there is little doubt that some Victorian actresses did supplement meagre theatre incomes with sexual labour, Davis (1991:100) foregrounds how the elision was largely metaphorical since it hinged on deep-seated assumptions that women occupying public spaces were sexually available and that 'the actress and the prostitute were both objects of desire whose company was purchased through commercial exchange'. Even though the DBEs conferred in 1921 and 1925 to the actresses Geneviève Ward and Ellen Terry had alleviated some of these assumptions, their residual impact continued to organise a hierarchical division between theatre and revue in which the scantily clad figure of the chorus girl remained a ready target for accusations of sexual laxity. Given Neagle's history as a chorus girl and the sexualised publicity and roles of her early career, it was unsurprising that some eyebrows were raised when she was given the lead in *Victoria the Great*.

However, some of the negative sexual associations were somewhat mitigated by fan magazines that register the element of performance that underpins chorus work. And they also observe how Neagle preferred costume roles because 'she found it more difficult to play a modern chorus girl' (*Film Weekly* 2 May 1936: 25). Publications also link the chorus line to a professional work ethic, rather than to sleazy glamour. Mapping her rise to success, *Picturegoer* describes her as 'good-looking, enthusiastic, a hard worker' (30 May 1936: 15) while *Film Weekly* reports the hours of trapeze training required by the 1936 variety theatre saga *The Three Maxims*. Two years later cameraman Fred Young describes her as 'tireless' and 'giving all her attention to the job' (*Film Weekly* 13 August 1938: 22). But more importantly, the popular and critical success of *Victoria the Great* vindicated the decision to cast Neagle in the Victoria role and established her credentials as a versatile British actress who could perform both sexualised glamour and straight-laced regality. This change of image was consolidated through a royal stamp of approval for Neagle's performance. This came in the guise of the unprecedented access to Windsor Park granted to the production of *Sixty Glorious Years*, the 1938 sequel to *Victoria the Great*. The *New Yorker* magazine even went so far as to describe *Victoria the Great* as 'something almost official, a kind of state document' (23 October 1937). All in all, the Neagle star persona was infused with a regal aura that facilitated a transformation from slightly suspect ingénue starlet to iconic English femininity. Crucially, with regal discourse inserted into the star persona, Neagle was no longer just an English film star; rather, she became a star that embodied English identity.

The complexity of this embodied identity has been central to recent Neagle scholarship which traces the star's position in the mesh of a racialised imperial hegemonic Englishness. Following Dyer (1997: 124), both Dolan (1996: 78–82) and Street (1997: 127) trace how recurring references to 'blonde hair' and 'an English rose complexion' within fan and trade literature function to reiterate the whiteness of English national identity. In imperial and colonial contexts, this normalised white Englishness was pivotal to the 'othering' practices of a globalised, racial dichotomy. In this instance, the Neagle persona works in the ideological production of essentialised racial differences. Moreover, Neagle's white, English rose appearance is frequently associated with a Celtic ancestry. Contemporary writings repeatedly circulate the story that she was born Marjorie Robertson, 'the daughter of a sea-captain, a typical British bulldog of

Figure 3.1 'Iconic English femininity': Anna Neagle as Queen Victoria in *Sixty Glorious Years*, directed by Herbert Wilcox (1938).
Source: The Steve Chibnall Collection.

Scottish descent', while her stage name, Neagle, 'was her mother's maiden name – an Irish name that used to be pronounced Nagle' (*Film Weekly* 2 May 1936: 23–4). All of which, as Neagle suggests in her autobiography, 'makes me an odd candidate for the critics' "English Rose"' (Neagle 1974: 35). Yet, it is not as odd as Neagle suggests in that the star persona can be seen to embody British Unionist ideals while simultaneously conflating them with white hegemonic Englishness. Thus, the body of Neagle came to articulate a unified formation of Englishness in which the multiple and long standing tensions that can be traced from the Act of Union are magically resolved. And as Street points out, this version of Englishness was 'essentially narrow and class-specific, particularly in the London series of inward-looking society dramas which ignored unmetropolitan notions of Britishness and repressed questions of class conflict' (1997: 127).

Dolan (2000) suggests that this narrow, seemingly unified identity locked into Second World War contradictions between patriotic duty and dominant ideas about proper femininity. During the war, expectations that women would volunteer for occupations previously deemed to be men's work were frequently perceived to be in direct opposition to formulations of respectable femininity. Released just one year after the death of its subject, the Amy Johnson bio-pic, *They Flew Alone* (1941), is resonant with these ideologically laden tensions. By the early 1940s, following the success of the Victoria cycle, the Neagle persona was already linked to jingoistic patriotism. This intersects with the film's representation of Johnson as a patriotic heroine whose rise to international glory came through a consistent refusal to be confined and regulated by traditional ideas of femininity. In *They Flew Alone*, Neagle plays Johnson as a post-suffragist modern woman who fights for women's right to be aviators and engineers and who subsequently champions women's wartime entry into military service. Thus through the Neagle/Johnson dyad, the narrative produces a temporal displacement that (re)locates the exigencies of war to the inter-war period and which (re)formulates demands that women take up previously sacrosanct male occupations as already existing opportunities for women that had been wrought in the inter-war period through heroines like Johnson. Given the gloss of truth attached to the bio-pic genre, this displacement is shored up by the patriotic appeal of the Neagle/Johnson dyad. Effectively, the narrative of *They Flew Alone* aligns an already transformed, modernised femininity with a patriotic desire to enter those very occupations demanded by the war effort. With 'white tie' scenes that showcase Neagle in luxurious gowns and jewels this transformation does not come through the loss of feminine accoutrements or at the cost of glamour. While not overtly propagandist, *They Flew Alone* can be read as playing a part in managing a wartime tension between patriotic duty and anxieties about proper *British* femininity.

Having established the specifics of Neagle's dominant image, we now discuss how two key technological developments – the coming of sound and colour – were used to further enhance her persona and which can be taken as exemplary registers of her position as a star associated with conservative modernity.

Voice

Neagle's rise to national stardom is inextricably linked to the coming of sound since her 1930 break into the film industry comes just one year after what is generally considered to be the first British 'talkie', Hitchcock's *Blackmail* (1929). The qualification is highly relevant since Wilcox has always claimed to have produced the first British sound film, *Black Waters*, in 1929 (Wilcox 1967: 84). Wilcox's claim is usually disqualified because the film was shot in America with an American crew (Low 1985: 77), and its distribution was severely limited because on its release only three cinemas, two in London and one in Coventry, were equipped with sound technology. But, regardless of any attribution of 'firsts', Wilcox's claim is important because from the outset he recognised the importance of the 'talkies' and he played a highly significant part in the transformation of the British industry following the coming of sound. Crucially, the 'talkies' were at the forefront of his thinking when he spotted Neagle's star potential. It is easy to forget how the rise of the 'talkies' had destroyed the careers of many established stars by placing voice at the forefront of star appeal, and conversely, had created opportunities for many others. It seems that early film makers were quick to recognise 'the capacity of the human voice to bring a quality of feeling and texture of meaning to the medium of film that may not be possible to convey through the visuals alone' (Smith 2007: 164). Clearly then, Neagle's star appeal should not be reduced to the visual and equal attention must be paid to the aural, a dimension of cinematic stardom that can be conveniently approached through the frameworks of accent and timbre.

In terms of acting performance, accent is never straightforward because it encompasses both the star's everyday accent used for some characters and those adopted accents used for others. With Neagle, the latter was always problematic and frequently exposed the limitations of her acting abilities. Even by the standards of the day when on-screen working class or non-English accents were highly stylised versions of middle class norms, Neagle's attempts at Cockney or Irish voices in films such as *Nell Gwyn* or *Irene* (1940) are poorly achieved and unconvincing. Moreover, they are inconsistent from scene to scene as Neagle's accent shifts between the pitfalls of overplaying to that of being virtually non-existent. Yet, this appears to have created no major hostility among audiences who continued to flock to her films. No doubt the pleasures of spectacle mobilised by her films far outweighed the limitations of performed accents. Yet, equally, the accidental reminders of Neagle's own accent that also inform the majority of her films may well be crucial here. While her accent is undoubtedly middle class, its particular inflections are far more inclusive than many others in that it avoids the clipped, strangulated extremes of those voices that dominated British screens (and radio) of the time. When compared to the crisp accents of contemporaries such as Celia Johnson, Googie Withers or even Margaret Lockwood, Neagle's accent is less formed and less specific. To put this another way, Neagle's accent is seemingly more neutral, less exclusive, in its manifestation of middle class voice. But conversely, it is sufficiently precise to secure a difference between those few authentic working class voices such as George Formby and Gracie Fields who forged a path between music hall and screen. As stars both were defined by their northern accents as much as by the singing and comedic talent that underpins their success. These northern accents secure working class identities for both Fields and Formby, even long after stardom had taken them out of the economic boundaries of working class culture. Also, it positions their identities as local, rather than national: as exclusively northern, rather than inclusively British. So although both Formby and Fields are nationally regarded stars, their accent prevents them from being representative of nation, unlike Neagle, with her ostensibly neutral accent. It is worth noting that the humanisation of the monarchy suggested by the 'Regal Neagle' configuration cannot be isolated from this inclusive middle class voice. Little wonder then that Pathé News employed Neagle to narrate their coverage of the 1947 wedding of Princess Elizabeth and Prince Philip.

Listening to that narration brings into sharp relief the particular timbre of Neagle's talking voice, which, like her singing voice, is 'sweet and fragile' and 'as unmistakable in its way as Dietrich's' (Braun 1973: 37). Whether speaking or singing, the gentleness of Neagle's voice is striking. In a culture that equates femininity with a gentle voice, Neagle can be seen (or heard) as a physical articulation of feminine ideals. On some occasions therefore, the essentialised femininity of Neagle's voice compounds the gendered formulations of nurturing heroines such as Edith Cavell and Florence Nightingale. In other roles, it offers a corrective to threats to the gender dichotomy posed by strong feisty women such as Amy Johnson or Odette Hallows who were famed for their incursions into masculine terrain. In these cases Neagle's voice secures a biological, essential femininity. This no doubt offers some rationale for the popular success of many Neagle films that were able to portray a progressive femininity grounded in inter-war feminist politics while also making it safe because it is no more than a superficial overlay to an unchanging and untrammelled biological female core.

In many ways, the tonal register of Neagle's voice is comparable to that of her contemporary, Greer Garson. In an extended analysis of *Random Harvest* (1942) that builds on Silverman's (1988) psychoanalytic approach to the female screen voice, Smith employs the concept of the sonorous envelope: the maternal voice that 'surrounds, sustains and cherishes the child' (Smith 2007: 72). Smith argues that Garson's voice mobilises a maternal voice fantasy of pre-oedipal plenitude and bliss. This fantasy then operates as a counterpoint to the prevailing terrors of the blitz (as in *Mrs. Miniver*, 1942) or as a powerful corrective to widespread social prejudices against the psychic turmoil of the shell-shocked soldier (as in *Random Harvest*). Garson's voice can thus be seen as a tranquil point of maternal reassurance in the midst of a chaotic social order. Following Smith it is easy to recognise that Neagle's voice is similarly crucial to the psychic economy of her films. With Neagle, the rich variety of genres and styles that characterise her films averts any risk that Smith's argument is simply applied as a reductive formula. Instead, Smith's formulation of the sonorous envelope can illuminate how Neagle's voice adds a layer in addition to the visual spectacle of films such as *Nell Gwyn* or *Maytime in Mayfair* (1949). In Neagle's darker narratives there are moments when the steadied measure of her gentle voice sustains a glimmer of warmth and hope even within the bleakest scenario. Most notably in *Odette*, the sonorous envelope mitigates two modes of violence; that of a mother separated from her children and that of a woman enduring sustained and brutal torture by Nazi oppressors.

Alternatively, Smith's argument opens the way to greater understanding of loss in strong dramas like *They Flew Alone* and *Piccadilly Incident*. Both of these films hinge on the death of the heroine, and in each case, the emotional economy of loss is magnified because the reassurances of voice are terminated. But the very different narrative trajectories of each film ensure that the economy of loss is deployed to very different ideological purposes. With *They Flew Alone* the death of Amy Johnson allows for a shift in the gender dimensions of ulti-mate sacrifice in service of nation, while also making it an ordinary sacrificial gesture that typifies 'The People's War'. Because *Piccadilly Incident* stages an account of inadvertent bigamy arising from the dislocations of the Second Wold War, the convenient death of its displaced heroine, played by Neagle, is almost inevitable in a highly clichéd Wilcox production. Yet, this does not produce a tidy resolution since the bigamist husband (Michael Wilding) and the unfortu-nate woman who thought she had married a widower, have a baby. Under English law this baby was born out of wedlock and remains a bastard, and as the critic for *Monthly Film Bulletin* remarks, 'the film ends on a bitter note' (September 1946: 3). This bitterness is a logical comment on an unsatisfactory legal system that constitutes both the category of the illegitimate and those legal and social penalties that accrue from the category. But there is also an emo-tional charge to the comment that coincides with the loss of Neagle's comfort-ing acoustics. Through the death of its heroine, the bitterness of legally sanctioned injustice is aligned with the psychic economy of maternal loss.

The widespread familiarity with Neagle's voice that stems from her many performances means that her star persona is also inflected through the dynamics of the sonorous envelope. This has particular implications for Neagle's position as a British national icon. While the longevity of Neagle's career can be attrib-uted to Wilcox's astute tutelage it is also the case that her star persona chimed with a period of social and economic disruptions shaped by entry into, and exit from, the Second World War. As noted above, Neagle's persona offered a point of certainty that resonated with a variety of rapid changes in the construction of British national identity, the organisation of gender and the ideological management of consumerism. Crucially, that point of certainty can be seen as imbued with the psychic reassurances associated with voice. The Neagle star image was never simply a visual phenomenon since it was also an acoustic dynamic tapping into British cultural fantasies of maternal reassurance and emotional fulfilment in a climate of chaotic uncertainty.

Colour

Just as Wilcox used sound to foreground aspects of her image which had coa-lesced into the 'Regal Neagle' formula of English femininity, colour also pre-sented opportunities to add visual inflections which were presented by the new technology of Technicolor. Neagle's reputation for being able to showcase gla-mour as well as exemplify lady-like decorum is reflected in different ways by her association with colour film at key points in her career. In the 1930s Her-bert Wilcox was keen to experiment with colour at a time when three-strip Technicolor had been successfully developed in the USA, guided in its applica-tion by Natalie Kalmus, head of the consultancy service which was a require-ment for any company which used the process. The release in the United Kingdom of Hollywood's *Becky Sharp* (1935), the first feature-length film in three-strip Technicolor, was the occasion for much commentary in the trade

press as to the efficacy of the use of colour in narrative cinema. While many
were enthusiastic about colour, the dominant response was that care should be
taken to avoid it being too distracting from key elements of a film's story. The
varied performance of many processes that were being demonstrated in the
early 1930s, including Dufaycolor, Spectracolor and Raycol, resulted in uncertainty as to how far colour should be embraced by all producers, especially
since Technicolor was more expensive than producing films in black-and-white.

Neagle however played a major role in legitimising the use of colour in her
roles as Queen Victoria in *Victoria the Great* and *Sixty Glorious Years*. The
Coronation of King George VI and Queen Elizabeth on 12 May 1937 provided a
showcase for four different colour processes. The event was filmed in Technicolor, Dufaycolor, British-Realita and Kinechrome. Of these films, the Technicolor version was received with most enthusiasm, described as 'a thing of
beauty', although Dufaycolor was praised for its ability to convey 'the dark
tones, particularly the glossiness of the horses' (*Kinematograph Weekly* 27 May
1935: 3). Soon after the Coronation, announcements for the release of *Victoria
the Great* appeared which advertised that the final reel of the Diamond Jubilee
was in Technicolor, the rest of the film being in black-and-white. The Coronation was attended by representatives from the British Empire, and the films
showcased colour as appropriate for the pageantry of imperial display. Wilcox
also emphasised this association with colour by choosing to highlight Victoria's
imperial role in the last colour reel of *Victoria the Great*. The trade press, with
an eye on the box-office, was enthusiastic, with the *Kinematograph Weekly*
reviewer describing the Technicolor reel as 'brilliant if not perfect' (28 September 1937: 24). Many commentators, however, found this to be a gimmick that
distracted from the film's overall image of decorum, good taste and Englishness.
Writing in the *Spectator*, for example, Basil Wright commented that 'The rather
vicious brightness of the Technicolor Diamond Jubilee forms an unfortunate
ending to a good-looking film' (24 September 1937: 499). Critic James Agate
was similarly unimpressed, pronouncing that:

> At the end it breaks into colour, with an effect like that of a picture book
> on which a six-year-old has been messing about with a box of paints. The
> result is to make the last half-hour of the picture look like something
> enamelled on pottery and marked 'A present from Blackpool'.
>
> (1946: 185)

Comments such as this equate colour with vulgarity, which was a common
assumption, and Agate also here links colour with class, a discourse which can
be traced back to early discussion of colour in the silent period.

Not deterred by the ambivalent comments on the last reel of *Victoria the
Great*, Wilcox immediately made *Sixty Glorious Years* entirely in Technicolor.
The issue of colour again received a somewhat mixed reception, although the
film was generally regarded as being very fine and the comments on colour are
not quite so critical. Since the whole film is in colour it lacks the spectacle of

surprise which the sudden addition of a colour reel represented in *Victoria the Great*. Also, by the time of release, Technicolor was gaining ground in technical and critical terms. A handbook on British Technicolor films singled out Technicolor's appropriateness for conveying 'a magnificent cavalcade of British history' (Huntley 1949: 30). Neagle returned again to the use of colour for historical pageantry in *Elizabeth of Ladymead* (1948), in which she plays four different characters from four different periods. Eastmancolor was used for *King's Rhapsody* (1955), based on Ivor Novello's mid-European royal romance with music, in which Neagle stars with Errol Flynn.

These examples exhibit the generic proclivity for colour as royal spectacle, as being able to convey the exoticism of empire, travel and the variety of history. As an adjunct to Neagle's star persona, these generic forms consolidated her position as a regal ambassador for British cinema. What is interesting about Wilcox's approach was that he used new technology to capitalise on the appeal of her established image, and colour provided the perfect means of enhancing the 'private life' approach to monarchy which had proved to be so popular with *Nell Gwyn*. While black-and-white reinforced dominant codes of realism, colour offered the spectacle of domesticating royalty, inspiring comments such as Huntley's appreciation of 'the reposeful chromatic pattern of the interior set in Apsley House, as against the bright outdoor colours of the Highland scene' in *Sixty Glorious Years* (Huntley 1949: 30). This approach extended the range of spectacle as interior, 'domestic' scenes acquired a greater sense of intimacy through colour.

The other key dimension of Neagle's association with colour privileged consumption, fashion and glamour. *Irene*, produced by Wilcox for RKO in the USA and based on a musical, featured the world of fashion retail and contained a Technicolor sequence for the 'Alice Blue Gown' number. While the majority of the 'London series' of romantic comedies were shot in black-and-white, they highlighted opulent décor and glamour, particularly through Neagle's costuming and references to consumerism such as when the character played by Neagle in *Spring in Park Lane* is thrilled to receive nylons from her uncle on his return from abroad. While glamour associated with Neagle is foregrounded in these films, it is important to note how this was always differentiated from its American counterpart, which was associated with brasher, more overtly sexualised feminine imagery, as in *I Live in Grosvenor Square* when Neagle's English demeanour (as exemplified in costume, speech, mannerisms) is contrasted with the American showgirls who entertain the American Air Force stationed in the United Kingdom.

The most obtrusive use of colour for Neagle was in *Maytime in Mayfair*, a romantic comedy which, as Dolan has argued, deploys the star as a means of alleviating some of the film's more excessive modes of display: 'Through the Neagle persona, English restraint is aligned with the conspicuous consumption of the film, and English "conservative modernity" is constituted in terms of conspicuous consumption' (2007: 48). The film takes place in London's fashion world and can usefully be aligned to the contemporary context of shifts in post-war patterns of consumption and consumerism as represented by the 1951

A scene from "SPRING IN PARK LANE"
A Wilcox-Neagle Production — An Eagle Lion Films Release
Printed in U. S. A

Figure 3.2 Opulent décor and romantic glamour: Michael Wilding and Anna Neagle in
Spring in Park Lane, directed by Herbert Wilcox (1948).
Source: The Steve Chibnall Collection.

Festival of Britain (Dolan 2007). Natalie Kalmus was responsible for the colour
design, in association with Joan Bridge, and many of her standard 'colour
consciousness' tenets for the use of colour are evident in the film.[3] Technicolor's
tendency to score colour design (the alignment of colours with the leading
female performer and creating a structural design for each film according to
dominant 'warm' or 'cool' moods and themes as represented by colour) is evident. For much of the film Neagle wears 'cool', 'quiet' colours of blue or white,
and when she is working as the manageress of the fashion house she wears
black, accented with a white collar tempered by a pattern or in a soft fabric.
The designs for Neagle's character Eileen exemplify an approach which is consistent with her image as a capable, sensible woman. In the film she coaches

Michael (Michael Wilding) into the world of fashion when he inherits the company where she works as manageress. His interest in fashion is, however, determined by his attraction for her, and we never feel that he has a genuine interest in the gowns designed at the house. Neagle's outfits are therefore not distracting, but that is not to say that colour and fashion are not a significant aspect of her performance. On one occasion, when she goes to the rival Davenport house for a job, she wears shades of violet and mauve which are replicated in the flowers which appear in the same shot. This is a typical way for a Technicolor film to 'score' colour by creating a link between the costume of the lead performer with flowers. In keeping with the film's theme costume and flowers are the main ways in which colour is obtrusive, although as noted above, Neagle's costumes are only marked by more saturated colour on a few occasions and usually when she is not working. In this sense colour is never allowed to disrupt the presentation of 'safe' femininity.

There are three sequences outside of the main story time of the narrative, and for each colour is used in striking ways. The Vogue fashion show in which women 'emerge' from covers of the magazine to showcase different outfits is reminiscent of the colour fashion sequence in Cukor's *The Women* (1939). The second is a fantasy sequence from Michael's point of view, when he dreams of Eileen dancing down a staircase. Again the colours for her are not bright or brash. For stronger hues of green, pink and blue, other models appear and are accompanied by jazz music which connotes seduction and sexuality. Again, we see Neagle's image being differentiated from more sexualised femininity, costume and colour. The third fantasy sequence is from Eileen's point of view when she has travelled to Paris with Davenport, owner of the rival fashion house. He tells her that he needs a name for a new perfume he is developing, and she suggests 'Maytime in Mayfair'. When he asks her what made her think of this, a daydream sequence begins of her dancing with Michael in an exterior setting with the predominant colours provided by flowers and lights. The sequence is shot in slow-motion which has the effect of emphasising the excess of her desire and longing to be back in London with Michael. Her dress, which is light-coloured, nevertheless becomes a spectacle by means of its voluminous, diaphanous material (an effect enhanced by the slow-motion), and with the light catching the sparkle of its sequins. It is significant that this sequence is conjured up by the mention of perfume, which creates a sensuous link between smell (the perfume) and the sight of colour (flowers and the suggestion of their scent). This equates colour with synaesthesia, in which one sense impression can be created by the stimulation of another, an idea that can be related to earlier discussions of the impact of colour film in silent cinema. Once returned to the world of normality and when Eileen returns to London to save the fashion house and marry Michael, she is once again seen in cool pastels.

As well as colour, costume and flowers being significant in *Maytime in Mayfair* the film emphasises Neagle's natural beauty in Technicolor. According to Technicolor cameraman Ran Rennahan, actresses with auburn or blonde hair photographed particularly well in Technicolor. Skin tones were also very important in discussions of what the process was capable of, and less make-up was generally worn because of the generally higher-key lighting needed for the cameras. These technical considerations meant that when shot in colour stars were in a way re-presented to audiences when they appeared for the first time in colour. While Neagle had already appeared in Technicolor, our first sight of her in *Maytime in Mayfair*, when she turns to Michael, is a medium close-up which emphasises her auburn hair, skin tones and lips. These colours are made more of an arresting spectacle than her costume as the audience is aligned with Michael's perception of her beauty. The emphasis on blondness which was a feature of discussions of Neagle in fan magazines was not disrupted by the colour change to auburn, particularly with its similar relation to dominant codes of whiteness and femininity. This impact is further underlined with an intertextual reference to Neagle as a film star when Michael later describes Eileen to a friend as reminding him of Anna Neagle. Flesh tones were a crucial register of Technicolor's ability to capture 'natural' beauty (Higgins 2007: 86–8). This was important for audiences who since *Victoria the Great* had got used to seeing Neagle primarily in black-and-white films, especially in her roles as national heroines and in wartime dramas. Colour was therefore used to reinforce the dominant codes which constituted her image. While there was certainly novelty value in seeing Neagle in colour, the careful ways in which it was used for her did not result in a fundamental change. She contributed to making Technicolor more respectable and less associated with Hollywood since it was deemed 'fitting' for a national screen heroine to be seen as *colourful* at a time when Britain was being ushered into the consumerist decade.

Conclusion

Neagle's enduring image can therefore be explained in the ways in which both she and Wilcox ensured that elements of the core persona were never seriously disrupted by developments in the film industry, be they technological or in terms of generic development. To recover a sense of the intensity of her popularity it is crucial to locate the dynamic between 'safe' femininity, conservative modernity and a very specific cultural imagining of the nation at critical historical junctures. While there is no doubt that this was based on a somewhat exclusive formula of the 'Regal Neagle', it is also the case that elements of her image were precisely about stressing her presence as a star who possessed an emblematic sensibility as embodying quintessential English femininity with which a very large percentage of the audience identified. We have shown that the construction of this particular identity can be explained by attention to specific attributes such as her voice, which avoided regional specificity in favour of a tonal register which aligned her with a particular conception of the nation as united, and which was enveloped by security and reassurance. In a similar way colour functioned to demonstrate how Neagle could be further differentiated from American stars and crude impressions of Technicolor which aligned the process with sexuality, vulgarity and Hollywood. In these ways she maintained the loyalty of the many British cinemagoers who voted for her in numerous popularity polls. Whether or not this defies the understanding of contemporary critics, for millions of cinemagoers during a key period in the development of British cinema and at a time when cinema admissions reached their all-time peak, Anna Neagle was a star they paid to see again, again and again.

Notes

1 Janet Thumim (1992: 66) usefully notes that fan and industry accolades are never neutral and that they are underpinned by multiple investments and motivations.
2 Nick James, editor of *Sight and Sound*, followed the publication of the BFI's 'Ultimate Film' listings in www.bfi.org.uk/features/ultimatefilm/feature.html. For full details of the listings see www.bfi.org.uk/features/ultimatefilm/chart/complete/php.
3 For Natalie Kalmus's article on 'Colour Consciousness' which outlines her main approach to the design of motion pictures in Technicolor, see the reprint of her article, first published in a technical journal in 1935, in Dalle Vacche and Price (2006: 24–9).

Bibliography

Agate, J. (1946) 'Victoria the Little', originally in *The Tatler*, 29 September 1937 and reprinted in Agate's *Around Cinemas*, London: Home & Van Thal.
Braun, E. (1973) 'Images on a chocolate box', *Films and Filming*, 20.2, November: 31–9.
Coulson, A. A. (1967) 'Anna Neagle', *Films in Review*, 18.3, March: 149.
Dalle Vacche, A. and Price, B. (eds) (2006) *Color: The Film Reader*, London: Routledge.
Davis, T. C. (1991) *Actresses as Working Women: Their Social Identity in Victorian Culture*, London: Routledge.
Dolan, J. (1996) 'National Heroines: Representing Femininity and the Past in Popular Film and Literature, 1930–55', unpublished thesis, Lancaster University.
——(2000) '*They Flew Alone* and the "Angel of the Air": crossings between respectability, Nation and Empire', *Visual Culture in Britain* 1.2, December: 25–42.
——(2007) 'Post-war Englishness: *Maytime in Mayfair*, utopian visions and consumer culture', in C. Hart (ed.), *Approaches to Englishness: Differences, Diversity and Identities*, Kingswinsford: Midrash Publishing.
Dyer, R. (1979) *Stars*, London: British Film Institute.
——(1997) *White*, London: Routledge.
Harper, S. (2000) *Mad, Bad and Dangerous to Know: Women in British Cinema*, London: Continuum.
Higgins, S. (2007) *Harnessing the Technicolor Rainbow: Color Design in the 1930s*, Austin: University of Texas Press.
Huntley, J. (1949) *British Technicolor Films*, London: Skelton Robinson.
Low, R. (1985) *Filmmaking in 1930s Britain*, London: Allen & Unwin.
Neagle, A. (1974) *There's Always Tomorrow*, London: W. H. Allen.
Silverman, K. (1988) *The Acoustic Mirror*, Bloomington: Indiana University Press.
Smith, S. (2007) 'Voices in Film', in J. Gibbs and D. Pye (eds), *Close-Up 02*, London: Wallflower Press.
Street, S. (1997) *British National Cinema*, London: Routledge.
——(2002) *Transatlantic Crossings: British Feature Films in the USA*, London: Continuum.
Thumim, J. (1992) *Celluloid Sisters: Women and Popular Cinema*, London: Macmillan.
Wilcox, H. (1967) *Twenty-Five Thousand Sunsets*, London: Bodley Head.

4 The Hollywood woman's film and British audiences

A case study of Bette Davis and *Now, Voyager*

Mark Glancy

As the study of British cinema has proceeded apace over the past few decades, film scholars and critics have usually conceived of it as a separate and distinct entity from Hollywood. Accounts of the industry focus on the beleaguered production sector and its struggles against the Hollywood behemoth. The most celebrated film-makers are those who worked mainly within the native industry, and patriotically resisted the allure of the world's film capital. The most note-worthy films are those with a style or narrative elements that set them clearly apart from Hollywood norms. British cinema, in other words, is defined in opposition to Hollywood and, with a few notable exceptions, the two are seldom seen to share common ground. However, it is not necessary to define British cinema solely in relation to film production, film-makers or even films. It can also include audiences and their cinema-going habits, experiences and pre-ferences. This perspective opens up some new and overlooked avenues, espe-cially with regard to the relationship between British audiences and Hollywood. Over the past 100 years, Hollywood films have been a staple of the British cinema-going diet, but we know comparatively little about this phenomenon. Have audiences also seen Hollywood and Britain in oppositional terms? Did they resent or enjoy Hollywood's dominance of British screens? And what meanings and pleasures did they find in films made 5,000 miles away, in foreign settings and by foreign film-makers? These issues have been explored in groundbreaking studies of British audiences, including Helen Taylor's *Scarlett's Women* (1989), Jackie Stacey's *Star Gazing* (1994), Annette Kuhn's *An Everyday Magic* (2002), and also within Harper and Porter's wide ranging *British Cinema of the 1950s* (2003). But the study of British audiences, as cinema-goers and as fans of Hollywood films, is an ongoing project and one that requires detailed investigations of specific time periods and audience groups, as well as key films, stars and genres.

Of all of the areas that might be taken up for study, the woman's film raises particularly compelling issues. One reason for this is that the genre is so closely associated with Hollywood, especially in a longstanding critical dichotomy that points to Hollywood as the embodiment of lowbrow cinema (characterized by lush production values, excessive emotions, escapist plots and a star system that valued glamour over acting) and at the same time heralds British cinema as a middlebrow alternative (characterized by realism, social relevance and fine acting). We now recognize that these characterizations are highly selective, and that they were promoted by a particular school of criticism that flourished in Britain during the 1940s, but it remains little known just how far these critical values seeped into the popular film culture of the decade. Another reason for studying the woman's film is that, for all of the attention that the genre has received in recent decades, its appeal to audiences is often considered in comparatively narrow terms. For example, Jeanine Basinger's noteworthy account of the genre, *A Woman's View* (1993), explores 'how Hollywood spoke to women' with the implicit assumption that the woman's film spoke only to American women and not to men at all.

This chapter seeks a wide range of critical and audience responses to the Hollywood woman's film in Britain, focusing specifically on Bette Davis, a star now inextricably linked with the genre, and one of her most popular films, *Now, Voyager* (1942), which is now held as a 'definitive' example of this genre (Shingler 2007: 152). It would be misleading, though, to imply that this star and film were chosen as straightforward representatives of the Hollywood woman's film. For many, Davis was a serious actor rather than a 'mere' star and, far from being dismissed as a lowbrow entertainment, *Now, Voyager* met with some considerable critical appreciation when it was first released in Britain in September 1943. Indeed, this star and this film have been chosen precisely because they test the perceived boundaries between 'quality' and 'popular' cinema, between Britain and Hollywood, and between the cinema-going tastes of men and women. These boundaries will be explored by considering the opinions of a wide range of film critics, and by using audience surveys and commentaries that allow comparisons between distinct audience groups.

Any understanding of Davis's British reputation, however, must begin at a more general level and in October 1936, when she arrived in London and announced that henceforth she would seek work as an actor there. At this point Davis had appeared in 25 Warner Brothers films within just four years. Her contract had a further three years to run, but she insisted that she would not return to the studio, charging that it had forced her to make too many films, to play parts unsuited to her, and to work unreasonably long hours (*The Times*, 15 October 1936: 4). She already had a reputation as a somewhat contrary star. In 1935, she remarked to the British magazine *Film Weekly* that it 'pays to be a type in Hollywood' and to 'remain more or less the same little woman in every picture' (29 March 1935: 7). It was clear that she had greater ambitions for herself, and her rebellion against Warner Brothers was a first step toward achieving them. Her complaints about Hollywood were likely to fall on sympathetic ears in Britain, and not only because she had chosen London as her new base. The popular film culture of the mid-1930s was dominated by Hollywood films, and articles about Hollywood stars were the mainstay of magazines such as *Film Weekly* and its chief competitor, *Picturegoer*. Although the films and stars were popular, the same magazines routinely derided Hollywood as an industry; it was resented both for underestimating the public's taste and for preventing the British film industry from prospering. The studio system was considered crassly commercial; a factory system that made films in the manner Henry Ford made cars. Davis's rebellion was thus presented sympathetically by *Film Weekly*, which portrayed her as a victim of 'the Frankenstein monster of Hollywood' (19 June 1937: 12–13). Yet when Warner Brothers sued Davis and the case went to the High Court, the revelation that Davis's salary reached £600 per week weighed against her. She lost the case and returned to work at the studio.

Davis was not yet among the first tier of stars and her rebellion against Warner Brothers did not significantly improve her standing. A 1934 survey conducted by the Granada Cinemas chain indicates that Davis did not figure at all among the '50 favourite female film stars' (*Bernstein Questionnaire Report* 1934: 1). In Granada's next survey, conducted in 1937 and after her rebellion, Davis appeared at number 30 on the list of '50 favourite female film stars', but she also came at number 12 on the list of most *disliked* female film stars (*Bernstein Questionnaire Report* 1937: 1, 6). That Mae West, Greta Garbo, Katherine Hepburn and Jean Harlow topped this unfortunate ranking is revealing. A significant portion of the audience disliked women who played assertive, sexually aware characters, and Davis's best-known roles, as a vulgar Cockney waitress in *Of Human Bondage* (1934) and as a fading, alcoholic actor in *Dangerous* (1935) fell within these parameters. Her struggle with Warner Brothers may have added to the impression of Davis as a career-orientated, defiant, independent woman. Certainly, a publicity campaign initiated on her return to Warner Brothers appears designed to soften her image. When *Picturegoer* told her 'life story', as a serial running over three issues, it culminated with her joy at seeing her husband's name – rather than her own – up in lights on a marquee (13 February 1937: 24). Similarly, a profile in *Film Weekly* emphasized her happy marriage and her devotion to her husband, the bandleader Harmon Nelson: 'The maid never mentions the name of Miss Davis; neither does the gardener, the cook, nor the neighbours. She is Mrs. Nelson at home' (19 June 1937: 12–13). At a time when the most popular female stars were Norma Shearer and Myrna Loy – both known for playing genteel, wifely, dignified women – this was a logical strategy to improve Davis's image, even if it was largely ineffective.

It was at the end of the decade that Davis's standing markedly improved. Many of her mid-1930s films had been typical Warner Brothers fare: modestly budgeted, contemporary and rather gritty dramas such as the off-beat crime film *Satan Met a Lady* (1936), the prize fighter melodrama *Kid Galahad* (1937) and the gangster films *The Petrified Forest* (1936) and *Marked Woman* (1937). These were not star vehicles, and in fact Davis did not always lead the casts, which included Humphrey Bogart, Edward G. Robinson, William Warren and other second-string Warner stars of the 1930s. Her turning point was *Jezebel* (1938). The story of a headstrong, defiant southern belle who comes to regret her indiscretions, this was by any measure a woman's film. Henceforth, Davis only appeared alongside major male stars if the film was a lavish costume drama – *Juarez* (1939) with Paul Muni, *The Private Lives of Elizabeth and Essex* (1939) with Errol Flynn and *All This and Heaven Too* (1940) with Charles Boyer – but in the majority of her films she was the primary star, and she was billed above dependable but less imposing co-stars such as George Brent, Paul Henreid, John Loder and Claude Rains. Like *Jezebel*, her later films centre squarely on her character's desires and dilemmas, as well as on Davis's own performance as an actor. She is a young heiress dying of cancer in *Dark Victory* (1939), a selfless unwed mother in *The Old Maid* (1939), a vengeful adulteress in *The Letter* (1940), a scheming and reckless killer in *In This Our Life* (1942) and of course a neurotic young woman who finally breaks free of her oppressive mother in *Now, Voyager*. As Cathy Klaprat has observed, the alternation between virtuous and vampish roles prevented audiences from becoming bored with her films, while her ability to play women of different countries and centuries, and women with repellent or attractive moral qualities, demonstrated her range as an actor (Klaprat 1985: 375).

It was a strategy that served Davis well on both sides of the Atlantic. Arguably, though, her status in Britain was greater than in the United States. In popularity polls conducted by *The Motion Picture Herald*, she came among the top ten stars at the British box-office for six consecutive years, from 1942 to 1947, peaking in 1945 as Britain's second-highest box-office draw (Ramsaye 1946: 784). This was a feat unmatched by any other woman in that decade, and it was significantly better than Davis's record in the United States, where Betty Grable and Greer Garson outshone her in a parallel set of rankings (reprinted in Basinger 1993: 509–10). Davis's appeal to British audiences may have stemmed in part from her continuing defiance of the conventions of stardom: she was regarded as a less glamorous and more ambitious actor than her peers. This was apparent in the number of films that she made, the range of roles that she took, and also in publicity that cast her as a hard-working and patriotic model of wartime femininity. *Picturegoer* noted approvingly that, when filming *Now, Voyager*, Davis came to the set and read her lines to co-star Gladys Cooper even when Davis herself was off-camera. Most stars, it was noted, 'leave that kind of thing to a "stooge"' (25 July 1942: 10). When Davis donned a nurse's uniform and made a brief appearance in the combat film *Winged Victory* (1944), the same magazine printed a photographic still capturing the moment, and commented, 'yes, the famous star, twice an Academy Award winner, became an extra the other day' (1 March 1941: 3). The film *Hollywood Canteen* (1944) highlighted her participation in entertaining the troops before they embarked for duty in the Pacific. If Davis's films and her publicity were especially appealing to British audiences, it may be because wartime exigencies were greater and had more of an impact on everyday life than in the United States. Certainly, the parallels between *Now, Voyager* and British films that portray wartime upheavals in women's lives and circumstances, such as *The Gentle Sex* (1943) and *Millions Like Us* (1943), become more apparent in this context. It is apparent, too, in British publicity for *Now, Voyager* that defined the film specifically as one that offered Davis her most challenging role.

The film's arrival in Britain was accompanied by a two-page advertisement in the trade paper *Today's Cinema*. This was dominated by a drawing of Davis in character as Charlotte Vale, and her coiffure, evening dress and pensive expression as she holds the telephone clearly signalled that *Now, Voyager* is a woman's film. The text, however, defined the film primarily in terms of Davis's achievements as an actor: 'An entire career points to this one magnificent achievement'. The next page is even more outspoken in this regard. A smaller image of Davis and Paul Henreid is surrounded by large cursive script reading 'Hail Bette Davis' (7 September 1943: 4–5). The attention given to Davis's acting is striking when this advertisement is compared with the film's American press-book. As Maria LaPlace has noted, much of the American pressbook focuses on consumerism, and products and tie-ins that are linked to Charlotte's transformation from repressed spinster to glamorous woman-of-the-world (1987: 141–42). The American pressbook also places significant emphasis on the melodramatic elements of the story-line and the centrality of a woman's experience within the fictional story. The American posters read: 'It happens in the best of families, but you'd never think it could happen to her'; 'Every woman has a right to one mistake ... and I'm not sorry for mine'; and 'Don't pity me ... in our few moments together I found the joy that most women can only dream of'. By contrast with the British advertising, there is far less emphasis placed on Davis as an actor, and none on the film as an achievement in a real woman's career.

The British trade papers followed the lead of Warner Brothers's advertising, and defined the film in ways that signalled that it would appeal to different segments of the audience. *Today's Cinema* referred to it as a 'psychological drama' and stated that it was 'finely appealing general entertainment', but also observed that it had 'especial attraction for femininity' (10 September 1943: 18–19). Similarly, the rival *Kinematograph Weekly* thought that the film was 'compelling drama and, at the same time, an irresistible woman's picture' (16 September 1943: 30). Both heavily praised Davis's performance; the former referring to it as a 'brilliant portrait' and the latter as a 'magnificent portrayal'. Beyond the trade papers, *Now, Voyager* entered into a distinctive critical milieu. The most prominent British film critics of the time were preoccupied, as John Ellis has observed, with an emergent style of British cinema that was informed by the tenets of documentary realism. Critics writing for a dozen or so mainly upmarket, London-based publications promoted the 'quality film' in the belief that they could lift audience tastes and influence the future of film-making. They approved of films that were imbued with the virtues of documentary realism – 'authenticity', 'restraint', 'sincerity', 'understatement' and a concern to portray the working class with dignity – and assumed that this was the progressive way forward for British cinema, both as an art form and as an industry. Hollywood, by contrast, was regarded as making films with an extravagance that was at odds with British understatement, and making films that aimed only at 'the lowest common denominator', an immature audience who sought nothing more than easy entertainment. The lines of taste were not drawn strictly by nationality. British films operating outside the prescribed parameters also drew scorn, and in some respects genre offers clearer lines of delineation. The excesses and escapism of Gainsborough melodrama, for example, drew scathing notices (Ellis 1996: 66–93). Either way, *Now, Voyager* had the potential to provoke the ire of the 'quality' critics. It was a lavishly mounted film, and its melodramatic story – involving a wealthy Boston family, a heroine who undergoes a remarkable physical transformation and an adulterous relationship on a cruise ship – had little in common with the prevailing notions of realism. Yet responses, even within the 'quality' school, were not consistent.

Interestingly, the most disparaging reviews from the 'quality' school came from the two leading film critics of the day, both of whom happened to be women. Dilys Powell and C. A. Lejeune made it clear that *Now, Voyager* was not to their taste. Powell commented on the 'precision and control' of Davis's performance, but regretted this was 'not paralleled by a greater austerity of form in telling the story' (*The Sunday Times*, 7 November 1943). Lejeune refused even to take the film seriously and instead offered a long-winded joke about opticians protesting against Hollywood's repeated suggestion that spectacles 'will cut down any heroine's love life' (*Observer*, 7 November 1943). A less prominent 'quality' critic, Joan Lester, was more appreciative, but she expressed her praise – 'I revelled unashamedly in the sentiment and the lovemaking' – in purely emotional terms (*Reynold's News*, 7 November 1943: 4). By contrast, many male critics – including 'quality' critics – not only admired the film, but were willing to consider its merits more seriously. The film found its most ardent admirer in Richard Winnington, who praised *Now, Voyager* in terms usually associated with the best British films:

> The consummate skill of Bette Davis makes valid each subtle development of the part; the curious spiritual quality she has, which seems to fuse with the camera lens, brings Charlotte Vale tenderly to life, an infinitely moving figure. Among other notable things is the delicate restraint of the lovemaking. These two [Charlotte and Jerry] talk and look like grown-up lovers. In a medium that is exclusively devoted to every permutation of human love, this happens to be so rare as to startle.
>
> (*News Chronicle*, 6 November 1943: 2)

He praised the director, too, for giving 'solidity' to the film's social setting, and for using Tchaikovsky's *Pathétique* symphony to 'underline and stress emotions' (ibid.). All of these qualities – fine acting, maturity, restraint, the authentic sense of place and the sensitive use of music – were considered hallmarks of the new British cinema, and they would be celebrated especially in the most admired of all 'quality' British films, *Brief Encounter* (1945). Indeed, parts of Winnington's review of *Now, Voyager* could be mistaken for the reviews of *Brief Encounter* that appeared two years later. Yet the connections between the two films have become less apparent over time, and obscured by critical and historical accounts that are more likely to see oppositions than links between Hollywood and Britain.

Davis's acting drew praise from almost all critics. Critical judgements about acting were informed by values that stemmed from a stage tradition. Actors' talent was apparent in their careful use of gestures, traits and mannerisms. A good performance, in effect, was one in which the actor's skills were apparent and yet he or she nevertheless created a convincing character (Gledhill 2003: 62–3). This favoured actors who played a wide range of roles, thereby demonstrating their skill in a variety of guises, and so Davis was well suited to these critical precepts. Critics often spoke of her 'mannerisms' as an actor, but this was usually a form of praise. Her 'little tricks and mannerisms' and her 'immensely expressive and many toned voice', as Paul Tabori commented in the *Daily Mail*, were what made *Now, Voyager* 'Bette at her best' (5 November 1943: 2). Davis's willingness to appear unattractive was especially commended. In the film's earliest scenes, she appeared 'grotesque' (*Kine Weekly*), 'lumpish' (*Today's Cinema*), 'a haunting creature' (*The Times*, 4 November 1943: 6), and 'plump, bespectacled and shapeless' (*News of the World*, 7 November 1943: 4). In the *Sunday Express* Ernest Betts explained that she was the 'most distinguished and popular actress on the American screen' precisely because she was an actor rather than a star:

> Bette has the extraordinary faculty of making an unattractive part attractive. … She is not a screen beauty, but she gives the impression of beauty. She can look glamorous, yet she does not need glamour to make you look at her. In fact, she is an actress. She conveys the secret emotions and everyday worries of ordinary people.
>
> (5 November 1943: 6)

Thus, even at the height of her stardom, Davis was regarded as working outside the norms of glamour, and so she appeared to be defying Hollywood, just as she had done on her trip to London in 1936.

While critical opinion was surprisingly homogeneous, the same cannot be said for audiences. Middle class audiences did follow the values and opinions of the critics, but this is what made them distinctive: no other audience group had tastes or interests that coincided so closely with critical views. Middle class responses to Davis's films can tracked through a wartime survey of film preferences conducted by Mass Observation. When discussing Davis's work, this survey's respondents were most likely to mention her status and skills as an actor: her performances were described as 'good dramatic acting', 'excellent', 'superb', 'meticulous', 'wonderful' and 'always worth seeing' (Richards and Sheridan 1987: 230, 233, 245, 257, 275, 285). Equally, the association between stage and screen was an important factor in middle class tastes. Among Davis's films, there was a strong preference for those that had been adapted from stage plays. *Watch on the Rhine* (1942) and *The Man Who Came to Dinner* (1941) were the most frequently mentioned in the survey, and each was adapted from a stage play that was still running in London's West End when the films opened. In fact, many of Davis's screen roles had been played on the London stage, and played by some of the English theatre's most respected actors: Gladys Cooper had starred in Somerset Maugham's *The Letter*, Edith Evans in John Van Druten's *Old Acquaintance*, Diana Wynyard in Lillian Hellman's *Watch on the Rhine*, Fay Compton in Hellman's *The Little Foxes*, and Coral Browne in Kaufman and Hart's *The Man Who Came to Dinner*. Within metropolitan and middle class circles at least, this was likely to enhance the status of the films. Critics made comparisons and so too did some of Mass Observation's respondents: 'I also saw the stage play in London, a radio operator in Newport commented about *Watch on the Rhine*, [but] I thought the film was better' (Richards and Sheridan 1987: 257). It is unlikely, in this context, that these films were regarded as belonging to the 'woman's film' genre. Although the survey had a nearly even gender mix (116 men to 104 women), men actually cited her films far more often than women: altogether 16 men placed one of Davis's films among their 'best liked' of the previous year, but only eight women did.

Mass Observation's survey was conducted in the same month that *Now, Voyager* was released in London, November 1943, and two months before it went on general release throughout the country. It was too early, therefore, to include a range of views on the film. Nevertheless, one man and two women cited it as one of their 'best liked' films, and each mentioned the acting as the film's most significant virtue. In such comments, a common feature of middle class responses emerges: the tendency to explain the pleasure taken from films in intellectual rather than emotional terms. For middle class audiences, the emphasis placed on Davis's acting skills, and the associations made with the stage, lent a legitimacy to tastes that might otherwise be regarded as lowbrow, unthinking or common. Of course, these were not average or typical cinema-goers. As Richards and Sheridan have observed, Mass Observation's respondents were a decidedly middle class, middle aged and middlebrow group, while the regular cinema-goers of this era were likely to be younger, to include more women than men, and to be either working class or lower middle class (1987: 220–1). Their opinions and views are more likely to be represented in the popular fan magazine *Picturegoer*.

Leslie Halliwell recalled that *Picturegoer* was the 'bible' of the avid cinemagoer in wartime (Halliwell 1985: 90). The magazine had a film critic of its own, Lionel Collier, but more emphasis was placed on a participatory fan culture, in which opinions were not passed down from metropolitan film critics, but were instead shared, discussed, debated and voted on. An annual poll asked readers to vote for the best performance by male and female actors in the past year, and Davis won the first-place 'gold medal award' twice (for *Dark Victory* in 1939 and *Now, Voyager* in 1944). Competitions allowed readers to express themselves in a variety of ways, including writing poems and drawing sketches of stars. Letters allowed readers to air opinions and exchange views. There was also a regular column, 'A Filmgoer's Diary', that offered the views of a supposedly ordinary, young, married couple named Ralph and Jane Denton. The Dentons may have been the editor's invention, but their 'diary' allowed for a discussion of films that was more informal and conversational than most film criticism. Davis, the Dentons once noted, was 'a somewhat ticklish subject' with *Picturegoer* readers; the editor apparently received ample correspondence from both her supporters and detractors (28 June 1941: 12). The issue was raised when Ralph Denton attempted to define the 'woman's picture' in relation to two of Davis's films, *The Great Lie* (1941) and *All This and Heaven Too*. Both had what Denton considered definitive characteristics of the 'woman's picture': they were 'primarily about a woman', they were 'concerned primarily with things that interest women' and they had a 'tearful trend'. The difference between them was one of quality. He thought *The Great Lie* was a 'great' film and therefore should not be confined to the niche of the 'woman's picture'. He was much less enthusiastic about *All This and Heaven Too*, which led him to suppose that it had a more narrow appeal and a predominantly female audience. A 'woman's picture', in short, was one that was not quite good enough to interest men (10 May 1941: 14). Neither this definition nor his opinion on *All This and Heaven Too* (1940) were accepted by the magazine's readers (14 June 1941: 12). Like so much of the writing in *Picturegoer*, the 'Filmgoer's Diary' highlights the fact that, while matters of taste and distinction were important to regular cinema-goers, the boundaries were not so clearly drawn, terms were open to debate, and standards shifted according to personal taste.

More extensive commentaries by *Picturegoer* readers were compiled by the sociologist J. P. Mayer, whose studies of cinema audiences in the 1940s were published as *Sociology of Film* (1946) and *British Cinemas and their Audiences* (1948). Through placing advertisements in *Picturegoer*, Mayer asked the magazine's readers to reveal their film preferences, and to comment on the influences that films had on their lives and whether that was manifested in their ambitions, behaviour or dreams. Such questions suited his thesis, that the cinema had a deleterious effect on audiences, harming the physical and mental health of children and inhibiting the imagination and individuality of adults. However, one need not share his basic supposition in order to find the responses fascinating, and highly useful as qualitative rather than quantitative information about the popularity of stars and films.

Many of Mayer's respondents expressed their admiration for Davis's acting, but where middle class admirers (responding to Mass Observation) wrote about Davis's performances in terms of her skills and technique, many *Picturegoer* readers valued her performances for the feelings and emotions that they stirred. Interestingly, men commented on this as openly as women did. A 19 year old student, whose father worked in a factory, commented on the intense feelings that *Now, Voyager* summoned in him, especially in the scenes prior to Charlotte's transformation:

> Bette Davis makes me feel strangely uncomfortable sometimes when watching her. Especially did I feel this in *Now, Voyager* – particularly at the beginning when she was so awkward with herself. But then after the change, I felt alright again. Perhaps Miss Davis has more 'hold' over me than any other screen performer.
>
> (Mayer 1948: 191–4)

A 21 year old clerk regarded Davis's performance in *Now, Voyager* 'as one of the most enthralling episodes in my movie experience'. The 'huge emotional benefit' that he got from this 'great acting' made him want to study drama himself (ibid.: 112–13). A 24 year old farmer was so moved by the romance in *Now, Voyager* that he hoped he would one day find for himself the form of 'true, lasting and perfect love' portrayed by Davis and Henreid (Mayer 1946: 208).

Class distinctions among fans are also apparent in the terms employed to discuss their preferences. Working class fans expressed their feelings directly and without shame. For example, a 21 year old woman, working in a factory, explained very plainly why Davis's films are her 'favourite type': 'I am very emotional especially if a film is sad. Before I realise it tears are springing into my eyes. ... I feel as if I can place myself in the circumstances of those who are playing the part' (Mayer 1948: 72). By contrast, fans in lower middle class professions were more concerned to make it clear that, while they were moved by Davis's films, they remained discriminating viewers. A 21 year old woman, working as a newspaper reporter, noted her enjoyment of *Now, Voyager*, but drew a distinction between its 'love story' and 'the sloppy cheap sentimental type' usually associated with Hollywood (ibid.: 108–12). Others characterized their enjoyment as a guilty secret or an indulgence. A 23 year old woman, working as a typist, admitted that she 'revelled in *Now, Voyager*' and added, 'I hope my more cynical type of friends will never hear me say this but I love a very sad film with a bit of weeping now and again' (ibid.: 209–10). Similarly, a 19 year old woman, working as a clerk, said:

> With true femininity I enjoy a good love-story and if it is the sorrowful type which ostentatiously does not end happily every after, such as *Now, Voyager*, I can give myself up entirely to the luxury of the moment and indulge my emotions, weeping at the touching scene before me.
>
> (ibid.: 69–70)

Now, Voyager, for these lower middle class office workers, was a source of pleasure, but one that had to be discussed defensively (in the first example) or as a fleeting indulgence (in the second and third examples).

For a wide range of Mayer's respondents, and especially the socially aspirational, Davis served as a sophisticated, worldly role model. In a wider study of post-war, female British film fans, Jackie Stacey has argued that fans' emulation of stars took different forms (1994: 162–8). One was 'copying appearances', such as hairstyles, make-up and fashions. This was actively encouraged by British fan magazines, which informed readers how they could recreate Hollywood glamour despite the rationing and austerity of the 1940s (e.g., *Picture Show*, 29 January 1944: 14). Another form of emulation was 'imitating behaviour', which involved mimicry or assuming the personality of the star. Both forms were directly relevant to Mayer's thesis, and he asked questions such as 'what have you imitated from films in mannerisms [and] dress?'(1948: 14). Not surprisingly, then, there are frequent comments on this topic. While many women state that they follow Hollywood styles and try to recreate them for themselves, few comments relate this to specific stars. By contrast, 'imitating behaviour' is discussed much more specifically, and Davis is a clear favourite. One type of imitation involved memorizing scenes from Davis's films. An 18 year old woman who worked as a cashier indicated that she wrote down the dialogue from *Dark Victory*, *Now, Voyager* and *Watch on the Rhine*, so that 'if I wish to relive the scenes in any of the films, all I have to do is read over my writing'. This was a part of a strong admiration for the star; the respondent states that 'the greatest wish of my life is to meet Bette Davis' (Mayer 1946: 220). Another 'imitator' also relates strong feelings. This 22 year old man, working as a clerk, commented that he saw each of Davis's films four or five times while they played at his local cinema, and that 'I've often caught myself' using her 'clipped phrases and highly dramatic movements' in conversation (Mayer 1948: 104–5).

Imitating the distinctive Davis style was a means of gaining social confidence. A 16 year old girl, working as a library assistant, commented that she often imitated the 'haughty laughter of Bette Davis' as a means of distinguishing herself from 'girls who giggle' (ibid.: 123). A 20 year old civil servant admitted to drawing on Davis's expressions and mannerisms when she needed to demonstrate a 'quick wit' to her co-workers during 'office chatter' (ibid.: 91–2). A 23 year old factory worker revealed that when she faced a difficult decision, she thought of her two favourite stars and asked herself, 'what would Bette Davis or Greer Garson do in such a situation?' (Mayer 1946: 262) For J. P. Mayer, statements such as these were evidence that films had the effect of 'levelling down' individuality. 'Count the Bette Davises, the Greer Garsons or David Nivens you may meet every day when you travel to your office!' he exclaimed with some dismay, but his concern comes across as snobbery rather than genuine social observation (ibid.: 265). More recently, the playwright Alan Bennett has offered a much more incisive opinion of why Davis was so frequently imitated in the 1940s. In his memoirs, *Untold Stories* (2005), Bennett recalls that his two aunts, Kathleen and Myra, lived in their home town of Leeds, worked at routine jobs as shop assistants, and remained unmarried well into middle age. But they liked to think of themselves as 'women of the world' and took Bette Davis as their model of the modern, sophisticated woman, who could drink, smoke, banter and hold her own in social situations:

> The supreme exponent of brittle sophistication was Bette Davis, and for my aunties in particular she was someone to emulate. With her clipped tones, raised eyebrow and mocking smile Bette was a standard bearer for shop assistants everywhere and in the 1940s you could find her presiding over the counters of the smarter shops.
>
> (Bennett 2005: 166)

Their favourite film was *Now, Voyager* and, looking back decades later, Bennett understood the relevance that it had for them in the mid-1940s, as

Myra joined the WAAFs (and embarked for India on a cruise ship) and Kath-leen joined the ambulance service. For a generation of women who faced unforeseen opportunities and upheavals, Davis offered a road map through the social changes, or at least a model of confident, independent femininity.

Decades later, and after *Now, Voyager* had been shown on television numerous times, it came to be regarded 'one of the all-time great weepies' (*Radio Times*, 31 March 2007: 69) and as 'the epitome of what used to be called the woman's picture' (*Guardian* [The Guide], 31 March 2007: 53). These labels were meant as nostalgic praise for a familiar, favourite film. Ironically, though, the label of 'woman's film' was one that, within Britain at least, Warner Brothers and many of the film's admirers had resisted in the 1940s. There is no mistaking the fact that this was a maligned and denigrated genre; that films in which women were central, and their experiences of paramount importance, were regarded as trivial and overly sentimental. Among the audience commentaries now available, it is apparent that only working class audiences were able to discuss their enjoyment of the genre in unfettered and emotional terms, and this included men as well as women. Lower middle class audiences were more cir-cumspect when discussing the pleasures offered by the woman's film. Most pre-ferred to discuss the star rather than the genre. For many, Davis's screen persona offered a useful social touchstone in the midst of war; one that was particularly useful for consisting of highly imitable mannerisms and phrases. For others, Davis's reputation as an actor could lift her films above the level of the woman's film. Davis was a prime candidate for this form of amnesty. Since the mid-1930s, her reputation was separate from the prevailing prejudices and ste-reotypes that many Britons associated with Hollywood and stardom, and during the 1940s her acting style and many of the roles she played were well suited to a critical culture that valued the theatre over and above films. Thus, middle class audiences, who sought cultural capital by following critical opinion, could appreciate Bette Davis in their own careful fashion. While responses to Davis's films must be filtered through a class lens, it is clear that the films had a wide and multifarious appeal. Responses to *Now, Voyager* in particular demonstrate the many ways in which a woman's film could be recovered and enjoyed by all. The story of Charlotte Vale's transformation may have been written and filmed thousands of miles away, but in cinemas up and down Britain, it nevertheless 'spoke' to British audiences as powerfully and intimately as any film could.

Bibliography

Basinger, J. (1993) *A Woman's View: How Hollywood Spoke to Women, 1930–1960*, New York: Alfred A. Knopf.
Bennett, A. (2005) *Untold Stories*, London: Faber and Faber.
Bernstein Questionnaire Report (1934) London: Granada Cinemas.
——(1937) London: Granada Cinemas.
Ellis, J. (1996) 'The quality film adventure: British critics and the cinema, 1942–48', in A. Higson (ed.), *Dissolving Views: Key Writings on British Cinema*, London: Cassell.

Gledhill, C. (2003) *Reframing British Cinema, 1918–1928: Between Restraint and Passion*, London: British Film Institute.

Halliwell, L. (1985) *Seats in All Parts: Half a Lifetime at the Movies*, London: Granada.

Harper, S. and Porter, V. (2003) *British Cinema of the 1950s: The Decline of Deference*, Oxford: Oxford University Press.

Klaprat, C. (1985) 'The star as market strategy: Bette Davis in another light', in T. Balio (ed.), *The American Film Industry*, Revised Edition, Madison: the University of Wisconsin Press.

Kuhn, A. (2002) *An Everyday Magic: Cinema and Cultural Memory*, London: I.B. Tauris.

LaPlace, M. (1987) 'Producing and consuming the woman's film: discursive struggle in *Now, Voyager*', in C. Gledhill (ed.), *Home is Where the Heart is: Studies in Melodrama and the Woman's Film*, London: British Film Institute.

Mayer, J.P. (1946) *Sociology of Film: Studies and Documents*, London: Faber and Faber.

——(1948) *British Cinemas and Their Audiences: Sociological Studies*, London: Dennis Dobson.

Now, Voyager Pressbook (1942), British Film Institute Pressbook Collection.

Ramsaye, T. (ed.) (1946) *The 1945–46 Motion Picture Almanac*, New York: Quigley.

Richards, J. and Sheridan, D. (1987) *Mass Observation at the Movies*, London: Routledge and Kegan Paul.

Shingler, M. (2007) '*Now, Voyager* (1942): melodrama then and now', in J. Chapman, M. Glancy and S. Harper (eds), *The New Film History: Sources, Methods, Approaches*, London: Palgrave.

Stacey, J. (1994) *Star Gazing: Hollywood Cinema and Female Spectatorship*, London: Routledge.

Taylor, H. (1989) *Scarlett's Women: Gone with the Wind and Its Female Fans*, London: Virago.

Ingénues, lovers, wives and mothers

The 1940s career trajectories of Googie
Withers and Phyllis Calvert

Brian McFarlane

'I never wanted to play the Phyllis Calvert roles,' said Googie Withers.[1] Neither, though, did Phyllis Calvert.[2] Between them, however, they summed up some crucial ideological aspects of British cinema in its 1940s heyday. Calvert's films of the period fall fairly neatly into the category disparagingly referred to as 'women's films'; Withers was more often, though not exclusively, associated with British cinema's new realism, but it might be truer to say that her films are posited on the idea of a different kind of woman – and perhaps in consequence *appealed* to a different kind of woman.

Rationale

The more obvious comparison may seem to be between Calvert and Gainsborough colleague Margaret Lockwood. I choose Withers here because the roles she played were earthed in a reality that highwaywoman Lockwood never, in my perception, aspired to. Lockwood could flare her nostrils and narrow her eyes, bare her cleavage and secure the deaths of hapless others, and be altogether a bad lot, but to me she always seemed like a nice girl in fancy-dress as she held up coaches and poisoned husbands. However, I am aware that a considerable body of scholarship would take issue with me here (Harper 1994; Babington 2001), and that Lockwood was an enormous favourite in 1940s British cinema. Withers, though, whether playing a sluttish pub landlady or a prosaically married woman yearning for her criminal lover, or a determined lady farmer, always imbued her roles with a powerful sense of their actuality, of their place in the circumambient world. So in her gentler way did Calvert. Both, via divergent screen personas, seemed related to the changing social realities of the period, the period of highest achievement in British cinema. Roughly put, I see Calvert's image as dominant until war's end when it is displaced by the bolder Withers women. It is not that there weren't other notable women contributing to this fertile period – think of Sally Gray, Valerie Hobson, Jean Kent, the sublime Celia Johnson – but it is at least arguable that no two actresses between them say so much about what was expected of and available to women in 1940s Britain and British cinema.

Undeniably, Calvert was given less rewarding material to work on than Withers was. Years later, Calvert recalled how she hated being typecast as goody-goodies, but the on-screen evidence indicates how intelligently she played them. She stays in the mind for her no-nonsense avoidance of sentimentality as she represents a 'wholesome' image of 1940s wife and mother. She represents a femininity no doubt held desirable in wartime when so many women were for the first time encouraged to break away from domestic confines – and then, post-war, encouraged to go right back to them. Withers, in her magnificently brazen sensuality, was clearly never going to be party to such patriarchal manipulation; Calvert, for all her English-rose sweetness, commands respect for her characters, insisting on their individuality despite the daunting stereotypes they may have seemed on paper.

Parallelism

Furthermore, these two actresses pursued careers of surprising parallelism, more so than was the case with any of those other women named above. Both had careers spanning over seventy years; both started pre-teenage, as dancers rather than actresses; neither trained as an actress but learnt on the job. Calvert first appeared at the Lyric Hammersmith in November 1925, in *Crossings*, Ellen Terry's swansong, and subsequently did seasons with provincial repertory companies during the 1930s, where, she said, 'I learnt my craft' (cited in McFarlane 1997: 109). Withers, in response to a suggestion that, as a film actress, she never betrayed staginess, said: 'That is probably because I had no proper stage training except as a dancer' and that when she started doing plays 'probably I was bringing a film performance to the theatre' (cited in McFarlane 1997: 608).

These two dancers-turned-actresses both became consummate *film* actresses in the 1940s. Both started filming in the previous decade, Withers much more prolifically than Calvert who had more stage experience in these years. Both served film apprenticeships with the famous comics of the day, notably with George Formby and Arthur Askey. Both reached their cinema peaks in the 1940s, the war boosting their careers, albeit in different directions. In the post-40s decades, both did some notable film work, but stage and television gradually gained ascendance. Withers moved to Australia in the mid 50s with husband John McCallum, and returned to England for theatre and television but never filmed there again. Calvert's film career flickered intermittently into the 60s, with a final vivid appearance in *Mrs Dalloway* (1997), while Withers made three films in Australia, last in *Shine* (1996). In television, each made notable appearances and each had her own series, Calvert in *Kate* (1970–2), as an agony-column writer, and Withers in *Within These Walls* (1973–8), as the Governor of a women's prison.

The 1940s

In interview Calvert and Withers emerged as two strong-minded women with a clear sense of what they'd wanted from their film careers and how far these had matched their aspirations (McFarlane 1992). Despite similarities in career trajectories, clearly they projected contrasting images in their peak years in 1940s

cinema. There are some instances of imagistic overlap: Calvert's dual role in
Madonna of the Seven Moons (1944) for once gives her the chance to throw off
restraint in a way that aligns her with Withers, whose characters rarely knew
the meaning of restraint. And Withers was occasionally – in *On Approval*
(1944), for instance – allowed the more obviously 'feminine' softness typical of
Calvert's persona. Their essentially different screen images were already dis-
cernible in the films each made with George Formby, and a stint as leading lady
to the toothy, twanging Lancashire comedian was almost *de rigueur* as a hoop
through which pretty, promising young actresses were required to jump before
going on to more demanding fare.

   In *Let George Do It* (1940), Calvert's Mary works as a receptionist in a
Bergen hotel, while actually involved in undercover war work. She and George
eventually unmask bandleader Mendez (caddish Garry Marsh), as a spy. That
Calvert's character is called Mary is the first step in placing her as a thoroughly
nice girl: 'nicely spoken', hair discreetly permed, costumes uniformly simple.
She contrasts with Coral Browne's easy, insolent sexiness as Iris, showing off
her legs and soignée in ways unthinkable for Calvert's Mary, but there is a pleasing
crispness in Calvert's diction. Withers, in *Trouble Brewing* (1938), shows at 21
some of the assurance that would so mark her as a dominant leading lady of
the 1940s. Again a 'Mary', though suggesting something bolder and sexier, she
played a resourceful secretary (to nasty Marsh again). Even as early as this, she
exhibits a good-humoured persona that suggests she can look after herself in a
man's world and a capacity to take the initiative, as she does when she
encourages George to get his just reward. Very pretty and sassy, she is already a
welcome female lead. She'd had plenty of experience prior to this at Gainsborough (with which Calvert would become inextricably associated in the 40s) at
holding her own in improbably comic situations: as, say, Baroness Charlotte
Russo with a fake foreign accent which she drops to threaten Will Hay in
Convict 99 (1938); and as a fashion model stranded on a remote Scottish island
with Nazis and Arthur Askey in *Back Room Boy* (1942).

   Their performances in these ancient comedies suggest that, in like generic
circumstances, they were already displaying very different screen presences.
How they measure up to the demands of their Formby roles seems to signal
how their paths would diverge in the next crucial decade. There was a nice,
sensible girl, sensibly dressed and made-up to look like someone a man could
trust in Calvert's image; Withers, by contrast, exuded a sprightly capacity for
dealing with men and innuendo, an easy sensuality, which marked her as a
woman not to be trifled with. In the event, Withers would get the better, more
varied chances, but Calvert had arguably the harder task in making goodness
interesting. By coincidence, when she *did* get a chance to show she was not to
be trifled with, she ended by falling into the same on-screen arms as those
which rescued Withers from being too independent: the film was *The Root of
All Evil* (1947) and the arms belonged to John McCallum, whom Withers
married. In the 50s, both had become strikingly assured mature female leads:
Withers in *White Corridors* (1951) and Calvert in *Mandy* (1952).

Two contrasting images

At the end of *They Were Sisters* (1945), Calvert's Lucy, happily married to William (real-life husband Peter Murray-Hill), is sitting on the lawn of a charming country cottage, with William and the children of her sisters, dead Charlotte and hedonistic Vera. For her, the woman's goal is that of 'muddling through' as wife and mother, her childless state now rectified so that William can say, 'God's in his heaven, all's right with the world'. It's hard to imagine a Withers vehicle finishing on this note; it is even harder to imagine Calvert bringing off Withers' last moments in *Pink String and Sealing Wax* (1945). The camera, in a great forward tracking shot, follows her progress from the pub, where she has stopped sobbing, braced herself and gone out on to the street, then pulls back to reveal her walking resolutely to the railing at the cliff's edge. Finally, she rises up majestically and hurls herself over. These two images – the one a static long shot, the other tracking – encapsulate much not only of these two star personas but also of how 1940s cinema was dealing with the idea of women in society.

The good woman

'We all did one film for [director Leslie] Arliss and said "Never again"', said Calvert (quoted in Aspinall and Murphy 1983: 61), and she, unlike co-stars Lockwood, Stewart Granger and James Mason, never did. However, she acknowledged that it was Arliss's *The Man in Grey* (1943) that made her a 'household name', while expressing her frustration that she was always being required to play 'just the girl that all the troops wanted to marry' (cited in McFarlane 1997: 110). That remark indicates her awareness of how she was being presented and how her roles belonged so revealingly to the anxious times in which her career flourished. Sue Harper writes: 'Some career advantages would certainly accrue to those who produced images of women which were commensurate with government propaganda policy' (2000: 38). This may well have been the case for Arliss; it certainly was for Calvert.

Between her dealings with Formby and *The Man in Grey*, she had projected an often gentle, womanly demeanour, but with a suggestion of moral grit as if being attractively feminine didn't preclude a certain decisiveness of action. Post-Formby, she had female leads in the wartime thrillers *Neutral Port* (1940) and *Uncensored* (1942), stooged enjoyably with comedians Arthur Askey (*Charley's (Big-Hearted) Aunt*, 1940) and Gordon Harker (*Inspector Hornleigh Goes to It*, 1941), and appeared twice for director Carol Reed. In his *The Young Mr Pitt* (1942), she has an unrewarding role as the object of Pitt's affections. However, Reed had used her much more enterprisingly as Ann Pornick, the cockney maid, who eventually marries the eponymous *Kipps* (1941), whose childhood sweetheart she has been. Of cockney origin herself, Calvert is charming and spirited, doing a lower-class accent convincingly, and with a fresh open face that seems incapable of concealment. Her Ann matures subtly as the married woman, accruing firmness and moral strength, and, with baby in arms and a convincing gloss of maternity, she has the film's last frame. Of the films she made before the watershed *Man in Grey*, *Kipps* is the one that most significantly suggests what lies ahead for her. One commentator, praising the other stars (Michael Redgrave and Diana Wynyard), writes: 'Calvert, lit up with the unspoiled charm of Ann, is no less satisfying' (Moss 1987: 127). 'Unspoiled' and that last frame: the writing was on the wall. She may not have been a household name by the time she played hapless Clarissa in *The Man in Grey*, but she had shown real competence and a charming freshness in a half-dozen films since her Formby stint.

Undeniably, though, it was the Gainsborough melodramas of the mid 1940s that made her a star. Billed second, after Lockwood, she first appears on the steps of the wartime London auction-room in a WRNS uniform, poised and modern-looking. As Peter Rokeby (Stewart Granger) admires the portrait of Lady Clarissa Rohan, and the 1940s Clarissa tells him, 'I'm the last of the Rohans', the film flashes back to the Regency era when she was 'the lovely and amiable' student at Miss Patchett's school, to which Hester, raven-haired Lockwood, came as a sort of 'poor relation' to whom Clarissa was kind: 'I need a friend who won't spoil me', she tells Hester. It's as if Calvert is already aware that too much of being 'lovely and amiable' may be just that: too much of a good thing. There is warmth and openness in Calvert's Clarissa, along with more sense of possibilities than the screenplay is allowing her. When she succumbs to the marriage proposal of the sadistic Rohan (James Mason), Calvert conveys Clarissa's submission and timorousness in the grandeur of the Rohan seat as well as a touching growth of apprehension and unhappiness. The painter taking her portrait sees something regal in her: there is dignity in Calvert's bearing here and later when she goes to the theatre to see 'friend' Hester perform with Rokeby (Granger as the modern Peter's ancestor). The closer one looks at her performance in this key film, the more interesting her range proves to be. When Rokeby comes to the Rohan house as librarian, she convincingly suggests both Clarissa's attempts to keep him in his place *and* the fact that she is instinctively charmed by him – and the way in which this burgeons into love.

Critics generally were unkind to *The Man in Grey* and to the melodramas that followed. Subsequent scholarship suggests that only the public was right in making box-office successes of them (Harper 1994; Murphy 1989). Calvert moved with increasing authority through *Fanny by Gaslight* (1944), *Madonna of the Seven Moons* (1944), *They Were Sisters* (1945) and the admittedly idiotic *The Magic Bow* (1946). In each, she is the 'good woman', with the exception that 'half' of her in *Madonna*, as we shall see, reveals the side of her that is usually suppressed. *Fanny*, perhaps the classiest of the Gainsborough melodramas, contrasts Calvert in the title role with no fewer than three other cast members. Her gentle decorum is first played off against Jean Kent's Lucy, her childhood friend who becomes an actress, not settling for the conventional woman's lot of marriage and children. Calvert's demureness as Fanny is even more strikingly counterpointed against Margaretta Scott's vivid Alicia.

Scott incarnates a worldly sophistication and sensuality completely at odds with Fanny's simple goodness, and the contrast between Calvert on the one hand and Kent and Scott on the other is reinforced by the involvement of all three with James Mason's swinish Lord Manderstoke. Finally, Calvert's openness is opposed to Cathleen Nesbitt's snobbery as Kate Somerford, Harry's (Granger) older, bitter sister, who does her best to dissuade Fanny from marrying her brother.

In relation to these three, Fanny shows herself as a sort of ideal woman for the times. The others reflect aspects of the war-disrupted 1940s: Lucy in pursuing a career; Alicia in espousing a woman's equal rights to sexual adventurism; and Kate as purveyor of an outmoded social system. Calvert's Fanny will have to earn her own living, and in circumstances less glamorous than Lucy's; she will eventually accompany Harry to Paris as his mistress, in which role she appears innocent and happy, the image of a woman fully in love; and in the film's last episode she routs the class-based interference of Kate Somerford. Across a social range that has embraced the aristocracy, 'symbol of a dark, unspeakable sexuality' in several of these films (Harper 1996: 207), the demimonde (actresses in 'supper rooms'), working-class pub and laundry, Fanny

Figure 5.1 'A sort of ideal woman for the times': Cathleen Nesbitt confronts Phyllis Calvert in *Fanny by Gaslight*, directed by Anthony Asquith (1944).
Source: The Steve Chibnall Collection.

acquires, in Calvert's very skilfully shaded performance, an increasing confidence that grows from an emerging self that has resisted corruption and mere ease, arriving at a credible maturity. Marcia Landy writes of Fanny's function as 'mediator' between extremes of 'aristocratic excess and repressive sexuality as associated with the middle class' (1991: 214). Calvert's playing creates a viable alternative, making devotion plausible, and as interesting as the showier extremes. As Robert Murphy sums up: 'Less sweet, less privileged than Clarissa, she comes to represent the average British housewife, turning her hand to any sort of work to survive ... and blossoming into a full-blooded woman determined to fight for her share of happiness' (1989: 48).

If restraint, not necessarily aligned with repression, is often characteristic of her roles, or of other major contemporary English actresses (think, most notably, of Celia Johnson in *Brief Encounter*), one needs only to turn to her two other 1944 films to appreciate her capacity for diverse responses, while still working within the over-arching paradigm of the 'good woman'. In *Two Thousand Women* (1944), director Frank Launder wanted Calvert to play the nun who falls in love with an airman, the part finally played by Patricia Roc, but Calvert held out to play Freda Thompson, the cynical, outspoken journalist, displeasing Launder as a result, but clearly enjoying the opportunity to exchange quips with, and about, Jean Kent as sexy Bridie. Of Bridie's dealings with the German officers running the internment camp for women, Freda observes: 'The rat is about to enter the trap after the oldest cheese in the world'. Without actually undermining her 'good-woman' image, she essays here more than gentle compliance, is even glimpsed in knickers and bra in one scene and, in another, exhibits a chic sophistication in evening dress.

But it is her other release that year, *Madonna of the Seven Moons*, which gives her most histrionic range in suggesting the complexity of the 'good woman' who, under pressure, gives vent to another side of her personality. As Maddalena, she is a virtuous upper-class Roman matron, whose libidinous other self emerges when the disturbing return from school in England of her ultra-modern daughter, Angela (Patricia Roc), full of new ideas and exuding sexual freedom, triggers off repressed needs in herself. There is no doubt something schematic about the way the Maddalena/Rome/matron/stately mansion is posited against Rosanna/Florence/mistress/thieves' kitchen, but Calvert persuades us that Maddalena and Rosanna are two parts of a single over-taxed sensibility. She is as convincing as the free-spirited Rosanna, in whom the urge to respectability is muted (the repression is not all on Maddalena's side!). Critics of the period derided the film as novelettish tosh, resisting what it might reveal about dichotomous demands made on women, and the resultant inner conflicts. They also showed a literal-minded tendency – as if everything should, or could, be judged on a criterion of 'realism' – which precluded responsiveness to the production design that renders the two different ambiences inhabited by the protagonist. Or of the costume design: how the sensuality of the uninhibited Rosanna (in free-flowing skirt and low-cut blouses) is hinted at in the clinging white evening dress (clearly uncorseted) Maddalena has worn at the ball in

Rome. Or the film's last image of the dead heroine with her husband's cross and her lover's rose on her bosom. Finally, as a 'woman's film', the remark by the old mother in the thieves' kitchen that 'fair's fair' – woman's sexual needs are as legitimate as men's – encapsulates *Madonna*'s claims to be considered a progressive text.

Though *They Were Sisters* offered Calvert a wholly sympathetic, conventional 'good-woman' role, she made it as intelligently forceful as its diagrammatic constraints would permit: the kind, maternal but childless sister ultimately taking on her sisters' unhappy children. It is hard to imagine another actress of the period so skilfully suggesting the fundamental nurturing kindness, along with a readiness to speak out strongly when occasion requires (as in her courtroom denunciation of Mason's sadistic Geoffrey). There is little to be said about *The Magic Bow*, allegedly based on the life of Paganini (Granger again). Calvert and Lockwood both sought to get out of it and only Lockwood succeeded, leaving Calvert with a colourless leading-lady role. She is graceful in period costume, but her role is no more than a romantic, well-born young woman being jostled into a marriage she doesn't want by her ambitious mother, and resisting this. There is perhaps a 1940s echo, with a woman daring to resist her pre-ordained future, and there are characteristic Calvert touches of spirit, leading her mother to say, 'You're behaving like one of the people.'

Her other 1946 release, Thorold Dickinson's well-intentioned, somewhat simplistic tract, *Men of Two Worlds*, took Calvert into very different narrative territory – and her first sortie into Technicolor. The film traces the return of Kisenga (Robert Adams), a black African pianist, to his native country, where District Commissioner Randall (Eric Portman) is the voice of enlightened paternalism. Calvert, appointed doctor to the territory, arrives looking crisp, middle-class and professional. She is persuasive as a working woman, dressed in slack suits and blouses (except when she turns up in evening dress for drinks with Randall), and able to take on Portman in their scenes of confrontation. She is also contrasted again with Cathleen Nesbitt's foolish traveller maundering about 'the soul of the people'. Much of the impressiveness of Calvert's *oeuvre* has depended on such contrast with other female characters, out of which her own persona was forged. Jeffrey Richards quotes Dickinson on the subject of Portman and Calvert in the film: 'They did their best but they had never visited East Africa and for the most part struggled against the usual stereotypes of white colonials' (1986: 122). Maybe, but it at least gives Calvert the rare challenge of playing a professional woman and, like Withers in *White Corridors*, she enacts medical procedures as if she knows what she is doing.

But the key film from the point of view of showing her as a woman determined to make her way in the man's world of business is Brock Williams' *The Root of All Evil* (1947), released in the same year that Withers set herself up as a farmer in *The Loves of Joanna Godden*. Both recall Michael Curtiz's *Mildred Pierce* (1945), in which a woman cuts a swathe through unsatisfactory men and achieves striking business success. Calvert plays Jeckie Farnish, who realises her father's indolence has been responsible for their farm's failure and who, as their fortunes plummet and her engagement to a rich young man ends, announces: 'From now on I'm going to manage the farm.' She is 'going to turn a somer-sault … from now on it's going to be head over heart. There's only one unforgivable sin – poverty'. Following this low point, there is a newly purpo-sive look to Jeckie, articulated through increasingly smart costumes (admired by girls in the street), a more sophisticated hair-do, commented-on smoking, and no-nonsense diction as she deals with men both supine and aggressive. As well, there is a sharper contrast made with her sister Rushie (Hazel Court in 'the Phyllis Calvert part'). Rushie settles for a conventional marriage, but Jeckie will eventually have to attend to Rushie's bromide, 'Life's not all business'. A brief affair with a suave visiting man (Michael Rennie), who nearly runs her down in his car (almost certainly a 'roadster'), hardens Jeckie further. Though there is feminist interest in Jeckie's enterprise, there is no question of her being allowed to get away with her money-making schemes, as a man might, and she finally finds comfort in the arms of Joe Bartle (John McCallum) and is forced to say, 'I've come home and I'm sorry'. Withers, similarly placed at *Joanna Godden*'s end, is not required by Ealing to be so abject.

The decade ran down for Calvert, as for Withers, both of them at Gains-borough in less rewarding vehicles. The stewardess Calvert plays in *Broken Journey* (1948) requires not much more from her than a display of efficiency, with a hint of restraint masking repressed feeling, as a woman who was once in love with a liar and cheat, but now has pilot James Donald in the offing as compensation. It isn't worthy of the solid filmography she had built up, and neither are the roles she had in Hollywood.

The tough woman

I've spent so much time on Calvert because it seems to me her 1940s career has been undervalued. There has never been any doubt, however, that Withers was a one-off in 1940s British cinema; her importance to the decade's view of itself needs less arguing. As already suggested, in her late 30s/early 40s comedy roles, she was already asserting the idea of a woman who knew where she was going. Even in the small role of Margaret Lockwood's friend at the start of Hitch-cock's *The Lady Vanishes* (1938), she is found doing leg exercises, unperturbed when a waiter enters her hotel room; she is cynical about Lockwood's proposed marriage, seeing it as no sure recipe for happiness; and, in a swaggeringly checked coat slung over her shoulders, she persists to the last moment in trying to talk Lockwood out of her plans for a 'secure' future.

So what was Withers' own future in the heyday of British films? Contrasting with Calvert's roles which, despite slippages, over-all reinforced what was desirable for women in her great period at Gainsborough, Withers racked up a string of outstanding performances at Ealing as women who were not about to be kept tidily in their places. Prior to Ealing, she did two patriotic films, Michael Powell's *One of Our Aircraft is Missing* (1942) and Vernon Sewell's *The Silver Fleet* (1943). That most unreliable autobiographer, Powell, who 'discovered' Withers in 1930s quota quickies, tells us that 'She broke down and cried when I gave her the part [in *Aircraft*]. She had never played anything but comedy, but she had Dutch blood ... and I knew she could do it' (Powell 1986: 391). Withers repudiates this account, saying she was just delighted to get so strong a role. It was her first important part in an 'A' feature and, though she doesn't appear until 70 minutes into the film, she is talked about well before that, and shown as authoritative in a man's world. She is wearing a turban which shows her face to great advantage; she is very beautiful; and her femininity emerges when she responds just a little to having her hand kissed by one of the RAF officers who have parachuted into occupied Holland. Later, at dinner, she is dressed in more conventionally female gear and says, 'It's nice to be a woman again, even if it's only for half an hour'. Withers has no more than 20 minutes' playing time in this wartime thriller, but she effortlessly commands the screen during that time and stays in the mind when it is over. When she asks the senior RAF man (Godfrey Tearle), 'Are you in command?' he replies, 'No, you are.' In more than one sense (she will spirit the fliers out of Holland) he is absolutely right, and there is something oddly touching when he kisses her as they leave.

In *The Silver Fleet*, again set in occupied Holland, she has – for her – an unusually recessive role. Elegantly dressed, she is represented first as understanding wife and mother, Helene, unaware that her apparently collaborationist husband (Ralph Richardson) is secretly undermining the Nazi cause. We know he is a patriot because the film is told via Helene's reading his journal after his death, but she 'is narratively an outsider who knows less than the audience' (Geraghty 1996: 235). There is an early mirror shot as she tries to wrest the truth from him, but the role offers her more scope as she grows angry with him, culminating in the moment when she locks her bedroom door against him and sits appalled, no longer able to trust him. If this role brought Withers nearer to the archetypal female protagonist of the 'woman's film', in her four great Ealing roles men would get shorter shrift. In her last pre-Ealing film, the delectable high comedy *On Approval*, she plays heiress Helen Hale, young, beautiful and so charming it's hard to believe she can be interested in the middle-aged fortune-hunter played by director-star Clive Brook. Here she is contrasted with brilliant comedienne, Beatrice Lillie (who indeed would *not* have been contrasted with Lillie?), beside whom Withers at first seems ingenuous. However, once the two women (and the men whose company they are testing) are installed on a remote island, Withers exhibits a new assurance in dress and posture, establishing herself as the practical one of the two. She has rarely been more irresistible as the camera lovingly tracks her sashaying round the house.

Dead of Night, Pink String and Sealing Wax, The Loves of Joanna Godden, It Always Rains on Sunday:[3] did any other British actress ever get such a rewarding quartet of roles in the space of a couple of years? This Ealing quartet is to Withers' career and *réclame* as a film actress what Calvert's earlier couple of years at Gainsborough were to her, their dominant screen personas being fashioned. In the celebrated omnibus horror film, *Dead of Night* (1945), she had the good fortune to be directed by Robert Hamer in her episode, 'The Haunted Mirror'. Withers as Joan, stylish, capable and sophisticated, tells of buying for her fiancé Peter (Ralph Michael) a mirror which reflects to him those recesses of his psyche which he has repressed. Peter Hutchings has argued very persuasively for considering the film as 'an intense and obsessive meditation on issues arising from the transition from a wartime to a post-war society' (1993: 26). It is through the intervention of the Withers character that the mirror which unmans Peter enters his life; it is through her enterprise that its baleful effect is finally exorcised. But as Charles Barr suggests, its 'ending is extremely ambivalent. It is by her sudden insight and strength that she saves him from re-enacting the violence stored in the mirror world and in himself' (1977: 57) but, in doing so, perhaps restores them to a somewhat anodyne relationship, in which she will always be the more resourceful partner.

Of Withers' role and performance in *Pink String and Sealing Wax* (1946) I have written at length elsewhere (McFarlane 2005: 58–61). I referred above to her superb last moments in this film, and I want to add here only that, though the screenplay undoubtedly has to punish Pearl Bond for the murder of her disgusting husband, it cannot distract our sympathies. I wrote in the earlier account:

> Pearl has an energy and intelligence more forceful than anyone else in the film; her tragedy is to find no outlet for them and the viewer's reward for emotional investment in her situation is to be far more moved by her finally taking charge of her own fate than by the ostensibly 'happy' outcome for the law-abiding Victorian family.
>
> (ibid.: 61)

Sensual, brazen and strikingly beautiful, by the time she appears a good deal of tension and repression has been established, and at reference to Pearl the film cuts to a woman in the street waylaying a man called Dan. Saying her husband is 'too drunk to notice', she throws herself into Dan's arms. Her sexual availability is established in the shadows outside before she takes her place proprietorially behind the bar. She stands up to her drunken husband; exchanges invective with other women in the pub; and invests her meeting with Gordon Jackson's youthful David with the symbolic significance of innocence and experience. With the collusion of Bianca Mosca's costumes and Stanley Pavey's cinematography, Withers establishes images of erotic potency and magisterial authority. Victorian values may seem to win out eventually but her boldly self-serving strength is the film's great positive.

The Loves of Joanna Godden (1947) is Withers' most explicit articulation of a feminist agenda. 'I'd like to meet the man who wouldn't take orders from me,' she tells neighbouring farmer Arthur Alce (John McCallum) as she rebuffs his embrace and decides to take on running her late father's farm. 'What a tartar,' someone says of her. 'I know what I'm doin',' she insists, and, helped by severe hairstyle and costumes, she compels belief in Joanna as a woman in charge, whether casting an appraising eye over sheep-dog trials or hiring a new shepherd (Chips Rafferty), with whom she talks knowledgeably about 'cross-breedin'. This is still only 1947, so there are also remarks like Arthur's: 'Jo, why don't you stop trying to be a man. It's all very well being a woman farmer if you don't stop being a woman', but, though Arthur is attractively presented and though he and Joanna will be together at the end, the film's heart doesn't truly seem to be in these sentiments.

Arthur's marriage to Jo's sister Ellen (Jean Kent) founders on Ellen's failure to engage sympathetically with his life and its difficulties. When his flock is wiped out, Ellen says, 'We'll be poor?', to which he replies, 'The two of us pulling together … no bounds to what we can do'. But Ellen, expensively educated by Joanna, knows what she wants: 'lots of nice things'; and her selfish superficiality throws Joanna's seriousness of purpose into relief. The contrast is finally reinforced when, Ellen having run off with another man, Joanna offers Arthur the use of her land for grazing. In shirt and tie, signifying that she has not surrendered her independence, her sense of equality with a man, she now accepts from Arthur the embrace rejected at the film's start, and he echoes his words to Ellen: 'No bounds to what we can do'. The film's feminist intentions may seem compromised by this conclusion; on the other hand, the film persuades us that these two people now understand each other. Further, there does not appear to be any etiolation of the forceful Withers image, but the forcefulness will now work in favour of a partnership.

David Thomson, no friend to British films, omits Phyllis Calvert altogether from his *Biographical Dictionary*, but does include Withers, and, writing of *Pink String* and *It Always Rains on Sunday* (1947), describes her as 'magnificent in two films by Robert Hamer' (2003: 945). And so she is. Pearl in *Pink String* is the showier of the two roles, but Rose Sandigate in *It Always Rains* is her crowning glory, a role written and acted with detailed, compassionate humanity. She is established at the outset as a bossy, grumpy housewife and (step-) mother, calling to the girls to bring early morning tea, boredom speaking in the lineaments of her body. But this is not a caricature of a bored housewife: she is justifiably tired from looking after a middle-aged husband, George (Edward Chapman), their son and his two grown-up daughters, flighty Vi (Susan Shaw), in whom she will recognise reflections of her own younger self, and more biddable Doris (Patricia Plunkett). Into the humdrum pattern of her Sundays erupts an escaped convict, her ex-lover Tommy Swann (John McCallum), who recalls the passion of their liaison, when she was still the pretty young barmaid at the pub where George is now darts champion. I doubt there was another British actress then or ever who could so convincingly have created the tensions of domestic prisoner and once-hopeful lover of the unreliable criminal-in-the-making – or so movingly the wife who, having made her bed, ends by gratefully lying in it. After Swann's departure, she expresses the most complex mix of pain, relief, disappointment, disillusion and despair. She knows life with George will neither rouse nor satisfy her passionate nature as Swann once did, but also knows how to value the fact that 'he's all right, he's decent to me'. Rose is, as Barr has noted, '[t]he definitive Googie Withers role' (1977: 68).

Figure 5.2 The eruption of passion into the humdrum domestic world: John McCallum, Patricia Plunkett and Googie Withers in *It Always Rains on Sunday*, directed by Robert Hamer (1947).
Source: The Steve Chibnall Collection.

Converging courses

Both women fetched up at Gainsborough in the later 40s and for neither was this a very rewarding period. Calvert's *The Root of All Evil* is interesting rather than distinguished and *Broken Journey* offers her a cardboard role. Her last film of the decade is *The Golden Madonna* (1949), which she co-produced for Independent Film Producers. By her own account, it was cut before release in such a way as to make it nearly incomprehensible, robbing the plot of key motivation.[4] Withers' late 40s Gainsborough films, *Miranda* (1948) and *Once Upon a Dream* (1949), are both lightweight romantic comedies, entertaining enough in their undemanding ways, and Withers plays in both, stylishly coiffured and coutured, with appropriate sophistication. At one point in the later film, she announces that she won't be treated as a 'chattel' any more. As if anyone would ever have dared!

Though the gap between them narrowed as their respective roles in *White Corridors* and *Mandy* manifested, Calvert's range could scarcely have encompassed Withers' tough *film noir* figure in Jules Dassin's *Night and the City*

(1950). Withers in the 40s had the best opportunities and did them wonderful justice; Calvert shows in *Mandy* just how much more she might have done than the 'Calvert roles' she was lumbered with. Even here, though, a certain consistency is maintained: Withers in *White Corridors* is primarily a professional woman, a doctor, fighting to save a small boy's life; Calvert, on the other hand, is still a wife and mother, albeit one with the bit between her teeth, fighting for a life for her deaf child. Between them and the roles they played in the 40s, it is fascinating to consider the kinds of rewards and punishments that were handed out for various kinds of female behaviour; and the ways in which these were fashioned into narratives meant for popular entertainment. Re-viewing their 1940s films today, it is clear that the conventional 'woman's film' was usually safer in Calvert's hands, whereas with Withers you were far less sure that the status quo would be upheld by the time she had finished with it.

Notes

1 Interview with author, March 1990.
2 Interview with author, October 1989 and reprinted in McFarlane 1997.
3 Her other Ealing film, *They Came to a City* (1944) has not been available for this study.
4 Interview with author, October 1989.

Bibliography

Aspinall, S. and Murphy, R. (eds) (1983) *Gainsborough Melodrama*, London: BFI.
Babington, B. (2001) '"Queen of British hearts": Margaret Lockwood revisited', in B. Babington (ed.), *British Stars and Stardom: From Alma Taylor to Sean Connery*, Manchester: Manchester University Press.
Barr, C. (1977) *Ealing Studios*, London/Newton Abbot: Cameron & Tayleur/David & Charles.
Geraghty, C. (1996) 'Disguises and betrayals: negotiating nationality and femininity in three wartime films', in C. Gledhill and G. Swanson (eds), *Nationalising Femininity: Culture, Sexuality and British Cinema in the Second World War*, Manchester: Manchester University Press.
Harper, S. (1994) *Picturing the Past: The Rise and Fall of the British Costume Film*, London: BFI.
——(1996) 'The years of total war', in C. Gledhill and G. Swanson (eds), *Nationalising Femininity: Culture, Sexuality and British Cinema in the Second World War*, Manchester: Manchester University Press.
——(2000) *Women in British Cinema: Mad, Bad and Dangerous to Know*, London: Continuum.
Hutchings, P. (1993) *Hammer and Beyond: The British Horror Film*, Manchester: Manchester University Press.
Landy, M. (1991) *British Genres: Cinema and Society, 1930–1960*, Princeton, NJ: Princeton University Press.
McFarlane, B. (ed.) (1997) *An Autobiography of British Cinema*, London: Methuen.
——(ed.) (2005) *The Cinema of Britain and Ireland*, London: Wallflower Press.

Moss, R. F. (1987) *The Films of Carol Reed*, Basingstoke: Macmillan.

Murphy, R. (1989) *Realism and Tinsel: Cinema and Society in Britain 1939–1948*, London: Routledge.

Powell, M. (1986) *A Life in Movies*, London: Heinemann.

Richards, J. (1986) *Thorold Dickinson: The Man and His Films*, Beckenham: Croom Helm.

Thomson, D. (2003) *The New Biographical Dictionary of Film*, London: Little, Brown.

6 A landscape of desire

Cornwall as romantic setting in *Love Story* and *Ladies in Lavender*

Rachel Moseley

As the train draws out of Plymouth, and begins to edge across Brunel's bridge over the Tamar, the passengers in my carriage, as one, look up from books and laptops and watch out of the window as we cross the river into Cornwall. After we pass through Saltash on the other side, the landscape seems to change rapidly, moving through verdant valleys and forests, across desolate and dramatic moorland, through the scarred industrial landscape of the mid-Cornwall clay country and, finally, into the softer landscape of South East Cornwall. Then, the long awaited glimpse: 'Can you see the sea yet?' I've made this journey 'home' so many times now, and in recent years it has become a routine dash down the M5. Making the journey by train rekindles the childhood excitement of looking for the sign on the little road bridge which marked the shift from Devon (England) into Cornwall (somewhere exciting, somewhere different), and I look backwards to see the Cornish coat of arms on Brunel's Bridge. There is something about the crossing of this border; Cornwall is almost entirely cut off from mainland Britain by the Tamar, has its own flag, language and claim to independence. Making this crossing has always been a bit like leaving England and travelling abroad, into another land. Cornwall is, at once, both home and away.

Of course, I am not the first to romanticize this journey. As the Great Western Railway extended into Cornwall and Brunel's bridge traversed the Tamar in 1859, the GWR's publicity for the journey into the South West solidified constructions of Cornwall as somehow both familiar and foreign. Thomas (1997) examines this early construction of the county, citing GWR-produced publicity and travelogue writing. Mais tells us that the GWR takes us:

> over the Tamar and into foreign territory: the simple truth is that Cornwall is far more different from any other part of the British Isles than most foreign places are. It is the only entirely foreign place you can reach without changing from train to boat after leaving London.
>
> (Mais 1928: 28)

Similarly, the GWR's own *The Cornish Riviera* in the same year tells us that 'Brunel's Royal Albert Bridge ... is the means, and an almost magic means, of transporting travellers from a county, which if richer than others is yet unmistakeably an English county, to a Duchy which is in every respect un-English' (cited in Thomas 1997: 120). Thomas comments that 'the railways companies … (re)constructed Cornwall as a land of romance and residual values in a changing, modernising world' (109), and produced it as 'the domestic exotic' a place that held together the comfort and safety of home with the thrill of the exotic other, in a move which drew upon Cornwall's Celtic traditions and geographical peripherality (120). Such images of the journey into and out of Cornwall suggest its construction as a pastoral, romantic space of retreat and return (Gifford 1999), and as simultaneously familiar and strange, England and not-England, home and abroad. In this chapter, I explore the use of the Cornish landscape in constructing desiring femininity in two British woman's pictures set within what Westland (1995) has termed 'the passionate periphery': the wartime melodrama *Love Story* (1944) and the more recent woman's/heritage film *Ladies in Lavender* (2004).

Imagining Cornwall

Cornwall is Britain's most south-westerly county; surrounded by the Atlantic Ocean on one coast, and the English Channel on the other, its industrial history has been in tin mining, china clay quarrying, farming, fishing and, of course, tourism. It has a thriving independence movement and there is a significant project to revive the Cornish language. The climate is milder than that of the rest of the British Isles, with its peninsulas having their own, sometimes sub-tropical, micro-climates. At the same time, Cornwall sees some of the wildest and most dramatic weather in the British Isles, with the Atlantic Ocean and gale force winds battering its craggy coastlines. Its landscape is one of contrasts, from the high and rugged cliffs of the North coast and Penwith peninsular, to the gentler coves and warmer waters of the Lizard. The landscape is dotted with reminders of Cornwall's Celtic and industrial histories: ancient standing stones and the fragments of mine chimneys and engine houses make the land-scape, potentially, a profoundly Romantic one.[1] Cornwall has a long history as a space of creative inspiration for artists and writers, from both within and with-out the county (Deacon 1997: 8; Brace 1999: 142), and strong within this visual and literary culture are veins of Romanticism, the connection between people and landscape, the gothic and the mystical (stories of hauntings, witchcraft, mythical creatures, empty spaces and abandoned houses, a landscape imbued with feeling), smuggling and piracy (see, for example, Baker 1973 and Rawe 1994), all of which flow into cultural constructions of Cornwall as a romantic space. The county has also, of course, been the setting for too many films, tel-evision serials and documentaries to list. Cornwall, then, has been constructed as a 'romanticised periphery' (Deacon 1997: 7) and mystical place, but its ima-gining is polarized and Cornwall is simultaneously familiar/exotic/foreign, bucolic/dangerous/backward, ordinary/extraordinary, prosaic/romantic, fantastic/mystical, home/escape. In simultaneously holding together all of these potentialities Cornwall is a liminal space, a space of possibility (King 1996: 220–1).

There is a growing body of work in Cornish Studies exploring Cornish history, identity and culture (Payton 1999) but also moving into the arts (Westland 1997: 2). Writers such as Westland (1995) and Kent (1995, 1997, 2003) have begun the exploration and deconstruction of the romanticization of Cornwall in literature, film and television, and I hope that this chapter will continue that task. Ella Westland suggests the significant relationship between love and landscape in which 'passion and place are interdependent' in the Cornish romantic novel and notes the way in which by the 1790s:

> artists had prepared enthusiasts to experience the serene and sublime in regions like the Lake District, the Scottish Highlands ... The transformation of Cornwall in the English imagination depended on rocky shores and surging seas taking their place with dark summits as approved sites for romantic sublimity.
>
> (Westland 1995: 154)

In the light of the dominant construction of Cornwall as a Romantic landscape, then, I want to consider this figuring of passion and place in relation to the representation of desiring (and desirable) femininity in the woman's picture, and to begin by examining the associations developed between Cornwall and the desirable, dangerous woman in the post-war film, *Miranda* (Ken Annakin, 1948), to introduce some key themes and concerns.

Miranda as Cornwall

Miranda, like *Love Story*, is little commented upon in critical writing on British cinema, even in work which focuses on Gainsborough Studios, perhaps because both films are 'neither here nor there' (Cook 1996: 51), neither costume drama, nor 'home front' film (like the oft discussed *Millions Like Us* (1943)) proper. In its focus on the desires of its central female protagonist and her conflict with cultural restraints (Landy 1991: 16), though, we can consider it a woman's film. *Miranda* is the story of a Cornish mermaid, Miranda Trewella (Glynis Johns) brought back to London by holidaying doctor Paul Martin (Griffith Jones) as his 'patient', and the chaos that ensues during her stay in his marital home. Miranda is openly desiring of the men around her; as Sue Harper notes, she represents a threat to normal women and to bourgeois society, suggesting that 'society finds female desire a disquieting phenomenon' (1996a: 97, 2000: 157). In the end, though, Miranda's voracious sexually is shown to have been channelled appropriately, as what she wanted – and got – was a baby. Justine Ashby reads this commercially successful film in terms of readjustment to shifts in gender identities and roles post war, in the context of 'the more relaxed sexual mores and the significant increase in illegitimate births that were two of the social legacies of the war'. Further, she points to the 'way it tentatively acknowledges that post-war Britain must come to terms with more liberated attitudes to female sexuality' (2000: 170). I want to extend this reading by thinking about how *Miranda* connects Cornwall, typically feminized in its imagining (Thomas 1997: 117), with desiring and desirable femininity. In this way, I will tease out the nexus of tropes around visuality, femininity and desire that underpin both *Love Story* and *Ladies in Lavender*, to examine their use of Cornwall to figure the problematic relationship between women and desire.

From the start, Miranda is immersed in the Cornish landscape, exotic and dangerously desirous. Paul heads off to Cornwall without his wife Clare (Googie Withers). He sees it as prosaic: 'If I were in search of *that* kind of adventure, I shouldn't go to *Cornwall*', while Clare is more cautious: 'Oh, you never know what you might find down there ... ' As he winds his fishing reel, wondering what he might catch, there is a wipe to a shot of a pretty Cornish fishing village from the sea, accompanied by the sound of gulls and a lush, sweeping string score. Our first glimpse of Miranda – her tail, glittering in the sunlight as she dives – instantly suggests the magical, through the use of a harp (which, along with the percussive celesta often signals the mystical) in the score. In a dramatic reversal of his expectations, *she* catches *him* and he descends into her mysterious, shadowy, underwater cave. As he regains consciousness, the construction of Miranda as a fantasy is made clear, as she sings her mesmerizing siren song and the image gradually comes into focus. This table-turning is important in thinking about the association between Cornwall as a feminized landscape and desiring femininity: Miranda constantly reverses the touristic and gendered gazes as she looks at him and strokes his legs appraisingly. 'I love tall men,' she says. 'The last two I caught were so short I had to throw them back again!' 'There's a dreadful shortage of men below sea,' she continues, adding that there must be plenty above, and so the plundered becomes the plunderer. Later, though, transported to London on a train journey (which through its montage of location shots of Cornwall from the carriage and dramatic repetitive brass and woodwind score signals the impending arrival of the passionate periphery at the centre as a threat), Miranda, despite her attempts to turn London into a tourist space, is herself endlessly 'produced' by the men around her: as a desirable fashionable and immobile woman by Paul, as 'art' by Nigel (John McCallum). It is, then, this struggle over the desiring, controlling gaze, which is the central trope of the woman's pictures which figure Cornwall in relation to the desiring feminine, and I explore this below. In this film, Cornwall and Miranda, rather than the rural South East, function metonymically as Britain (there are strains of 'Rule Britannia' at the opening and close of the film) and suggest that Miranda is, like Cornwall, both part of the nation, and simultaneously a troublingly different and independent thing. Miranda is constructed as exotic (she is a world traveller, eats raw fish and drinks salt water) and mesmerizingly attractive, but also as just an ordinary girl (she reads Vogue, loves clothes and wants a baby). Miranda, like Cornwall, is both British (signalled clearly by Johns' polite, if husky, received pronunciation) and foreign (Nurse Carey (Margaret Rutherford) likens herself as a young woman to Miranda, when she once danced a Mazurka, 'a foreign sort of dance'). The 'passionate periphery' is acceptable when in its proper place, but is troubling when brought to the centre; there is a desire to domesticate it (the underwater sequence of the opening credits turns out to be a fish bowl) but this may be impossible (Miranda gradually eats the goldfish). Cornwall is strongly associated here with a passionately desiring, independent and troubling femininity, and the film is at pains to contain her. In the rest of this chapter, I explore the tensions produced in the meeting of visuality, the Cornish landscape and female desire.

Picturing Cornwall: gender, desire and the 'prospect view'

Laviolette, in his analysis of Cornish landscape images, comments that people generally imagine landscapes from a distant and elevated viewpoint, and argues that not only have the majority of Cornish landscape paintings offered such views of dramatic coastlines, but that literary Cornish landscapes offer similar panoramic views that eschew the detail (1999: 107, 113, 119). Similarly, in their discussion of 'rural cinema', Fowler and Helfield comment that while in landscape painting 'the rural space is most frequently "pictured" by way of the panoramic or widescreen, deep focus image ... the pan and deep-focus lens combining to produce an ideal panoramic view or a rural space that suggests a colonial capturing of a land', some may offer a different perspective, not a 'magisterial gaze', but a more intimate, eye level perspective suggesting a more equal relationship between the beholder and the object of the gaze (2006: 8–9). These typical landscape perspectives can be usefully linked to conventions of representation in the Romantic arts. Jackie Labbe convincingly draws out the gendered associations of the sublime and its associated 'prospect view', masculine in its focus on 'disinterest, reason and the ability to abstract', given the Romantic assumption that the male mind welcomes eternity and infinitude, while the female welcomes confinement and detail (1998: ix). The elevated prospect view is the vantage point from which art might be composed, and Labbe questions who has access to it. The prospect view of the Romantic landscape, she suggests, is 'a metaphor empowering to one gender, yet debarred the other' (1998: x). She comments that in contrast many female Romantic writers situate themselves within the landscape, offering a detailed perspective (which she calls 'the landscape view') (1998: 3). She also comments very suggestively on Wordsworth's perspective in his *Guide to the Lakes*, in which the sublime, which is awe-inspiring and resistant to perceptual organization, becomes 'the picturesque', a perspective which relies on the viewer's control. The picturesque, she suggests, offers 'a detached appreciation of painting-like scenery, suitably rough yet contained by an assumed frame' (53). In what follows, then, I argue that one of the central representational tropes of the woman's film set in Cornwall, is the negotiation of the prospect, landscape and picturesque views in the figuring of the desiring woman.

Love Story

In *Love Story*, concert pianist Lissa Campbell (Margaret Lockwood), discovering she is unfit to join the WRAF due to a fatal heart condition, goes to

Cornwall to enjoy the time she has left. There she meets Kit (Stewart Granger), a former airforce pilot, who, as the result of his selfless heroism, is going blind. Both keep their illness from each other until near the end of the film when they are reunited and Kit, cured by an operation that Lissa convinced him to risk, returns to the airforce. Judy (Patricia Roc) plays Kit's friend, secretly in love with him, who is directing a production of *The Tempest* at a Cornish amphitheatre. She has convinced him not to risk the operation, knowing that this will mean his future reliance on her. The film tends to be discussed primarily in relation to the role of women in British 'home front' cinema (Landy 1991), sometimes in conjunction with discussion of the central character's status as a wilful, creative but terminally ill female musician (Harper 1988, 1996b; Laing 2007). Lant discusses the film in relation to its rural/coastal iconography and wartime context, pointing out the familiar structure in the film in which aerial shots are male, and the 'land-bound' look is female (1991: 53). Many accounts comment on the way in which Lissa, inspired to compose the film's theme, the 'Cornish Rhapsody' (composed by Hubert Bath) by the Cornish landscape, is in this way associated with nature and the elements (see also Donnelly 1997: 165). Laing (2007), in particular, offers a wonderful extended close reading of the film in which her careful analysis of the musical structure of the Rhapsody enables her to make a convincing argument about the close relationship between Lissa's composition and the construction of the landscape as eternal and unchanging (125). Her analysis of Lissa draws upon the Romantic gendering of the musician figure (113), and she argues that Lissa's 'elemental' emotions are harnessed in the service of recuperating Kit for the war effort (125–6). I want to extend and complicate these accounts of the film through a focus on the relationship of Lissa and Judy to the Cornish landscape, film aesthetics and the play between the Romantic prospect and picturesque views.

As Trezise comments, the movement westwards is a powerfully romantic one, and he points out the tendency to 'romanticize the point where the land of Britain ends and the ocean begins' (2000: 15). The focus in this film is on the most westerly and potentially romantic Cornish landscape (Penwith, with its Celtic stones and engine houses), and it is easy to see this in relation to Lockwood's star persona and her association with roles as exoticized, eroticized and wilful women (Cook 1996; Landy 1991), even if this is retrospective. It is this Romantic landscape which inspires Lissa's composition of her 'Cornish Rhapsody', as she stands on a high promontory at the end of Cornwall. Robert Murphy comments that 'the concentration on bright, airy Cornish location photography prevents any build up of claustrophobic tension' (1989: 48), but in fact, while the film makes some use of location shooting on the Penwith peninsular and around the Minack Theatre at Porthcurno, it also makes significant use of both rear projection and studio/backdrop shooting, which, as I will show, produces quite a different effect, particularly in how we might read the desiring woman. Pam Cook, in her discussion of *I Know Where I'm Going!*, has commented on the potentialities of rear projection in cinema, suggesting that it may act as 'an additional reminder that this is an imaginary landscape, while the use of documentary inserts ... emphasises that we are watching a pastiche of images' (2002: 33). While the combined use of rear projection and documentary images at times works in a similar way in *Love Story*'s figuring of the Celtic Cornish landscape, I argue that the use of rear projection and studio/ backdrop shooting in this film also works to contain and limit Lissa's relation-ship to the Cornish landscape she has attempted to escape into, and that this is intensified by her 'picturing' through Kit's point-of-view.[2] When Lissa finds out about her illness, she tells her manager Ray (Walter Hudd): 'I want to be *in* life for the little time that's left, not outside watching it as I always have ... I'm going out into the sunshine, I want to walk in the wind and watch the waves breaking against the Cornish rocks!' What Lissa desires is freedom from her 'endless train journeys and practice' indoors, and physical and emotional immersion in the Cornish landscape, but already in Lissa's speech is a combi-nation of imagined 'prospect' and 'landscape' views, in which she is both observer and part of the landscape. Her active role as prospect observer, in which she can abstract and create, though, is delimited by the way the film figures her in relation to landscape.

On Lissa's first trip out into the Cornish countryside, she is figured in a long location shot, fully immersed, a tiny figure in the landscape. She is then given a location point-of-view shot of the moorland cliff top ahead from the driver's seat, in an unstable moving documentary image that effectively expresses her liberation. At this point there is a cut to a medium close-up of Lissa, driving and singing the traditional Cornish 'Furry Dance', a stable and static image against a blurry rear projection of the landscape. As she arrives at the cliff edge promontory, the camera is positioned behind her and we are given a location shot of Lissa, whip in hand, looking out over the expanse of sea and cliff: here she is figured in relation to the classic (masculine) prospect view of the explorer and creative artist (although always, of course, already pictured by the camera). A further long location shot of Lissa against the panoramic coastal view is fol-lowed by a close-up of her face, with rear projection. After a final brief, lib-eratory location shot as she runs across the cliff and the camera pans to catch up with her, she arrives at a (significantly lower) promontory and is pictured in medium close-up sitting among the rocks. While Lissa has apparently achieved her desire of freedom in the Cornish landscape, she is now pictured in a studio set with a painted backdrop, 'wind' blowing her hair and the (previously recorded) sounds of gulls, waves and wind. She is allowed a precipitous view of the waves crashing on the rocks below, before Kit arrives, climbing up the cliff. At this point, the camera's view of Lissa is transferred precisely to Kit's optical point-of-view, and their ensuing encounter at the cliff edge is shot entirely through rear projection. Lissa is clearly associated in a particularly contained and controlled way with the Cornish landscape, which is both feminized and made crucial to the war effort. Kit has found 'Molly' (molibdinum, an essential element) deep in the cliff: 'If she's the girl I think she is, she's a rare piece.' The ensuing 'prospect view' of the Romantic Cornish landscape, with rugged cliffs, crashing waves and engine houses, is directed by Kit. As Lissa runs off to

Figure 6.1 Prospect view: Lissa against the Cornish coast.
Source: *Love Story*, directed by Leslie Arliss (1944).

another promontory and begins to compose her Rhapsody in her head, she is pictured again in a studio set approximating the cliff top.

While *Love Story* increasingly works to contain Lissa within studio sets and rear projection, taking her out of the 'free' Cornish location shots, there are also tensions in this film whereby the image of Lissa 'resists' this positioning. Kit's point-of-view shot of her here does not ring true, for instance, as the eyeline match is incorrect. As she composes, she has a location point-of-view of the waves to inspire the chromatic rise and fall which will represent the waves and the wind, intercut with a studio close-up, followed by a shot of gulls as she imagines their cries as music. From her prospect view, she controls the land-scape, picking out its details and turning them into carefully composed Romantic art, in a combination of the (masculine) prospect and (feminine, detailed) landscape views.[3] As the theme that will become the signifier of her meeting with Kit on the cliff top comes to her (Laing 2007: 121), Kit's voice interrupts her process with a jolt: 'Keep still, can't you? How can I fix you in my mind if you keep on leaping about?' At the moment that Kit attempts to immobilize her, pictured on the cliff top, her creative process is interrupted and she is denied a further location point-of-view shot. 'You're going straight into my box of special memories,' he says. 'You won't find it crowded there, and I'll often bring you out.' As she agrees to their date the following day, he pictures

Figure 6.2 Prospect view: Lissa against the Cornish coast.
Source: *Love Story*, directed by Leslie Arliss (1944).

her securely, framed between the rocks in the studio set, and we have a brief location glimpse of her disappearing out of the frame. Later, her new acquaintance Tom (Tom Walls) an elderly Yorkshireman conscripted to 'pep up' the mine, comments 'Appen he'll be adding you to his collection, eh?' 'Happen he won't,' Lissa replies. 'In my own small way I'm quite a collector myself.' Like Miranda, Lissa, closely related to the landscape, attempts to turn the tables on the male 'collector'. I am not arguing that Lissa is entirely contained by the landscape aesthetics of this film; rather, I am suggesting that there is a constant play between location and studio/rear projection, which expresses Lissa's desire for liberation in the Cornish countryside, but simultaneously indicates the impossibility of this within the terms of the narrative, in relation to her illness and the war. Kit and Lissa's subsequent donkey trap rides around the Cornish coast are shot against rear projection, with the few location point-of-view inserts either motivated by Kit (who for example points out the 'Merry Maidens' stone circle, said to be women turned to stone for dancing on a Sunday and immobilized women if ever there were any), suggesting Lissa's impending death (she sees independently a cliff top church and graveyard) or reminding them of the war (the injured servicemen they encounter in the lane). This pattern can be traced through the film, with Lissa's visual containment gradually increasing as location shots disappear, until her final, climactic performance of

Figure 6.3 Lissa contained within the studio set: Kit's point of view.
Source: *Love Story*, directed by Leslie Arliss (1944).

the rhapsody is entirely contained within the Royal Albert Hall. Judy (who smokes and wears trousers), in contrast, is far more frequently and consistently figured in relation to and within location shots around the 'Porthmerryn' open air theatre and surrounding cliffs.

There is no end to this oscillation between control and escape in relation to the Romantic landscape. The end of the film pictures Lissa once more atop the Cornish cliffs, waving to Kit as he flies back to war and playing with her wedding ring. While this image has been read as one in which Lissa is brought properly into line for the war effort, married, landbound (Lant 1991; Laing 2007), my reading of the patterning of location shooting complicates this, for here Lissa is filmed entirely on location and in the powerful position of the prospect viewer. There remains the question, then, of how one might read the opening of the film which, as Laing suggests, powerfully connects landscape with music and emotion (Laing 2007: 118–19) The opening credits play over a series of long-held location shots taken, we might imagine, from the back of the donkey trap we see in the film. These images of the Cornish landscape used in the film, are clearly images which are moving through and away from that space and as such, in conjunction with the orchestrated version of Lissa's rhapsody (minus, as Laing points out, her piano (2007: 118)) are imbued with a sense of tragic loss. Indeed, as the shot travels over a hill, with the open

Cornish sky in the frame, we cut back to an image we have just seen, giving the sense of moving backwards and leaving all over again. What prompts this sense of loss which opens the film? Should we, in fact, read it as the ending? Undoubtedly it is the loss of the love story, so closely tied to the landscape, and perhaps the potential loss of rural England in wartime. It is also perhaps, the loss of Lissa's fantasy of escape and artistic freedom. This is a film about female desire and subjectivity, contained by the film's landscape aesthetic.

Ladies in Lavender

Ladies In Lavender, while clearly a heritage film in terms of pace, narrative and aesthetic (Higson 1996), is also a woman's film, in its sensitive and complex portrayal of an older woman's passion for a younger man.[4] Elderly sisters Ursula (Judi Dench) and Janet Widdington (Maggie Smith) live in their deceased father's house in Cornwall, in the mid-1930s. Their lives are suddenly disrupted by the arrival of young Polish virtuoso violinist Andrea Marowski (Daniel Brühl), who is washed up on their beach after falling overboard en route to America, and the presence of Olga Danilof (Natascha McElhone), sister of the maestro violinist Boris Danilof, who is on a painting holiday in the area. The mise en scène of this film powerfully expresses 'the inner life' (Monk, cited in Higson 1996: 241) of its female protagonist, through the relationship it constructs between desire, music and landscape. The film carefully connects the foreignness and exoticism of its two primary objects of desire (Andrea and Olga) with both the Cornish landscape and Ursula's desire for passion, romantic love and a different life, the possibility of all of which, the film suggests, has passed. The film is set in a composite Cornwall, which, while a much gentler setting than *Love Story*, still retains the possibility for drama. The credit sequence clearly establishes the contrasting characters of the sisters and their relationship to their surroundings, as well as introducing the brief and barely perceptible slow-motion which is used throughout to emphasize Ursula's direct and desiring gaze at Andrea. As they walk out onto the beach from behind a cliff, they are encapsulated within and framed by the beach, with no open space in shot, frozen for a few seconds. With the contrast in the image lowered, they become one with the landscape. Ursula runs down to the water to paddle as her sister declines and sits to watch, the camera cutting on Ursula's movement to a low, eye level view of the water and sky from behind her as she plunges in. There is a sudden shift with this cut to saturated colour and bright sunshine, in contrast to the faded image that preceded it. Ursula, the film suggests, is at heart a vibrant and passionate woman. The shift to a low level, detailed, feminine landscape view (Labbe 1998) is also important in relation to the representation of Ursula as desiring, as throughout the film the dramatic images that signal her desiring subjectivity, such as those of crashing, stormy waves which precede Andrea's 'magical' near drowning and arrival on the beach, are consistently shot from this low level, immersive position which affords the viewer a detailed, rather than panoramic landscape view. These are not presented as point-of-view shots, however, but rather as metaphorical representations of Ursula's desire or state of mind. It is at the moment, after the storm, when Ursula ascends to an elevated prospect view, that she is given a troubling point-of-view shot of the beach and Andrea's lifeless body. She stands on a stone pulpit, a Romantic classical fragment, looking out to sea, in a clear echo of the conductor's podium at Andrea's London performance at the end of the film (Figure 6.4). This may be the proper cultivated woman's 'little elevation [in] her own garden' (Hannah More cited in Labbe 1998: 67), a Romantic, encircled and genteel space appropriate to the lady, but as Labbe suggests, following Mary Wollstonecraft Shelley, 'the garden can also open a less decorous space structurally designed to subvert, obstruct, or transgress gentility' (1998: 66). Certainly, it is Ursula's 'prospect view' from her simultaneously English cottage/exotic Cornish subtropical garden, which both prompts the disruption to the sisters' peaceful status quo, and activates her desire. Cornwall, as a wild and marginal land, frequently suggests an erotic undercurrent (Hughes 1997: 69). As she sees his face, an attenuated, drawnout piano fragment of theme from the central piece associated with Andrea – the 'Fantasy for Violin and Orchestra' – briefly plays. This then, as it moves from diegetic to non-diegetic status throughout the film, comes to signal Ursula's desire for Andrea (Laing 2007: 69), its minor

Figure 6.4 An elevated prospect view.
Source: *Ladies in Lavender*, directed by Charles Dance (2004).

tonality and rise and fall echoing the mournful cry of the gulls and the sound of the waves, and strongly signalling loss in relation to the Cornish landscape and Ursula's desire. Her only independent prospect view, when she leaves the garden, is interrupted by Andrea's arrival. Ursula is also endlessly pictured as the desiring woman at the window identified by Pidduck (2004), who suggests that this recurring moment 'captures a particular quality of feminine stillness, constraint and longing', and is 'a generic spatio-temporal economy of physical and sexual constraint, a sumptuous waiting barely papering over an elaborate yet attenuated register of longing' (25–6). From her station at the window, though, Ursula is frequently pictured gazing into the lush and windblown Cornish landscape, where constantly moving tamarisk and cordyline suggest the barely contained restlessness of Ursula's desire.

Olga (who the film suggests may be Russian, and can communicate fluently with Andrea in German) functions as an openly expressive, vibrant and unfaded representation of the passionate young woman Ursula longs to be and might have been, and the film connects them strongly through editing and visual rhymes, as for example when Olga creeps into the garden, and the two women's postures are mirrored as they watch and listen to Andrea play (Figure 6.5). We are introduced to Olga after a cut from Ursula's desiring gaze at the

Figure 6.5 Mirrored postures of the young and old woman.
Source: *Ladies in Lavender*, directed by Charles Dance (2004).

sleeping Andrea, through two punctuating close, detailed landscape shots of lichen covered rock and rushing waves, as she paints the ladies' house as a picturesque composition from her own elevated prospect view (their abode is pictured in this way, from this perspective, throughout the film). We only see a glimpse of her hair (unruly like Ursula's, only blonder, brighter), and her palette of primary watercolour pots, which match the bright, saturated reds and greens of her exotic jacket, an unfaded echo of Ursula's paler printed frocks. Because we do not see her fully, she remains in control of her elevated view and composition of it. She is frequently associated with such a positioning, but as she becomes the object of desire of Doctor Mead (David Warner), this control is wrested from her and she herself, the independent painter, becomes the painted, contained within his picturesque view of her, the Cornish landscape and the romantic fragment of the ruined folly on the distant headland (Figure 6.6). As Newlyn painter Stanhope Forbes suggested in 1913, Cornwall is seen as naturally 'pictorial': 'Here every corner was a picture and ... the people seemed to fall naturally into their places and to harmonise with the surroundings' (Laviolette 2003: 142). This, it seems, is also true of the desiring woman in the Cornish landscape, her desiring, composing gaze brought under control by her own picturing or confinement to the detailed, landscape view. Nevertheless, because

Figure 6.6 The woman artist contained within the view.
Source: *Ladies in Lavender*, directed by Charles Dance (2004).

Olga gently resists Andrea's advances, the film's romance can remain between Ursula and Andrea, if only in fantasy, and through the powerful signalling of its impossibility through landscape and music.

Conclusion

These woman's pictures set in Cornwall share several thematic and representational tropes, not least of which are the association of the Romantic Cornish landscape with female desire and its impossibility, and the play with picturing as a means of its containment. In its potential for the 'domestic exotic', the use of Cornwall as a romantic setting for the British woman's film brings into play the foreign and the familiar in ways that are suggestive for the expression of female desire, which, it seems, remains problematic. In wartime Britain, the specific associations of Cornwall as a British region made it an appropriate backdrop and cipher for the representation and negotiation of new and more liberated female sexualities and desires. More recently, *Ladies in Lavender* returns to this regional setting in its exploration of the desiring subjectivity of an older British woman. Like these troubling, desiring women, Cornwall is problematic, liminal and in negotiation with its Britishness. The use of Cornwall as a setting in relation to desiring femininity produces an image of rural, regional Britishness which is ultimately as unstable as it is affective.

Notes

1 As Rustin points out, the Romantics were preoccupied with crumbling ruins and depictions of lost civilizations (2007: 50).
2 While the use of rear projection, studio inserts and location stand-ins is determined by the exigencies of shooting schedule and actor availability, it also forms a significant representational trope in this film.
3 Lissa's music is a powerfully Romantic composition, in its direct expression of feeling inspired by landscape, flowing melody, use of chromaticism, modulations and wide dynamic range. Many thanks to my piano teacher, Sue Bradford, for her insightful comments on the Cornish Rhapsody.
4 Claire Monk (in, for example, 2002: 181) has usefully pointed out the connection between the heritage film and the female audience.

Bibliography

Ashby, J. (2000) 'Betty Box, "the lady in charge": negotiating space for a female producer in postwar cinema', in J. Ashby and A. Higson (eds), *British Cinema, Past and Present*, London: Routledge.
Baker, D. V. (ed.) (1973) *Haunted Cornwall*, London: New English Library.
Brace, C. (1999) 'Cornish identity and landscape in the work of Arthur Caddick', in P. Payton (ed.), *Cornish Studies Seven*, Exeter: University of Exeter Press.
Cook, P. (1996) 'Neither here nor there: national identity in Gainsborough costume drama', in A. Higson (ed.), *Dissolving Views: Key Writing on British Cinema*, London: Cassell.
——(2002) *I Know Where I'm Going!*, London: BFI.

Deacon, B. (1997) '"The hollow jarring of the distant steam engines": images of Cornwall between West Barbary and Delectable Duchy', in E. Westland (ed.), *Cornwall: The Cultural Construction of Place*, Penzance: The Patten Press.

Donnelly, K. J. (1997) 'Wicked sounds and magic melodies: music in 1940s Gainsborough melodrama', in P. Cook (ed), *Gainsborough Pictures*, London: Cassell.

Fowler, C. and Helfield, G. (eds) (2006) *Representing the Rural: Space, Place and Identity in Films about the Land*, Detroit: Wayne State University Press.

Gifford, T. (1999) *Pastoral: The New Critical Idiom*, London: Routledge.

Harper, S. (1988) 'The representation of women in British feature films, 1939–45', in P. M. Taylor (ed.), *Britain and the Cinema in the Second World War*, Basingstoke: Macmillan.

——(1996a) 'From *Holiday Camp* to high camp: women in British feature films, 1945–51', in A. Higson (ed.), *Dissolving Views: Key Writing on British Cinema*, London: Cassell.

——(1996b) 'The years of total war: propaganda and entertainment', in C. Gledhill and G. Swanson (eds) *Nationalising Femininity: Culture, Sexuality and British Cinema in the Second World War*, Manchester: Manchester University Press.

——(2000) *Women in British Cinema: Mad, Bad and Dangerous to Know*, London: Continuum.

Higson, A. (ed.) (1996) 'The heritage film and British cinema', in A. Higson (ed.), *Dissolving Views: Key Writings on British Cinema*, London: Cassell.

Hughes, H. (1997) '"A silent, desolate country": images of Cornwall in Daphne Du Maurier's *Jamaica Inn*', in E. Westland (ed.), *Cornwall: The Cultural Construction of Place*, Penzance: The Patten Press.

Kent, A. M. (1995) 'Smashing sandcastles: realism in contemporary Cornish Fiction', in I. A. Bell (ed) *Peripheral Visions: Images of Nationhood in Contemporary British Fiction*, Cardiff: University of Wales Press.

——(1997) 'The Cornish Alps: resisting romance in the clay country', in E. Westland (ed.), *Cornwall: The Cultural Construction of Place*, Penzance: The Patten Press.

——(2003) 'Screening Kernow: authenticity, heritage and the representation of Cornwall in film and television, 1913–2003', in P. Payton (ed.), *Cornish Studies Eleven*, Exeter: Exeter University Press.

King, J. (1996) 'Crossing thresholds: the contemporary British woman's film', in A. Higson (ed.), *Dissolving Views: Key Writings on British Cinema*, London: Cassell.

Labbe, J. M. (1998) *Romantic Visualities: Landscape, Gender and Romanticism*, Basingstoke: Palgrave.

Laing, H. (2007) *The Gendered Score: Music in 1940s Melodrama and the Woman's Film*, London: Ashgate.

Landy, M. (1991) *British Genres: Cinema and Society, 1930–1960*, Princeton, NJ: Princeton University Press.

Lant, A. (1991) *Blackout: Reinventing Women for British wartime Cinema*, Princeton, NJ: Princeton University Press.

Laviolette, P. (1999) 'An iconography of landscape images in Cornish art and prose', in P. Payton (ed.), *Cornish Studies Seven*, Exeter: University of Exeter Press.

——(2003) 'Cornwall's visual cultures in perspective', in P. Payton (ed.), *Cornish Studies Eleven*, Exeter: Exeter University Press.

Mais, S. P. B. (1928) *My Finest Holiday*, London: GWR.

Monk, C. (2002) 'The British heritage-film debate revisited', in C. Monk and A. Sargeant (eds), *British Historical Cinema*, London: Routledge.

Murphy, R. (1989) *Realism and Tinsel: Cinema and Society in Britain 1939–49*, London: Routledge.

Payton, P. (ed.) (1999) *Cornish Studies Seven*, Exeter: University of Exeter Press.

Pidduck, J. (2004) *Contemporary Costume Film: Space, Place and the Past*, London: BFI.

Rawe, D. R. (1994) *Haunted Landscapes: Cornish and West Country Tales of the Supernatural*, Truro: Lodenek Press.

Rustin, S. (2007) *Romanticism*, London: Continuum.

Thomas, C. (1997) 'See Your Own Country First: the geography of a railway landscape', in E. Westland (ed.), *Cornwall: The Cultural Construction of Place*, Penzance: The Patten Press.

Trezise, S. D. (2000) *The West Country as a Literary Invention*: *Putting Fiction in its Place*, Exeter: Exeter University Press.

Westland, E. (1995) 'The passionate periphery: Cornwall and romantic fiction', in I. A. Bell (ed.), *Peripheral Visions: Images of Nationhood in Contemporary British Fiction*, Cardiff: University of Wales Press.

——(1997) (ed.) *Cornwall: The Cultural Construction of Place*, Penzance: The Patten Press.

7 'A prize collection of familiar feminine types'

The female group film in 1950s British cinema

Melanie Bell

In 1989 the actress Virginia McKenna recalled her experience of working on the 1956 British film *A Town Like Alice* as one of the most positive experiences of her career; delighting in a film which offered 'a cast full of marvellous actresses' some substantial film roles at a time when they were in short supply in mainstream cinema (in McFarlane 1997: 382). This film is unusual because the narrative centres on a small group of women of different ages and with different life experience, that are drawn together as a result of extreme circumstances. As the story unfolds the women's relationships with each other assume priority in contrast to those with men, which are comparatively small-scale. Films that focus on groups of women are relatively rare in mainstream cinema so how might we account for this scarcity? Certainly patriarchal structures play a part, requiring women to be individualised – that is, disconnected from other women – their social embeddedness deriving from heterosexual processes such as marriage that position them in relation to individual men and the family. Popular film can play a role in this process. Classic narrative cinema typically prioritises a (male) hero-protagonist on whom narrative interest can centre. Hollywood's star system favours star vehicles, which clearly work against group dynamics. As Yvonne Tasker has argued, 'glamorous stars ... in spectacular isolation' are the norm in Hollywood, particularly for female stars, a strategy that has effectively 'marginalized representations of female friendship' (1998: 139), a dynamic that emerges when groups of women are portrayed. For Jeanine Basinger '[t]he notion of a group of women working together is a film rarity' with the more common representation of women as 'petty rivals' (1986: 224) clearly fulfilling patriarchy's requirement for individualisation.

Women in groups, where they do appear in mainstream cinema, seem to do so under particular social circumstances. William Wellman's *Westward the Women* (1951) for example, which follows a group of Chicago women travelling to California to meet prospective husbands, highlights female solidarity and independence and concludes with the women's right to enter into marriage on absolutely equal terms with men. Despite its nineteenth century setting the film is clearly a response to changes in the way that 'the family' was understood in American society in the post-war period.[1] Within a British context the Second World War gave rise to a crisis in gender roles with women increasingly replacing men in the workforce. British cinema produced a number of female group films during this period of 'crisis': *Millions Like Us* and *The Gentle Sex* (1943), *2,000 Women* (1944), *Great Day* (1945). These films responded very directly to changed social circumstance and the reality of female conscription, internment and the demands of a female-dominated Home Front.

Given the relative paucity of what might be termed 'the female group film', the fact that it emerges under particular circumstances and the pull of patriarchal structures, the question arises: how does popular film represent groups of women, and at a particular point in time? This chapter will explore these questions through a case study of 1950s British cinema with a particular focus on two popular group films: *A Town Like Alice* (1956) and *The Weak and the Wicked* (1954). Both films were commercially profitable, achieving box office success at a time when British cinema was struggling to respond to both rapid social change and declining cinema audiences. Clearly there are points of connection between films which deal with groups of women, and the 'woman's film'. For Maria LaPlace the latter is 'distinguished by its female protagonist, female point of view and its [engagement with] love, emotion and relationships' (1987: 139). Certainly these are all elements that are readily applicable to the female group film, which is populated by female characters and where events are presented from a female perspective. On closer inspection, however, the two are not exactly synonymous. The idea of a solo protagonist that gives the 'woman's film' its individualistic slant would appear to be antithetical to the premise of the group film. Further, to what extent is the 'traditional realism' of women's experience shaped or extended by the particular social circumstances that gave rise to the female group in the first place? A film such as *The Gentle Sex*, which emerged during the crisis of war, is less concerned with depicting 'love, emotion and relationships' than the rigours of military training as experienced by a group of female conscripts. In this respect it seems likely that films that deal with groups of women have an affinity with, but are not reducible to, the 'woman's film', and I aim to tease out some of the differences in my subsequent analysis.

Within the British context, domestic cinema has proven rather more hospitable to the female group film than Hollywood. In part this can be explained by the tradition of ensemble-playing in British cinema. Britain's lack of a star system (relative to Hollywood) and the close relationship between theatre and cinema, has meant that ensemble pieces have historically been a mainstay of indigenous film production – a vehicle for showcasing the breadth of Britain's 'great acting' talent.[2] Although typically this has favoured men (the war genre being the most obvious example) women occasionally benefit from the tradition and rather more space is found in British cinema for groups of women. For example, films such as *She'll Be Wearing Pink Pyjamas* (1985) and *Bhaji on the Beach* (1993) are more contemporary instances of the female ensemble film that emerged in response to the particular social circumstances of, respectively, second wave feminism and multi-culturalism. In this respect a case can be made for the female group film as a *type* of 'woman's film' that finds particular expression in mainstream British cinema.

1950s British cinema and the 'female group' film

The 1950s presents an interesting case study because it is commonly assumed to have been inhospitable to women's issues. For a long time British cinema's output from this decade was written off as moribund and dull; an endless parade of war films and trite comedies with gender politics reduced to 'the hegemony of the tweed jacket' (Medhurst in Williams 2002: 6). Recent important studies have challenged this blinkered view: Harper and Porter (2003) understand it as an 'anxious cinema' uneasily negotiating the demands of modernity while Geraghty (2000) discusses the contradictory discourses shaping the 'new woman', but there is considerable work still to be done concerning gender politics. In this decade there was a sharp contrast between the official descriptions of women's lives as wives and mothers within the companionate marriage and nuclear family, and the reality of increasing numbers of married women in the workforce, their wages in part fuelling the growth in production and consumption of new household goods. The period can be seen as a transitional phase in female equality where the profound social changes of the Second World War were absorbed and worked through in the social fabric. Popular cinema did engage with women's problems and at times directly address female audiences, although output was never as prolific as the 1940s. The concerns of the beleaguered housewife for example are central to *Woman in a Dressing Gown* (1957) while *Young Wives' Tale* (1951) offers a satirical take on the competing demands of work and career from a female perspective.

The female group film, which had enjoyed some popular success in the 1940s, continued to find a space in a cultural landscape dominated by social problem films and the genres of war and comedy. The social problem film, which 'raise [d] topical social issues within a commercial cinematic form' (Hill 1986: 67), was perhaps most hospitable to the theme due to its backdrop of 'crisis' scenarios or 'extreme' circumstances – typically prison or girls' reformatory – which provided the setting for female group dynamics to flourish. Films such as *The Weak and the Wicked*, *Good Time Girl* (1948), *Yield to the Night* (1956) and *Turn the Key Softly* (1953) dramatise female relationships against a backdrop of incarceration, foregrounding the connections and differences between women. Related to the social problem genre were films that dramatised the changing social reality of contemporary Britain in the shape of the new welfare state, the NHS and the growth in social science disciplines. Set in a children's hospital ward *No Time for Tears* (1957) follows the fortunes of a female nursing group, while *Streetcorner* (1953) deals with the experiences of women police constables, both films providing narrative space for different types of femininity and female life experiences to be explored.

In the comedy genre, the commercially successful St Trinian's series dramatised the machinations of a large group of women. Inaugurated by the success of *The Happiest Days of Your Life* (1950) – where a girls' school is forcibly billeted at a boys' public school leading to a classic 'battle of the sexes' scenario – subsequent St Trinian's films (*The Belles of*, 1954; *Blue Murder at*,

1958) focused on the spectacle of the destructive female group. Schoolgirls both young and old band together to challenge any and every established social order (the police, the education system and the army) in what Harper has aptly described as 'a rueful celebration of unruly females' (2000: 87). At the end of the decade it was service comedies such as *Operation Bullshine* (1959) and *Petticoat Pirates* (1961) that continued the comedic treatment of sexual politics and female hedonism.

Outside a comedic framework, the 'realist' war film, which had previously been hospitable to the theme of women in groups, reverted in the 1950s to portraying male homosocial relations. Innumerable 'prisoner-of-war' and 'special mission' films (*The Colditz Story* and *The Dam Busters*, both 1955) dramatised the male group operating within a crisis situation. *A Town Like Alice*, which portrays the travails of a group of civilian women stranded in Malay after the Japanese invasion, is atypical as the only all-female group war film of the decade. Critical discussion of the film has focused on it either as an example of the British war in the East (Murphy 2000: 232) or as a star study of Virginia McKenna as the 'new woman' of 1950s Britain (Geraghty 2000: 168). Both approaches, although useful, have little to say on the subject of women in groups.

While my examples here have been necessarily brief and selective, they do highlight something of the breadth of British film production during the decade and how films featuring groups of women continued to be made, particularly in the newly emerging social problem/realism genre. In terms of audience address, neither *Alice* nor *The Weak and the Wicked* were promoted as 'a woman's film' nor were they targeted exclusively towards women, although women as a specific audience were addressed by some promotional literature. *Picturegoer*'s very positive review of *The Weak and the Wicked* described it as a 'romantic comedy melodrama' which, it suggests, is 'bound to hold and intrigue the "populars" of either sex' (27 February 1954: 19), while the press pack for *Alice* outlines numerous gender-specific publicity strategies. These range from special film previews for women's organisations to a press search for surviving male prisoners-of-war of the Japanese. Clearly there were a number of ways to approach the film and those viewing it at special 'women's previews' (where these took place) were certainly positioned to read the film as a 'woman's film' and anticipate that it would engage with women's experiences in particular ways. What appeal might these films have had for female cinema-goers? At a time when women's cinema attendance was slowly declining the appeal of the female group film was two-fold. Most obviously it prioritised women's concerns and the contemporary experience of being a woman. This could be done literally, as in *Streetcorner* where career women balance the demands of the public and private sphere, or it could be displaced onto 'extreme' settings such as the prison which likewise dramatise female life choices, a common feature of the woman's film. In addition, films that introduce multiple female characters allow for a range of femininities to be displayed. If, as Jackie Stacey argues, cinematic identification involves not only 'processes based on similarity, but also … the productive recognition of differences between femininities' (1994:

171) then the female group film – with its display of multiple femininities – is ideally placed to address those needs of female spectators.

The female group in war-time: *A Town Like Alice* (1956)

A small number of 1950s British war films engaged with women's contribution to the war effort, replacing a focus on the Home Front with the true stories of a select number of 'special women', either female resistance fighters as in *Odette* (1950) and *Carve Her Name With Pride* (1958) or, more unusually, the endurance of a female group in a hostile environment, as in *A Town Like Alice*. *Alice*, made for the Rank organisation, was based on a popular novel by best-selling author Nevil Shute, which was adapted by experienced screenwriter Bill Lipscombe and directed by Jack Lee, whose film-making experience was grounded in the British documentary tradition. The film was a commercial and critical success, winning BAFTAs for the central couple Virginia McKenna and Peter Finch, with McKenna's role voted the most popular female performance in both the British trade and fan press (Harper and Porter 2003: 252). The film focuses on the story of Jean Paget (McKenna), a young English woman working as a secretary in Malaysia at the time of the Japanese invasion. Told through Jean's post-war flashback, she is stranded alongside British ex-patriots at a Malay river depot. The invading Japanese army promptly dispatch the men to POW camps, but disposing of the women and children is problematic. Accompanied by Japanese guards the female group trek through the Malay jungle in search of a camp that will accept them. Half their number die on the journey until finally, bereft of male guards, they persuade the male elders of a Malay village to accept them into their community as workers, where they remain until the end of the war. During the women's extended trek, Jean meets and falls in love with Joe, an Australian POW (Finch). The film returns Jean to the post-war present where she learns that Joe survived the war and she flies to Alice Springs to be reunited with him.

   From the outset a cross-section of women are introduced and individuated. In the river depot scene Ebbey tries to sit on Mrs Frost's suitcase and belittles her husband, 'sickly' Mrs Frith hoards her medicines, while Ellen flirts with a man in return for a cigarette. Different character types are thus economically signalled: conservative/traditional British (Mrs Frost, 'you wouldn't catch me bowing to a Jap'); calm/capable (Jean, Miss Horsfall); bossy (Ebbey); flighty/sexy (Ellen); neurotic/anxious (Mrs Hammond, Mrs Frith). The group is comprised of young, middle-aged and older women, some are married, others like Jean and Ellen are single, while some like Miss Frost are widows or spinsters. The teacher Miss Horsfall is defined by her profession, Ellen by her sexuality and Mrs Hammond by her children. Thus a range of feminine types are introduced, the group differentiated by age, experience, marital status and personality. An ensemble cast of British actresses are used and bring established character traits to bear on their roles, for example Jean Anderson (Miss Horsfall) often played the strong, reliable type while Nora Nicholson (Mrs Frith) specialised in 'dotty' older women. Among the younger actresses Virginia McKenna was, at this time, British cinema's 'English Rose', a leading star in the industry. Narrative interest is initially balanced across the seven women, with Miss Horsfall marked as the leader and Jean her deputy although, as the march progresses, Jean assumes the role of principal.

As the women make their journey across the harsh Malay environment, strong, mutually supportive relationships develop across the group. When anxious young mother Mrs Hammond is struggling to cope, Ebbey takes care of her baby so she can rest. All the women, at different times, take turns in carrying the weak and sick members of the group, both motivating their exhausted peers ('We'll never get over the mountains', 'Oh yes we will' and 'Come along my dear, try, try') and offering consolatory embraces and compassionate smiles when the journey gets particularly tough. At various points in the narrative supportive exchanges are shown to take place between all the women. While never extravagant these small-scale gestures are entirely in keeping with both the emotional tenor of the British war film and the dynamics of the group film where a dispersal of narrative interest across a number of characters means that such seemingly 'minimal' interactions hold great significance.

Figure 7.1 The female group including Virginia McKenna (far left) in *A Town like Alice*, directed by Jack Lee (1956)
Source: The Steve Chibnall Collection.

Mutually supportive bonds develop between seemingly mis-matched types. Elderly Mrs Frith is a hypochondriac and initially a drain on the group's resources but is afforded considerable space in the narrative. She offers Jean support as her relationship with Joe develops, comforts the younger woman following her grief at Joe's torture and finally reconciles Jean to the belief that prolonged hatred of an enemy is impossible to sustain. The figure of the older woman, typically marginalised in mainstream cultural representation, has here a central role to play as a mentor, confidante and provider of emotional support. Although initially signalled as 'dotty' (her illnesses shown to be imaginary), she turns out to be one of the most physically and psychologically robust members of the group. In one scene a young Japanese guard moves towards a hut where the women are sheltering one night, his movement suggesting that rape might be his intention. Mrs Frith appears at the doorway and with a curt 'Good Night' and challenging gaze, the captive dismisses the captor. The guiding role that Mrs Frith plays in relation to Jean is reciprocated. Jean partners Mrs Frith with Timothy, an orphaned child, knowing that through this relationship the older woman will learn to share and think beyond her own immediate needs.

In these respects the women experience the 'learning and growth process' that characterises the male-group war film (Basinger 1986: 75), although in *Alice* the age range is considerably broader, with older women playing a central role in the process. Although the women rely on each other, the supportive bonds are not shown as naturally occurring but achieved through negotiating conflict and dissent. Medicines are forcibly confiscated for example while disagreements break out over the distribution of quinine. On one level the film expands the traditional realism of women's experience as it is typically found in the 'woman's film' through a focus on extreme problems such as starvation, death, disease and exhaustion. On another level however these scenarios have clear parallels to the lives British women faced during wartime. The death of children, the forced separation from men, food rationing and general hardship would have all been within recent memory for many women in the cinema audience. In this respect the film functions as a form of 'displaced' Home Front film, relocating civilian women's experience into the 'othered' realm of the Malay jungle.

Alongside the portrayal of female agency and the strong female bonds that necessarily arise as a result of the women's predicament, there are a number of elements within the narrative that operate to limit the possibilities of active femininity and work to re-feminise the women in accordance with gender norms. First, the inclusion of children in the group foregrounds the role of women as maternal carers. Mrs Hammond's death leaves three orphaned children and, while care for the two oldest is shared across the group, Jean quickly assumes sole responsibility for the youngest child. Jean is thus recast in the role of mother, demonstrating her capacity to deliver childcare and her potential as a suitable partner for Joe.[3] Second, and related, is the relationship between Joe and Jean, which inserts romantic love into the female group and singles out McKenna's character as a protagonist. The relationship between them is developed in two key scenes where they meet secretly at night and discuss life 'back home'. Although brief these small-scale exchanges demonstrate great intimacy and while the women's interactions are primarily concerned with survival, Joe and Jean discuss a world outside and beyond the immediate reality. The structure of the narrative is such that these exchanges provide respite from harrowing scenes where the women and children die. The heterosexual couple are thus afforded a degree of privilege within the narrative, and the audience is positioned to invest in the successful development of their relationship.

In addition to motherhood and romance, the bodies of the women are decisively reaffirmed as female. As they trek through the jungle they become increasingly dirty and dishevelled, their faces grimy and streaked with dirt and hair ungroomed and limp. Tight belts have been removed, thus waists and therefore clearly 'feminine' figures have been lost while many of the women wear 'coolie hats' which cover their long hair – one of the more obvious signifiers of femininity. Jean, the most adaptable to her new circumstances, exchanges her skirt and blouse for a Malay sarong and shapeless long-sleeved shirt. Through the loss of such obvious gendered markers the women are less immediately recognisable *as women* and as Western women. In a key scene, occurring mid-way through the story, the women come across an abandoned colonial villa and discover that the water supply is still connected. An extended scene shows the women bathing and washing their clothes, while the children play in the garden with a water-hose.[4] Jean has removed her shapeless long-sleeved shirt, her tight-fitting sarong now emphasising her waist and, with her hat removed, an extremely long plait of blond hair is clearly visible for the first time in the film. The combination of loose hair and tight clothing begins the process of re-feminising her. Impatiently shrugging off her clothes, her naked lower limbs are depicted stepping into the shower, followed by a cut to a close-up of her face tipped backwards, the water flowing over her face, open mouth and throat, the final shot suggesting orgasmic ecstasy.

The scene suggests that the dirt, grime, coolie hats and – by extension – female agency are a temporary state, behind which resides an essential and sexually desirable femininity, one which is crucially coded here as white and English. As Dolan and Street argue in their discussion of Anna Neagle, references to 'blonde hair' and 'an English rose complexion' are used to establish the whiteness of English national identity (see chapter three in this collection). An integral component of McKenna's star persona was the English Rose image, connotations that are used effectively to re-establish this as a group of white English women. The setting is significant: the colonial villa is a safe space where 'true' English femininity is revealed. While all the women can embody English femininity, the sexual aspect of identity is reserved only for the younger women. The older women are not seen bathing, rather Mrs Frost stokes the fire, Ebbey washes clothes, while the oldest character Mrs Frith sits fully clothed soaking her feet in a bowl. The older women are positioned outside the sexual economy, the re-establishment of their femininity limited to activities considered, within patriarchal logic, 'appropriate' to their age.

These scenes, which re-feminise the women in accordance with gender norms, seem to function as a form of narrative compensation, designed to ameliorate what has effectively been a 'theft' of masculinity (i.e. agency, homosocial bonds). In this respect the film demonstrates something of the limitations or parameters that operate when women appear in groups in films. Furthermore, the unity and importance of the group, which has clearly been established by the time the women find permanent shelter in the Malay village, is undermined by the film's flashback structure which locates female agency and solidarity safely in the past. The final reel, set in the post-war present, focuses on Jean's reunion in Australia with Joe, thus prioritising that relationship. In the film's conclusion, no further information is given about the other women, thus the female group is almost 'suspended', belonging to a different time and place, and implicitly signalled as a temporary and aberrant state. However what has been depicted is the hardship faced by Jean, and all the women. Jean can thus enter into a post-war partnership with Joe on equal terms and in this respect the film's world-view is in tune with the ideology of the 'companionate marriage', which dominated debates in the 1950s.

In sum the narrative depicts romance, motherhood and the desirable female body alongside portrayals of female agency, supportive group bonds and a broad range of feminine types, which extends (atypically in mainstream cinema) to more positive representations of older women. This balancing of a number of elements that can broadly be termed 'progressive' and 'conservative' within the social logic of the period is consistent with the 'Janus-faced' convention of the woman's film (i.e. complicit with, and challenging, norms of gender) that was discussed in the introduction to this collection. It's a device that also met the needs of audiences who had a particular appetite in the 1950s for films marked by 'textual compromises and ambiguities' (Porter 2001: 408) as these provided space for them to negotiate some of the myriad changes taking place in society. It is likely that it is these two aspects – the bringing together of well-worn genre or narrative convention with audience preference for ambiguity – that accounts for the film's considerable popularity with audiences and critics.

The female group in prison

Social problem films were a mainstay of British film production in the 1950s. A combination of melodrama, thriller and realism, these films explored a wide range of contemporary social concerns including prostitution, juvenile delinquency, unmarried motherhood and homosexuality. The reconstruction of society in peacetime threw up a number of concerns around gender roles, sexuality and family life and the 'problem woman' was a central figure in the genre. The social tendency to criminalise female desire gave rise to a number of films with prison or reform school settings where women could be both punished for refusing the demands of normative femininity, and rehabilitated to their proper gender roles. In both *Good Time Girl* and *Yield to the Night* for example, the female protagonists desire freedom and autonomy and refuse the roles of daughter and wife, a rebelliousness which society works hard to contain.

Turn the Key Softly, the first British film to include scenes shot in Holloway women's prison, attends to the figure of the 'problem woman'. The film opens with three women on the day of their discharge and follows them through the course of that day and their readjustment to civilian life. The small group is comprised of young and flighty Stella (Joan Collins), the more mature middle-class Monica (Yvonne Mitchell) and a recidivist shoplifter Granny (Kathleen Harrison). The women are faced with a number of life choices, a common feature of the woman's film. Stella is torn between her desire for sparkly earrings and a 'good time', or the sensible option of marriage to a bus conductor and life in the suburbs. Monica likewise must choose between an unsuitable corrupt man, or a respectable life as a secretary. Although the majority of the action takes place after the women have been released, the opening scene is particularly interesting in relation to the theme of the group. It dramatises the re-acquisition of the women's feminine identities, which were lost after a prolonged spell in prison where gender norms have been put under pressure. Lined up in front of the discharge officer, the women first appear dressed in shapeless standard-issue prison uniforms and considerable narrative space is given over to the processes by which they are individuated and feminised. Reading from a discharge list the officer returns their civilian clothing and other feminine accoutrements in what amounts to a roll-call of femininity. Stella's comprises 'one skirt, one pair of stockings, one lipstick … two bracelets' while Granny's items ('one coat, one dress, one undervest – torn') reveals the older woman's poverty and her failure to maintain expected feminine standards. Monica's middle-class femininity is spared the humiliation of being paraded for the state's inspection. Hastily signing the release form before the officer has time to read out her personal items, she emerges from the changing cubicle in a smart, well-cut wool suit and discreet pearl earrings, eliciting various looks of approval and envy from the surrounding women. The scene functions in a manner similar to the bathing sequence in *A Town Like Alice*. Female bodies and, by extension, normative femininity has been lost through wearing androgynous clothing and the curtailment of women's attention to their physical appearance. The scene highlights the narrative requirement to re-assert the women as 'real' women: feminine, heterosexual and desirable.

These themes are taken up in *The Weak and the Wicked*, which provided British cinema-goers with the first prolonged dramatisation of life in a women's prison. Directed by J. Lee Thompson, the film was adapted from Joan Henry's popular account of her time in prison, *Who Lie in Gaol* (1952), and enjoyed considerable commercial success, despite the 'quality' film journal *Monthly Film Bulletin* disparagingly dismissing the film's 'prize collection of familiar feminine types' as 'two-dimensional creatures' (in Hill 1986: 183). Joan Henry had been a well-heeled society women but a gambling addiction culminated in a prison sentence and, upon her release, she drew on this experience for her novel. Thompson and Henry wrote the screenplay with Anne Burnaby, a resident script-writer with the film's production company ABPC. Burnaby had a reputation as an excellent writer, was remembered by Thompson as sexually ambiguous (Chibnall 2000: 53), and had an acute feminist awareness that often viewed contemporary gender politics through a lens of irony. The demands of commercial cinema and the need to secure an 'A' certificate meant that many of the more radical elements of the novel (prison violence and prostitution) were excised for the screen. The film opens with gambling addict Jean Raymond (Glynis Johns) being sentenced to twelve months for fraud. Once incarcerated she meets a number of women from a variety of backgrounds – first-time offenders and good-humoured recidivists – all with a different story to tell. After a spell of good behaviour she is transferred to an open prison, Askham Grange, where she develops a close friendship with a young woman, Betty (Diana Dors). After serving the remainder of her sentence she is released into the arms of her waiting boyfriend.

In a manner comparable with *Alice* the film's ensemble cast is drawn from a broad age range. It comprises character actors such as Olive Sloane as Nellie and comic actress Athene Seyler as Millie, alongside established younger stars; sexy good-girl Glynis Johns and Britain's blonde bombshell Diana Dors. The film's portmanteau structure weaves together a number of personal narratives which dramatise a range of feminine types and female life experiences. Four stories recount the women's lives through flashback. Jean has been imprisoned for fraud, Nellie, a repeat offender, for shoplifting, Millie for blackmail and Babs for child neglect. These central stories are complemented by other female types who extend the range of femininities. In the hospital ward pregnant inmates Pat and Andy are respectively cynical and terrified mothers-to-be, Betty (Dors) is naïve and easily led, while hot-headed 'foreigner' Tina has murdered an unfaithful lover.

In most cases men are responsible for the women's predicament and in this respect the film draws on the 'traditional realism of women's experience' that characterises the 'woman's film'. Betty has perjured herself to save her worthless boyfriend Norman; a futile gesture as he abandons her during her prison term. Babs, a single mother, is pressurised by her American boyfriend to leave her young children unsupervised at night while she goes dancing, and returns alone to find the baby has died. Jean prefers gambling and the excitement of the roulette wheel to a stable relationship with stolid Michael (John Gregson). Her incarceration is therefore as much because she refuses the socially expected role of wife as it is for unpaid gambling debts. As Anne Morey observes, men in the women-in-prison films have a central role to play 'as the agents who drive women to prison in the first place' (1995: 80) and are also instrumental in effecting their rehabilitation. The purpose of prison is to recalibrate problem women to take up their proper place in the gendered social economy. The male chaplain urges Jean to marry Michael on her release ('I wouldn't leave it too long my dear'), while in the open prison women learn the gendered skills deemed necessary for domesticity and marriage: dress-making, rug-making, knitting. For the prison Governor such activities will ensure that 'women are fitted for their return to the world'. Pregnant inmates, perversely, have their babies adopted after nine months, thus child-rearing – that most central of feminine skills – is withdrawn. Notwithstanding this contradiction, demonstrable proficiency in all other areas indicates that women have overcome their resistance to normative femininity. Prison is, as Morey observes, 'at once a means of regulating deviant behavior and an attempt to restore the outcast to society – on society's terms' (1995: 81), terms that are always shaped by the demands of patriarchy.

Despite the expectations placed on women regarding the feminine norms of heterosexual marriage, female friendships among this group of women move centre-stage. Judith Mayne's observation that the women-in-prison film is a genre 'where relationships between women are paramount ... [and] differences between women are stressed' (2000: 127) might stand as readily as a definition of the female group film and may account for its appeal for female cinemagoers. At the centre of *The Weak and the Wicked* is the relationship that develops between Jean and Betty after they are moved to the open prison Askham. They quickly become best friends with Betty admitting to Jean how important the friendship is to her. Shortly before Jean's release the two women

Figure 7.2 Female friendship centre stage: Glynis Johns and Diana Dors in *The Weak and the Wicked*, directed by J. Lee Thompson (1954)
Source: The Steve Chibnall Collection.

are granted an unsupervised day visit to a nearby town, and are shown laughing and enjoying each other's company while they share lunch, and visit the cinema and fairground. This scene of intimate female bonding is positioned alongside reminders of romantic love; a montage of heterosexual couples at play at the fun-fair, the film showing at the local cinema – *One Night of Love* – a reminder of what the women have been missing. Although the sequence culminates in Betty ostensibly running off to London to find Norman, what remains from the scene is a sense of how compatible the two women are.

Other attempts to balance the women's close friendship with recourse to heterosexual relationships are similarly treated in an uneven manner. When Jean is discharged, the women share an intense emotional good-bye, exchanging home addresses with Jean attempting to console a weeping Betty by promising faithfully 'I'll send you postcards and things, it won't be long … we'll keep in touch won't we.' She leaves the prison and is surprised (along with the viewer) to find Michael waiting for her. Their relationship had broken down and Jean had no contact with him during her time in Askham. Not present in the novel, and written into the screenplay to meet the demands of commercial cinema, there is throughout the film awkwardness to the handling of the heterosexual romance between Michael and Jean, and the ending feels similarly unconvincing and contrived, straining to balance out the more robust depiction of female solidarity. Commented on at length by a number of critics (Landy 1991; Chibnall 2000; Williams 2002), Landy argues that Michael's return is 'totally unmotivated', both 'a purposeful form of self-censorship' and 'a commentary on the interdiction of female relationships and sexuality outside the heterosexual matrix' (1991: 455). While Chibnall considers Landy's reading wishful (feminist) thinking (2000: 66) the scriptwriter Anne Burnaby, positioned as a sexual 'outsider', would have perhaps been better placed to portray with subtlety and skill those relationships that disrupted the heterosexual matrix above those that readily conformed to it.

The strength of the women's friendship suggests the possibility of lesbian desire. As Tasker has argued '[w]hile friendship between women is a source of strength … the question of the closeness of that friendship to lesbian desire is in constant negotiation' (1998: 152). Jean and Betty's day trip bears all the hallmarks of a date. We are positioned to read Betty's abrupt departure to London/Norman as being triggered by jealousy at the sight of happy heterosexual couples at the fairground. However, as Jean shares a swing-boat with a man (the two women have only enough money for one ride) there is a distinct possibility that Betty is jealous, not of Jean, but of the man. The film that the women watch, *One Night of Love*, might easily be Burnaby's ironic comment on what the women have been sharing during their time in prison. During the emotional farewell scene, Betty sobs inconsolably while Jean cradles her, suggesting the painful separation of lovers. The intensification of female friendships in the women-in-prison genre, and the narrative marginalisation of men, seems to particularly push away from heterosexuality and towards same sex desire, in a manner not readily found in the war genre for example. As Mayne has cogently argued, the

women-in-prison genre is one of the few established genres where lesbianism is not an afterthought or an anomaly. There is almost always a lesbian
character … and lesbian desire is represented across a wide range of activities,
from longing looks between female characters, to special friendships … to
sexual activity, to sexual coercion.

(2000: 118)

While the relationship between Betty and Jean is positioned at one end of a
spectrum of lesbian desire – articulated in popular culture via oblique looks and
coded references – other characters and expressions in the film are more overt.

Prison Officer Arnold (Joyce Heron) is the only individuated officer in the
closed prison and is coded as the stereotypical predatory lesbian through her
uniform, mannish stride and authoritative stance. The object of her affections is
a young, first-time offender, Miriam whose *femme* appearance (fair-haired,
slender, pale skin) contrasts markedly with Arnold's more butch persona. After
the obligatory bathing scene (which asserts the women's bodies as female,
mediated by the gaze of a patrolling female guard) the women cluster in the
boot room, selecting regulation-issue shoes. Arnold singles out Miriam for
attention: her eyes cast a lascivious gaze down the young woman's body, before
she settles an intense stare on Miriam's confused, flustered face. Arnold later
checks on Miriam through the cell-door spy-hole, the young women captured
and framed as the object of Arnold's gaze. While the depiction of the predatory
prison officer is clearly unsympathetic, a space is opened up where the male
gaze is displaced and it becomes permissible for women to look at other
women. While the dynamic between Arnold and Miriam is predicated on
uneven power relations, the close friendship that Miriam develops with a fellow
inmate Tina is shown as equal and mutually supportive. The two women
exercise together in the yard and communicate through their cell walls through
a series of coded taps. This infuriates Arnold who clearly has a (sexual) history
with Tina. Arnold intervenes between the two women in the exercise yard,
'don't get so close together', and warns Miriam to stay away from Tina as
'she'll only lead you into trouble'. The double-meaning of the dialogue invites a
reading of women's relations with each other as ambiguous and multi-layered,
functioning as both platonic and/or sexual. In all cases close female friendships
are marked as divergent. Miriam and Tina's coded communication contravenes
prison regulations, as does Betty and Jean's swapping of home addresses. But
The Weak and the Wicked, like many women-in-prison films, demonstrates the
interest women clearly have for each other. As an example of how women can
appear in groups in film it is noteworthy for the considerable narrative space it
affords to female relationships and the relative weakness of the heterosexual
dynamic.

Of the two films, *The Weak and the Wicked* is the more radical in its gender
politics as female solidarity takes precedence over the film's more conservative
elements. The relationship between Jean and Betty and their emotional farewell
for example is barely disturbed by the brief surprise appearance of Michael in

the final shot. Certainly the women-in-prison genre has the capacity to foreground female relations. Prison is a space where women's social embeddedness – derived from relationships with men and close family structures – is automatically disrupted and female bonds, by necessity, assume priority. A space is cleared where lesbian desire can be articulated. This ranges from the 'special friendships' enjoyed by a number of the women where traces of sexual attraction may be found, to an overt expression of sexual desire, although, in a stereotypical manner, this can only be attributed to the predatory and harsh prison officer. Conversely heterosexuality is afforded a more privileged position in *A Town Like Alice*. The inclusion of young children in this female group ensures that motherhood and caring remains a central role for the women, while an extended scene of the young women bathing reasserts the youthful, sexually desirable feminine body.

Conclusion

I have argued that women in groups do not readily appear in mainstream cinema because patriarchal structures (which clearly shape the film industry) position women in relation to men and the family. When these films do emerge, their presence demands our attention. In the 1950s the small but significant number of female group films produced by British film-makers can be seen as a response to social changes concerning the family, women's economic role and their relations to men. My discussion of *A Town Like Alice* and *The Weak and the Wicked* suggests that the female group is represented in a particularly selective way. Across the group, a wide range of femininities and female types are introduced (typically including older women) and women are positioned in relation to each other, as confidantes, mentors, friends and lovers. Robust female friendships, depictions of female ingenuity and at times lesbian desire are worked through. The appropriation of the male privilege or 'theft' of masculinity – agency, homosocial bonding and androgynous clothing – requires a form of narrative compensation, which takes the form of re-establishing the 'true' female body through fetishistic display, and re-inserting men (previously marginalised) into the narrative. The commercial successes enjoyed by these films suggests that their fairly complex portrayals of femininity, and their narrative contradictions and ambiguities, met the needs of British cinema-goers in the 1950s. Certainly the multiple femininities on display in these films – characters differentiated by age, marital status and life experience – would have extended the range of identification possibilities for female spectators. At a time when British cinema was producing fewer female-centred dramas, this is significant. These films emerged in the 1950s, a time commonly understood as dominated by debates concerning the reconstruction of the 'traditional' nuclear family, with sexual politics settled along traditional gender lines. The presence of these films stands as an important record that Britain was experiencing some social unease vis-à-vis gender roles and femininity during this period, and that women's social embeddedness in patriarchal society was clearly *not* assured at this time.

Notes

1 I am grateful to Sue Harper for this example of how the female group film responds to social circumstance.
2 Britain's established tradition of episodic, portmanteau or omnibus films, 'short story compendiums … where a number of personal narratives are presented, generally with some linking thread' (McFarlane 2003: 205), are well suited to ensemble casts. In contrast, Emanuel Levy argues that Hollywood stars are typically advised to eschew ensemble films as traditionally they rarely garner industry prizes for actors (2003: 121).
3 Jean is contrasted sharply with the other single young woman, Ellen, who is not shown caring for any of the children and, though she readily shares her medicines, is predominantly defined by a sexuality that is, at best, tolerated by the other women.
4 The scene is not without precedent in British cinema. In *2,000 Women* a similar female bathing scene is used and is discussed in some detail by Babington, who argues that ultimately voyeurism is 'demoted to the margins' (2002: 76). Conversely in *Alice* fragments of the female body (faces, lower legs, shoulders) are shown in close-up and medium shot. The camera is in this sense intrusive and voyeuristic, although the scene as a whole is interspersed with shots of the children playing in the garden and the baby being washed, placing bathing alongside other domestic activities.

Bibliography

Babington, B. (2002) *Launder and Gilliat*, Manchester: Manchester University Press.
Basinger, J. (1986) *The World War II Combat Film, Anatomy of a Genre*, New York: Columbia University Press.
Chibnall, S. (2000) *J. Lee Thompson*, Manchester: Manchester University Press.
Geraghty, C. (2000) *British Cinema in the Fifties, Gender, Genre and the New Look*, London: Routledge.
Harper, S. (2000) *Women in British Cinema, Mad, Bad and Dangerous to Know*, London: Continuum.
Harper, S. and Porter, V. (2003) *British Cinema of the 1950s: The Decline of Deference*, Oxford: Oxford University Press.
Hill, J. (1986) *Sex, Class and Realism, British Cinema 1956–1963*, London: BFI.
Landy, M. (1991) *British Genres: Cinema and Society, 1930–1960*, Princeton, NJ: Princeton University Press.
LaPlace, M. (1987) 'Producing and consuming the woman's film: discursive struggle in *Now, Voyager*', in C. Gledhill (ed.), *Home is Where the Heart is: Studies in Melodrama and the Woman's Film*, London: BFI.
Levy, E. (2003) *All About Oscar: The History & Politics of the Academy Award*, New York: Continuum.
McFarlane, B. (1997) *An Autobiography of British Cinema*, London: Methuen.
——(2003) *The Encyclopedia of British Film*, London: Methuen.
Mayne, J. (2000) *Framed: Lesbians, Feminists and Media Culture*, Minneapolis: University of Minnesota Press.
Morey, A. (1995) 'The judge called me an accessory: women's prison films, 1950–62', *Journal of Popular Film and Television*, 23.2: 80–7.
Murphy, R. (2000) *British Cinema and the Second World War*, London: Continuum.
Porter, V. (2001) (review), *British Cinema in the Fifties: Gender, Genre and the New Look*, *Screen*, 42.4: 405–8.

Stacey, J. (1994) *Star Gazing, Hollywood Cinema and Female Spectatorship*, London: Routledge.

Tasker, Y. (1998) *Working Girls*, London: Routledge.

A Town Like Alice pressbook (held at BFI Library).

Williams, M (2002) 'Women in prison and women in dressing gowns: rediscovering the 1950s films of J. Lee Thompson', *Journal of Gender Studies*, 11.1: 5–15.

8 Swinging femininity, 1960s transnational style

Marcia Landy

The brave new world of globality is identified with 'mobile' subjects and a lifestyle that differs substantially from the years prior to World War Two in Europe. Social and political changes took place in both Britain and Italy that altered the contours of these two nations, and cinema and television played a critical role in the cultural changes. This chapter compares a number of woman's films produced in Britain and Italy in the 1960s, involving dynamic images of the corporeal body, geography, music, fashion, landscape and media forms that underscore the transnational dimensions of 1960s cinematic culture involving portrayals of gender.

In Britain, altered portraits of femininity emerged in *Girl with Green Eyes* (1964), *The Knack ... and How to Get It* (1965) and *Darling* (1965), largely connected to the world of the metropolis, and actresses such as Rita Tushingham and Julie Christie became icons of swinging femininity (Geraghty 1997; Luckett 2000). These films resemble those made in other West European cinemas of the decade in their shared concern with the re-fashioning of the culture and politics of femininity within the emergent society of consumption. Such films are structured around physical journeys within and across regional and national borders as well as conceptual journeys across boundaries of social class, generation and sexuality; voyages in space and time that present a clear departure from the earlier woman's film which 'most often revolves around the traditional realms of woman's experience: the familial, the domestic, the romantic' (LaPlace 1987: 139). The popular British costume dramas of the 1940s do not 'foreground family as an issue' but instead create a fanciful site of sexual pleasure (Harper 1987: 190). A more hybrid generic form, the swinging 1960s film adopts a cinematic language that invokes different clothing fashions, hair-dos and mises en scène for addressing femininity (and masculinity). These films have been celebrated as dramatizing changes that 'had a fundamental effect on society and the environment' (Murphy 1992: 139). After years of privation, the decade ushered in an affluent society in which traditional attitudes toward gender and sexuality, the feminine body, courtship, the family, maternity and social class appeared to be crumbling in the wake of the permissive society. Legislation that allowed for modest changes in relation to marriage, divorce, homosexuality, family planning and abortion (Hall 2000:167–85) helped to reconfigure conceptions of the nation, its institutions and its inhabitants. The British cinema expressed these promises and threats to an emerging society and its culture in its films.

Corresponding changes were also manifested in Italy and identified with what came to be known as the Economic Miracle. In the late 1940s and early 1950s, Italy was largely a 'backward' country characterized by a low standard of living that was most marked in the south of the country where 'more than 2,700,000 families were classified as "poor" or "needy", equivalent to a quarter of the total population … [o]nly 7% of households had electricity, drinking water, and an indoor toilet. Illiteracy was still widespread' (Duggan 1998: 262). By the mid-1960s the economic situation had changed noticeably. Southerners began to migrate to the industrial north, to cities such as Rome, Turin and Milan, and participated in the growing prosperity exemplified in the production and purchase of Italian cars, motorcycles, and office and domestic appliances, and the growing popularity of Italian fashion was manifest both nationally and internationally.

Technological strides brought new social mores into existence, and changing modes of femininity suggested a national rebirth (Buckley 2000; Gundle 1999; Reich 2004). In the 1950s, a voluptuous and fecund figure of woman emerged, identified with Sophia Loren, Gina Lollobrigida and Silvana Mangano. Their narrow waistlines, full breasts, shapely legs and 'unruly' behaviour embodied a challenge to Catholic views on marriage, maternity and family. Moving into the 1960s, Monica Vitti's star image offers a cinematic portrait of femininity that grapples critically with these issues. Having made her name in the existential explorations of director Michelangelo Antonioni, she also appeared in more genre-defined films, including her first foray into Britain with the stylized spy thriller *Modesty Blaise* (1966). Vitti's comedy vehicle *La Ragazza con la Pistola* (*The Girl with the Pistol*, 1968) assumes a more explicit relation to transnational cinema, and is consonant with certain British comedies that highlight a conflict between tradition and modernity.

City lights: British 1960s style

The Knack and *Girl with Green Eyes* both involve young women who leave the provinces for the city. Urbanity is highlighted by encounters with the sights and sounds of city life, including street scenes of window-shopping. The treatment of femininity introduces the spectator to a world of fashion, food, gossip, dancing and physical pleasures with young men. The initiation of a provincial girl into the pleasures and dangers of sexuality is not a new motif. The difference from conventional woman's films comes with the portrayal of the young women as adventurers, not victims, who are escaping from moral constraints about marriage and sexuality to pursue an independent existence. In contrast to the male-orientated social realism of the class-conscious 'Kitchen Sink' films of the late 1950s and early 1960s, these films offer a celebratory vision of youth. Produced by Woodfall, the independent company associated with *Look Back in Anger* (1959), *A Taste of Honey* (1961) and *The Loneliness of the Long-Distance*

Runner (1962), the woman's films are indicative of a flirtation with the seductive but also threatening character of mass culture.

The Knack … and How to Get It portrays the swinging world of the 1960s in the context of mass culture, and the music employed on the sound track conveys the texture of this world. Directed by Richard Lester, the ex-pat American who directed the Beatles in *A Hard Day's Night* (1964), and scored by John Barry, *The Knack* was an important indicator of how British identity was departing from the traditions of British cinema in style and point of view. The innovations introduced in *A Hard Day's Night* are expanded in *The Knack*. Through the numerous shots of street life that portray its dynamic and contentious character, the film connects to the mod world of youth and the 'counterculture'. Thanks to the film's artistic designer, Assheton Gorton, the film is a 'mixture of styles', contributing to a mise en scène that creates 'new artwork made from used images' to incarnate the world of swinging London (Tuson 2005: 104).

The film's eccentric characters embody 'the opportunities afforded by the new climate of permissiveness' (Murphy 1992: 136). For Robert Murphy 'the real hero of the film is Colin, a shy, weedy schoolteacher [Michael Crawford], who, against all expectations wins the love of the innocent but canny country girl, Nancy played by Rita Tushingham, who comes to London looking for adventure' (1992: 136). Nancy is the film's adventurous protagonist – not its victim. Tolen (Ray Brooks), the antagonist, is a brash womanizing young man. While the film attacks the narrow-mindedness of the older generation, it appears critical of compulsive forms of heterosexuality incarnated in Tolen, conveyed through images of the multiple women he photographs, his motorcycle, vaunting of his dynamic sexual prowess and disdain for Nancy's naiveté ('Just come off the boat, have you?'). *The Knack's* visual and aural tracks convey a visceral sense of the emotional stakes in this changed milieu. Jump cuts, direct address to the spectator, mirror shots, the insertion of inter-titles, a range of voiceovers and fantasy sequences that counterbalance documentary sequences, all provide vivid insights into the world of the female protagonist.

Nancy's journey is introduced in parallel to three young men. Her wandering through the streets in search of a YWCA permits a perspective on London life as epitomized by 'ordinary' citizens who leer or express their discontent about youth and the collapse of moral values. There is an emphasis on female body parts – faces, breasts and legs – through advertising images on billboards and in the magazines that Nancy reads. One of the early sequences portrays Nancy window-shopping and then entering a shop; accosted by a salesman, she tries on clothes and hats but leaves with her same tweed coat and cap without purchasing an item. This sequence situates Nancy as a critical observer rather than as an enthusiast of fashion. Her goal of finding the YWCA becomes a trope for her independence from men, just as a large-sized bed becomes a trope for Colin's quest for 'the knack'.

The critical moment occurs when Nancy, being seduced by Tolen after a lengthy ride on his motorcycle, finds herself facing him alone in a wooded area of a city park. Telling him to 'keep off', degrading his vaunted sexual prowess, repeating 'Don't come near me' and screaming rape, she faints. The word 'rape' echoes on the soundtrack as a particular reproach to Tolen, who is frustrated in his intention. After a verbal confrontation with and chastisement of Colin, she and he retire to his bed to enjoy sex. Nancy has punctured the men's sexual posturing as she has punctured the tires of Tolen's motorcycle. The comedy ends on a utopian note with Colin and Nancy walking in the street at night and holding hands. She has 'educated' the schoolteacher into sexuality that entails a woman's pleasure as well as his own, but the film, in contrast to the romantic conventions of the traditional woman's film, is silent about the prospects of marriage.

In *Girl with Green Eyes*, adapted by Edna O'Brien from her own novel, Rita Tushingham once again incarnates the provincial girl coming to the city for adventure. Kate (Tushingham) arrives in Dublin from the Irish countryside, finds a job in a shop, and falls in love with a sophisticated writer and married man, Eugene (Peter Finch). The film depicts her struggle with a sexually repressive Catholic family background. Several scenes dramatize the oppressiveness of her violent father and his cronies who seek by means of verbal and physical abuse to separate her from a 'sinful' relationship. Her sexual difficulties are portrayed in her inability to expose her naked body to Eugene. After finally succumbing to sex with Eugene, she becomes possessive, re-enacting the role of a jealous wife and alienating him. The ending of the relationship drives her melodramatically to contemplate suicide, but with the aid of her friend Baba (Lynn Redgrave), she emigrates to London. The two actresses would play best friends making a journey to London again in a later Desmond Davis-directed film, *Smashing Time* (1967).

Figure 8.1 Mobile young women: Kate (Rita Tushingham) and Baba (Lynn Redgrave) on the boat to England in *Girl with Green Eyes*, directed by Desmond Davis (1964).

The film ends with an image of her with a group of young men outside a college in which she is enrolled. Her voice-over narrates the contents of a letter from Eugene expressing regret that he was unprepared for a relationship and that she was too immature to handle it. Thus, the film dramatizes several journeys: from the country to Dublin and from Dublin to London, and from fantasies of love and marriage to a world where she can discover freer forms of relationships. Tushingham's physical appearance over the course of the film reveals her transformation from a dowdy, impressionable and vulnerable girl to a self-confident young woman. The ending portrays her as entering a life that differs radically from her class and ethnic origins.

Although still focused on the mobile young woman, *Darling* presents a more obviously glamorous transnational milieu, skipping between London, Paris and Italy. The film made an international star of Julie Christie, who was to become an icon of the cinematic swinging sixties and a consummate image of its nomadic style. After interviewing well-known American actresses, the film's producer Joseph Janni and director John Schlesinger went with Christie instead who is recorded as saying 'I was embarrassed by the whole thing ... I wasn't terribly interested' (Callan 1984: 50). In spite of her qualms about stardom, Christie recognized the novelty of her role as 'a woman who didn't want to get married ... have children ... [but] wanted to have everything', and saw it as pointing women 'to a new way of living' (Callan 1984: 35). This tallied with her own persona developed through publicity of a woman who 'loves her freedom' (Callan 1984: 43). As Melanie Williams suggests, '*Darling*'s Diana gave expression to an emergent female identity that could not be contained within the film's moralizing framework and became instead the object of aspiration for young women' (Williams 2005: 39); an image of desirable swinging femininity repeated across newspapers, advertising, television, photography and haute couture. However, these dimensions of the film do not address its critical treatment of femininity as commodity to sell fashion and images of the easy life, nor its stinging critique of the era's penchant for spectacle.

From her voice-over narration, the audience learns that from childhood Diana was slated to be everyone's 'darling'. Her appeal resides in her protean character, her ability to present herself differently to the different audiences she confronts; a perspective different, if ambivalently so, from the conventional conflicts posed by the woman's film. The film capitalizes on her photogenic qualities. In retrospect, Christie complained, 'I looked like somebody who wasn't anything to do with me. That person on the screen was beautiful and not an awful lot more' (Williams 2005: 38). In the film's opening images, an enormous poster of Christie's face is being pasted over posters of suffering Africans, carrying the title 'The Ideal Woman'. From the standpoint of advertising, she is an ideal; from the perspective of the film, she is a product. *Darling* is punctuated with photographs of her similar to those in fashion magazines – her portrait plastered on walls – that highlight the film's preoccupation with filming her face and body. Her costumes designate her transformation from a playful, semi-conventional young woman who wants to be admired, to a seductive model whose appearance evokes the upper class elegance of the era. Her wedding outfit and hairdo are svelte but not overstated, and her daytime clothing in the palace conveys the expensive simplicity of royalty at home that reproduce images from numerous magazine articles on the lives of the rich and famous. Even the costumes that she wears with her companion in Italy, a gay photographer, have another audience in mind, namely, young international travellers that frequented the beaches and spas of the Mediterranean. Tourism was integral to the 'easy life' identified with increasingly nomadic youth.

Her visit to Paris evokes scenes from *La Dolce Vita* (1960) and her marriage to an Italian prince recalls the much-publicized European marriage of Grace Kelly to Prince Rainier. The ending of the film with her return to the prince is the final unhappy chapter of her journey. The plane carries her off, leaving the audience with the sound and image of a badly sung Neapolitan lyric by an ungainly and unfashionable London street woman: a concluding ironic allusion to the transnational dimensions of Britain in the heart of London. But however much the film offered a problematic image of the new woman, audiences saw *Darling* differently, in terms of its evocation of this 'new way of living [that] went beyond sexual behaviour to embrace an unconventional lifestyle with which Christie became strongly associated' (Williams 2005: 39). This international lifestyle was to penetrate Britain just as British fashion was to penetrate Europe.

Italy and Britain: a transnational journey

In the 1960s, Rome became a centre for international stars (British and American) as evidenced by the peplum epics, Italian westerns and films of Federico Fellini that focus on Roman high society and its international character. Among the factors responsible for the success of Italian cinema was the decline of Hollywood production between 1958 and 1968: the Italians took advantage of this low productivity to revitalize its own film industry (Bondanella 2002: 145). The Italian film industry extended its markets at home and abroad by distributing the auteur films of Michelangelo Antonioni and Fellini as well as popular genre films such as westerns and comedies. The practice of co-productions gained impetus from the mid-1960s: 'Between 1963 and 1964, the numbers alone of co-productions more than doubled, and for the rest of the decade they consistently outnumbered purely indigenous films' (Bergfelder 2000: 141). Though the British film industry was initially reluctant to entertain co-productions, 'Anglo-Italian arrangements were more common in the 1960s' (Bergfelder 2000: 145).

Co-productions were potentially profitable but they necessitated changes, with films and their stars having to appeal to audiences beyond national borders. These co-productions relied on stars that were familiar internationally, such as Sophia Loren and Gina Lollobrigida, and casts that were a mixture of national and transnational actors. British stars such as Christopher Lee, Barbara Steele, Terence Stamp and Richard Harris made the reverse journey to Italy. Remakes were popular, and adventure films returned earlier popular heroes to the screen, particularly in the epics that drew on classical mythology and history. However, Italian comic genres also achieved international success. Given the liberalization of sexual portrayals in this decade, the narratives became familiar to audiences of the time in Italy and abroad. These films were attuned to cultural and cinematic changes that made them accessible across national borders.

The comedy *La Ragazza con la Pistola* focuses on a female protagonist torn between traditional expectations of her social position and dramatic changes wrought by urban life. Directed by Mario Monicelli, *La Ragazza* is a journey film in which the central female character sets out from village life in southern Italy to Britain and, in the course of that journey, is transformed into a swinging single. This swinging world is presented as a counterweight to the constraints of a static traditional society whose women are feared and controlled. The comedy portrays outmoded forms of courtship, marriage and sexual behaviour. Vitti's comic performance, for which she received numerous prestigious awards internationally as well as in Italy (including the Nastro d'Argento for the best female performance in 1968), effectively mimics a rural naïve woman bound to her old world who then becomes a worldly and transnational embodiment of newly liberated femininity.

La Ragazza portrays Assunta Patane's journey from Sicily to Scotland, to the city of Sheffield, and ultimately to London. Monicelli's films have been identified with the post war *commedia all' italiana*, a genre with its roots in the *commedia dell'arte* that has been described as a 'tragicomedy bordering on the grotesque ... that lays bare an undercurrent of social malaise and the painful contradictions of a culture in rapid transformation' (Bondanella 2002: 145). Monicelli's comedies satirize cultural and social institutions, bureaucracy and the dead weight of the past. His casting of Monica Vitti as a voluble southern Italian woman contrasts to her serious and enigmatic middle-class image of femininity in Antonioni's films, but corresponds with her image of a woman confronting the imperative of change.

Like Antonioni's *Blow Up*, a UK and Italian co-production, *La Ragazza* is another instance of the transnational movement of Italian filmmakers in its use of international stars and of the British landscape and characters to satirize Italian cultural backwardness, using a female protagonist to question traditional values identified with southern Italy. Monicelli's comedy is not unique in this respect, for Pietro Germi in *Divorzio All'Italiana* (*Divorce, Italian Style*, 1961) and *Sedotta e Abbandonata* (*Seduced and Abandoned*, 1964), and Pier Paolo Pasolini's *Comizi D'Amore* (*Love's Meetings*, 1964) entailed similar explorations. The films that focused on the south of Italy are 'the ideal site to explore the manners and mores of a new society; for the south, in its very "backwardness," its cultural distance from modernity, provides the widest possible distance for the effect of comedy' (Restivo, 2002: 47). However, while the Germi films envision Rome as a location to portray a 'woman who steps outside of her culture to radically negate it' (Restivo, 2002: 47), the Monicelli film transports its female protagonist to the United Kingdom, but maintains a similar project of distancing her from her culture to dramatize her encounters with modernity.

Figure 8.2 Transnational femininity: Monica Vitti as Sicilian girl in swinging London in
        La Ragazza con la Pistola, directed by Mario Monicelli (1968).
Source: Author's personal collection.

The opening scenes of *La Ragazza* take place in a small village in Sicily. Assunta is enamored of Vincenzo Macaluso, but in this world women may look surreptitiously at men (through semi-open blinds) but are prohibited from having sex before marriage. Vincenzo is an exaggerated portrait of southern masculinity, a parody of the Latin lover, pampered by women, who spends his days with his cronies, hanging out in bars, ogling and, when he can, seducing women. This *gallo* lives to talk about his sexual exploits to other men and exposes the sexual politics of this Sicilian world as based on male dominance. Masculinity is 'based traditionally on the tendentious preservation of female chastity, the archaic code of honor, and sexual talk rather than action' (Reich 2004: 55). Women in this milieu are not passive. They legislate the sexual mores of the community, ensuring conformity to chastity and punishing those women who violate the codes that control female sexuality.

Monicelli's *gallo* does not merely indulge in talk about sex with women; he succeeds in having Assunta forcibly brought to him by his cronies (though they err in bringing the wrong woman). Assunta demands marriage and, after assuming his agreement, she passionately has sex with him. Unfortunately for her standing in the community, he runs away before fulfilling his promise. Thus Assunta becomes a seduced and abandoned Sicilian woman whose sexual purity has been violated and who has therefore become an outcast in her Southern community. The women in her village are insistent on the necessity of revenge, since Assunta's 'dishonour' affects them all. She becomes a 'puttana', a whore 'who has engaged in pre-marital and extra-marital intercourse' and 'failed to uphold the integrity of the family' (Reich 2004: 53). The word 'puttana' will echo throughout, a reminder of female exchange value that Assunta's sexual transgression has exposed. Assunta's only recourse after this public display of denunciation is to take money, a photograph of Vincenzo, his address in the United Kingdom and a pistol given to her by her family to pursue her seducer to clear her name. Initially dressed in the customary black outfit of mourning with her long hair bound in a braid reaching down her back, Assunta boards a train, travels by ship to the United Kingdom, and arrives by train along with other immigrants who have been hired as domestics.

Looking for a foreign servant, a woman offers Assunta a position as a maid, but she refuses. Unlike the other immigrants, she has not come for employment but for vengeance. While the film does not take as its central concern the role of immigration from Italy in the late 1950s and 1960s, it provides images of largely Mediterranean women hired for domestic work in foreign lands who exemplify the mobile world of the 1960s. Walking on the busy streets and accosting people for directions, Assunta finds the Capriccio Restaurant where Vincenzo is employed, with the intention of confronting and shooting him. He escapes with the assistance of an Italian fellow worker who then invites her to spend the night with him, an offer she rejects, but, having kept the address card given her by a woman at the train station, she accepts the position as maid.

Dressed as a domestic in a striped dress and white apron, she serves guests during a cocktail party given by her employers. In the midst of the party,

Assunta receives a phone call from Vincenzo, disregards the guests, stands in the middle of the room before the assembled group, berating him loudly in Italian for dishonouring her and orders him to make her an honest woman or she will shoot him. Her indifference to her audience is further indication of her immersion in a Sicilian milieu with its public drama of violated sexual honour that appears comic to this middle-class British audience. She removes her apron, walks out on the job and continues her journey of revenge to the city of Sheffield. A bus ride, highlighting the English landscape, takes her there. On a street, she encounters a young man, John (Anthony Booth) who, she notices 'has Italian shoes', and she enlists him in her quest for vengeance.

After a hair-raising ride in a fancy sports car, John takes her to a disco to find Vincenzo, where she is introduced to the swinging world by way of the fashions of the young people, along with their music and style of dancing. When a young man pulls her from her chair to dance, outraged, she orders John to defend her honour. Assunta's obsession with chastity, Sicilian style, is thus made to appear ridiculous. Also at the disco, Assunta learns of Vincenzo's whereabouts from a young woman who praises him as 'a real Latin lover', underscoring the presence of this stereotype in the British context. Angrily, Assunta calls the young woman a 'puttana', betraying her own internalization of Sicilian sexual values. Assunta accepts John's invitation to spend the night with him but under strict conditions of abstinence. Oneiric sequences of flashbacks to the village scenes of her dishonour are interspersed throughout the film and play a critical role in underscoring Assunta's internalization of the past. The flashbacks serve as counterpoint to the confusing world she confronts and resists in her travels. In the next phase of her journey, John leaves her at a coffee shop the following morning where she awaits Vincenzo. Clothed demurely in a black dress with a lace collar, clutching her purse with the gun, and sitting facing the door she accidentally drops the purse. The gun goes off, bringing all activity in the shop to a standstill, and the scene recapitulates the excessiveness of her behaviour in this unfamiliar world.

The first signs of her capacity for pleasure are revealed in her enthusiastic involvement with the fans at a rugby game where John is playing. But her enjoyment is truncated when she observes a wounded player being carried off the field. Thinking that one of the stretcher-bearers is Vincenzo, she races off to follow the ambulance. At the hospital, she runs madly through the corridors but mistakenly enters a room where she views an operation in progress and faints. As nurses lift her up, her gun falls to the floor and is picked up by a doctor, Tom Osborne (Stanley Baker), who assumes a central role later in her adventures. When Assunta comes to, she is asked by one of the nurses for her blood type and enlisted as a blood donor for the wounded athlete, Frank.

The third phase of her journey involves her relationship with Frank. Finding him sympathetic (having shared her blood with him), she accepts a ride from him and enlists his assistance in finding Vincenzo. Learning of Vincenzo's death from two men dressed in black (Vincenzo's cronies), at a cemetery she sobs loudly in traditional Sicilian style, falling on a grave bearing Vincenzo's photograph.

Ostensibly free, she leaves the cemetery with Frank who declares his admiration for her as a 'strong' woman and proposes marriage. Now engaged, Assunta's appearance changes. She has abandoned her traditional black clothing and is dressed in a short beige suit with a mini skirt and a pink scarf. Significantly the various stages of her journey are marked by her changing appearance and by encounters with men – not women. The male characters introduce her to relationships that differ markedly from her background. But her brief engagement to Frank ends when Doctor Tom takes her to a bar where she observes men in flamboyant garb, fondling each other. She comments that they are 'finocchio' (gay) and in Sicily, would be treated as criminals. This episode is another way the film satirizes Sicilian sexual mores.

In his role as mentor, Tom urges her to become independent, find work and learn English. Hair cut short, dressed in a striped mini dress with a white apron, she serves as a nursing auxillary and takes English classes. Her friendship with Tom blossoms, and it seems that she has abandoned her revenge. Wearing a curly red wig, short black dress and orange shirt to match her hair colour, she walks jauntily on a street reciting her English lessons; a model of female mobility. Her walk is disrupted when she looks into a window of a restaurant and sees Vincenzo who has only been playing dead and is with a woman. She runs home to get her gun, puts on her black raincoat, and when she finds him in the bushes with the woman, she fires a shot but hits Vincenzo's lover rather than the man himself. The woman, wife of a physician, is not seriously wounded, but Tom pressures Assunta to return to Sicily and confront her family and community. He takes her to the airport, but, despite his arrangements, she disembarks in London. The next time he sees her she is taking part in an anti-imperialist demonstration, and he saves her from arrest. Her appearance has again altered; her bright red hair has long curls, she wears jeans, a big silver belt and a colourful blouse. She shows Tom a poster for which she has modelled and takes him to a restaurant where she works as a singer. Her movements are self-confident. Taking a guitar, she sits on a table with legs crossed and sings an Italian lyric to the diners. Her education in social and sexual relationships is further advanced when she learns that Tom and his wife have decided to divorce, another lesson for her in modern relationships.

But the issue of Vincenzo and of her past still casts its shadow. He now seeks to reestablish relations with her despite her evasions. Having decided to take a boat to Jersey to escape, she drives to the pier and discovers that she must wait until the next day. Vincenzo tries to seduce her again by appealing to their common background, shared language and customs, though she tells him that she has changed. She dances with him, and he confidently accompanies her to her hotel room. Reluctantly, she allows him to enter, but she points her gun at him, whereupon he quickly responds, 'I'll marry you.' They fall on the bed together, but the next scene abruptly cuts to him on the bed alone (as Assunta had been at the beginning of the film). He hurries to the pier to discover that her boat has left. She sits on deck smoking a cigarette and reading a magazine, indifferent to Vincenzo and her former mission of revenge. The voice-over repeats the phrase that had been chanted several times earlier, 'the girl with a gun'. Standing on the pier as the boat recedes, Vincenzo's final words are 'she was a whore and she remains a whore'.

Vitti, a ubiquitous presence in the film, gives full reign to her comic abilities. The film is generous in close-ups of her facial expressions that reveal a range of responses from dismay, contempt, naïveté, rage, confusion and cleverness. Close-ups and medium shots call attention to her appearance and dramatize her gradual conversion. The film's comedy resides in her exhibiting, while exaggerating, the same standards of morality as Vincenzo and her Sicilian community. Vitti's performance as a transformed woman is attuned to new directions for modern women, in striking contrast to traditional Italian culture. *La Ragazza* reveals its awareness of international filmmaking, appropriating the British landscape to challenge dimensions of Italian culture that are anachronistic in the changing Western European metropolis of the 1960s. Transported to a foreign milieu, crossing national borders, Vitti's persona incarnates the effects of the 'economic miracle' that brought into existence new forms of social life and sexual morality that might free women from machismo, traditional forms of femininity, familial demands and social class. The film ends as Assunta continues to travel toward an uncertain future.

Conclusion

Several British and Italian films of the 1960s share a concern to investigate the nature and effects of physical and social mobility that emerged from experimentation with female characters through various forms of narration and uses of spectacle. The characters' encounters with the urban, technological and consumer objects of modernity and their increased movement across national borders also involve a crossing of cinematic borders in their styles through exploring the possibilities and perils of the virtual world of media. Departing from earlier expressions of the woman's film, these films highlighted alterations in the 1960s aesthetic and critical landscape with consequences for reconfiguring the female body, sexuality, marriage, maternity and female agency.

Bibliography

Bergfelder, T. (2000) 'The nation vanishes: European co-productions and popular genre formulae in the 1950s and 1960s', in M. Hjort and S. Mackenzie (eds), *Cinema and Nation*, London: Routledge.

Bondanella, P. (2002) *Italian Cinema: From Neo-Realism to the Present*, New York: Continuum.

Buckley, R. (2000) 'National body: Gina Lollobrigida and the cult of the star in the 1950s', *Historical Journal of Film, Radio and Television*, 20.4: 527–47.

Callan, M. F. (1984) *Julie Christie*, New York: St Martin's Press.

Duggan, C. (1998) *A Concise History of Italy*, Cambridge: Cambridge University Press.

Geraghty, C. (1997) 'Women and 60s British cinema: The development of the "Darling" girl', in R. Murphy (ed.), *The British Cinema Book*, London: BFI.

Gundle, S. (1999) 'Feminine beauty, national identity and political conflict in postwar Italy, 1945–54', *Contemporary European History*, 8.3: 359–78.

Hall, L. A. (2000) *Sex, Gender, and Social Change in Britain since 1880*, New York: St Martin's Press.

Harper, S. (1987) 'Historical pleasures: Gainsborough costume melodrama', in C. Gledhill (ed.), *Home is Where the Heart is: Studies in Melodrama and the Woman's Film*, London: BFI.

LaPlace, M. (1987) 'Producing and consuming the woman's film: discursive struggle in *Now, Voyager*', in C. Gledhill (ed.), *Home is Where the Heart is: Studies in Melodrama and the Woman's Film*, London: BFI.

Luckett, M. (2000) 'Travel and mobility: femininity and national identity in swinging London films', in J. Ashby and A. Higson (eds), *British Cinema, Past and Present*, London: Routledge.

Murphy, R. (1992) *Sixties British Cinema*, London: BFI Publishing.

Reich, J. (2004) *Beyond the Latin Lover: Marcello Mastroianni, Masculinity, and Italian Cinema*, Bloomington: Indiana University Press.

Restivo, A. (2002) *The Cinema of Economic Miracles: Visuality and Modernization in the Italian Art Film*, Durham, NC: Duke University Press.

Tuson, E-M. (2005), 'Consumerism, the swinging sixties and Assheton Gorton', *Journal of British Film and Television*, 2.1: 100–116.

Williams, M. (2005) 'Julie Christie: honey-glow girl', *Sight and Sound*, 15.12: 36–40.

9 The British women's picture
Methodology, agency and performance in the 1970s

Sue Harper

The term 'British women's picture' contains a range of issues which we need to unpick. It would be possible to discuss films made *by* women, *for* women or *about* women. In the first, the issue of female agency needs to be interrogated: the contributions made by women in different areas; art direction, costume design, scriptwriting and so on. I began this task in the second half of *Women in British Cinema* (2000), in which it became clear that female autonomy was determined by the managerial structures of the industry. Films such as *A Taste of Honey* (1961) and *Rita, Sue and Bob Too* (1986) were dominated by the ideas of their female writers, who had managed to find a voice in the production process. It was easier for women to develop their creativity in some periods than in others. In the 1950s, for example, it was possible for Muriel Box and Wendy Toye to develop directorial careers. With Box, it was family connections, combined with her own facility with the dominant realist mode, which advanced her career. With Toye, it was the cumbersome structure of the Rank organisation, plus the 1950s industry's preference for comedy, a genre in which she excelled. Another period in which female directors flourished was in the alternative cinema of the 1970s. Exasperated by what they saw as the venal mainstream industry, avant-garde directors such as Ariel Levy, Sally Potter, Annabel Nicholson and Laura Mulvey operated in a relatively unfettered manner, and produced explicitly feminist films.

It would be feasible to construct a narrative about films *by* women, but it would need to be scrupulously related to mainstream production and also to cultural and social developments. The danger of such a project is that it might lead us into an uncritical feminist approach, in which the mainstream industry is presented as a conspiracy against hapless females. I am chary of such an approach for two reasons: first because it encourages a victim-mentality among female artists and critics, and second, because it simplifies the inner workings of patriarchy. That is always intellectually fatal. Patriarchy, like all systems of social control, manifests (indeed *requires*) powerful images of the social groups over which it holds sway. In order to function properly, it also needs texts which show the pleasures of the losers as well as the winners in its system.

What about our second category – films *for* women? This can be a helpful way of analysing patterns in British cinema, as long as it is carefully historicised. 'Woman's film' needs to be understood as an industrial category – that is to say, a category devised by studios for a target female audience. Evidence of this type of targeting can be found in the advice to cinema managers in the trade journals, about how to select specific films. Films were frequently categorised according to the class likely to respond positively to the film. *Thunder Rock* (1943), for example, was presented as high-brow fare for the better halls: 'such fantasy is not for the hoi-polloi' (*Today's Cinema*, 18 September 1942). Trade journals also emphasised the gender of the target audience: *Clara Dean* (1932) was recommended as 'good programme booking, particularly for the masses with strong feminine and emotional appeal' (*Kinematograph Weekly* 26 May 1932). Trade advice about target audiences is plentiful until the early 1960s, but disappears thereafter. The second source of evidence about target audiences is the publicity material provided by studios, which gives clues about how the films were intended to function. The producers of Gainsborough costume melodrama were quite clear about the ideal viewers for their films. Publicity material on *Madonna of the Seven Moons* (1944) suggest that it be sold through the headline 'Split-Mind Disorder Gives Idea For Year's Finest Romance!' They urged that this would appeal to 'curiosity, that great feminine characteristic. Trade on this!' (Press books for *Madonna* held in BFI Library.) Similar material on *Caravan* (1946) and *The Wicked Lady* (1945) indicates that producers were more interested in the profit women could generate than in the textual pleasure they might experience.

What is notable about British cinema is that the market category of woman's film was relatively short-lived. As a discrete cultural form, it spread from the 1930s to the late 1950s. What took its place in the market was the 'family film', which foregrounded children and wholesome values, and which was an important aspect of provision throughout the 1960s and 1970s. Partly because of this emphasis on generational rather than gender distinctions, 'woman's film' was not an industrial category in Britain during the 1960s. This was for two reasons. First, audience demographics had changed, and second (and probably as a consequence of that), studios were no longer producing films predicated on a female perspective. Of course, in working with the notion of films *for* women, the question of the gendered nature of taste must also be addressed. It is clear from work that has been done on female film taste in the 1930s, 1940s and 1950s (Kuhn 2002; James 2009; Glancy 2009; Harper and Porter 2003) that female viewers in all three decades used films for far different purposes than their male counterparts. But after that, there is a paucity of evidence about film taste in general, but particularly about female film taste. This may be because fewer films were specifically aimed at female audiences, or possibly because evidence of their taste has been lost, or not thought valuable enough to keep.

The third category, and the one to which I want to devote the remainder of this chapter, is films *about* women. By this I mean films which are preoccupied by women's role, by their feelings (whether socially convenient or not), their appearance and their symbolic function. These films are neither celebratory of, nor admonitory towards, the gender group on which they focus. That is not to say that they are neutral: rather, one of their social functions is to draw a line between the sacred and the profane, for a particular (often narrow) historical period.

From this perspective, we can interpret films such as *Yield to the Night* (1956), *Sapphire* (1959) or *Darling* (1965) as *limit-texts*. Each of them distinguishes between the acceptable and unacceptable female libido, and draws a line in the sand: beyond this line, it is implied, females cannot advance without expecting disaster. Their heroines can be implacable in the pursuit of their desires, but if these are combined with a socially marginal position, then punishment will ensue. The heroine of the first film comes from the working class, which doubtless fuels her desire for luxury items. The heroine of the second is black, and is torn between her desire to conceal that and her desire to 'swing her legs'. The heroine of the third is from that most marginal class of all – déraciné individuals who would be intellectuals if only they were clever enough. It looks as though 'limit-texts' can only operate as such when they focus on the combination of sexual appetite with class-specific discourses – when their heroines challenge the status quo on a number of fronts.

Besides delineating film texts which police the boundaries, we also need to establish those which reside happily within them. Such films are *comfort-zones*, and provide a place where the viewer can relish the delights of the sexual status quo. They draw rigid distinctions between the genders in terms of their emotional repertoires, physical abilities and intellectual powers. Films such as *Millions Like Us* (1943), *Mandy* (1952) and *A Kind of Loving* (1962) make their audiences feel confident in their own abilities to ignore innovations in the sexual arena. The heroines of these films may be injured when they experience the pains of limitation, but their pains are akin to a religious wounding – stoically borne and ritually displayed in order to consolidate the social fabric.

A third category of films can be termed *gauntlet-throwers*. These are films which are intended to disrupt certainties about female identity and power, and which are innovatory in their sexual politics and sometimes (though not always) in their formal properties. Examples would be *First a Girl* (1935), *Black Narcissus* (1947) and *Orlando* (1993). Such risk-taking films make female viewers question who they are, and make male viewers question what they want. These films confer on both genders an impunity from the social dangers of desire, and offer them the possibility of imaginative transformation – of a world in which sexual difference is neither absolute nor damaging.

So far so good. Of course, the proportion of limit-texts, comfort-zones and gauntlet-throwers will vary according to quite short historical periods, and it is hard to determine which types of film produced most pleasure for their target audiences. All of them are partially determined by the sexual politics and cultural capital of their progenitors, though (as ever) much depends on the power which they managed to exert during the production of what is, after all, an industrial artefact. But our account must not rest there, or it will run the risk of being descriptive rather than analytical. British women's pictures can, in some periods, be categorised according to the cycles of industrial organisation. In *Women in British Cinema*, I suggested that in the 1930s, when the producer was the determinant in the last instance, it is perfectly feasible to construct a 'Korda woman' or a 'Balcon woman' from the evidence of the films over which they had an overweening influence. In the 1940s, the organisation of production companies was sufficiently autonomous to permit the emergence of (for example) a 'Gainsborough woman', an 'Ealing Woman' and so on. In the 1950s, as a consequence of legislative changes, the power passed to the distribution companies, and it is feasible to argue that the narrative functions of women in film could be categorised according to them – Rank, ABPC, British Lion and so on. This explanatory model, with its pleasing symmetry and simplicity, can no longer function from the early 1960s, when the studio system in Britain broke down and the links between production, distribution and exhibition were inexorably fractured. From that period, the way women appeared in British film was much more complex, and can be traced back to a combination of individual directorial authorship, new styles of female stardom, and to increasingly permeable membranes between social and cinematic discourses. To deal satisfactorily with the new ways of seeing and filming women, we need to focus on a precise historical period. But I shall return to that in a moment.

So far, I have skirted round the word 'representation' and evaded the problems it trails in its wake. It is now time to grasp the nettle. I want to argue that as an explanatory model, the notion of 'representation' is played out, because it is too tainted by the notion that it is culture's task to reflect social reality. The notion of *mimesis* denotes a real world, and it is easy to fall into the trap of seeing film as a medium which relates directly to that, and to make judgements accordingly. But we should not judge films according to the accuracy with which they deal with 'real' social experience, or else we will run the risk of ignoring the codes and discourses they deploy. No film can capture the quintessential experience of (say) women, gays or the working class. To argue that it should do so is sentimental. It is high time we abandoned the metaphor of art 'reflecting' reality. Perhaps the notion of *refraction* has some mileage – as when a stick is placed in water, and its line is jagged because of optical laws of which we are not consciously aware. The film can thus be seen as a sort of prism. Or perhaps we might revive the metaphor of a film as a 'window'. Each film, or set of films, can be said to offer a perspective out onto a world of emotions and artistic codes. And these 'windows' are determined by the coherence of their world-view and the adroitness with which they respond to visual fashions.

But to progress the argument further, we now need to develop a more precise historical focus, and map out the ways in which women appear in British film in a particular period. The 1970s is otherwise unrepresented in the periods studied in this book, and it offers tricky problems for students of women and film. It is an instructive case-study because the films challenge the mimetic argument in the profoundest way, and because the ideological and industrial transformations of the period are dealt with in an unpredictable manner.

The case of the 1970s

The 1970s was a period in which the social and sexual innovations of the 1960s – experienced by a few – were assimilated into the lives of the many. It is impossible to overestimate the transformation of personal life brought about by efficient and widespread contraception and the legalisation of homosexual acts. But we must also remember that the 1970s was a period of extreme economic instability in Britain. Crises brought about by strikes and events in Ireland called into question notions of traditional class ascription and national identity. There was a transformation in the way people thought about the world of goods, via increased commodification and the growth of consumerism. Most importantly of all for our topic, the increased visibility of the women's movement seems to have exacerbated anxiety among the more traditional members of society. On all fronts, there was a heightening of consciousness about the consequences of social and sexual change, and an intensification of a sense of impending transformation, which was seen as both exciting and dangerous.

British cinema did not respond to these social anxieties in a predictable way, but in a particularly indirect form. In any case, it was hampered from systematic engagement by a massive transformation in its economic and organisational structures. These threw out of kilter, and displaced from centre stage, that social-realist aesthetic and liberal ethic which had characterised mainstream cinema from the 1950s onward. This meant that, in the general melee, images of women were shaken free from their old moorings, and British cinema of the 1970s contained a wider variety of 'pictures of women' than had obtained hitherto. It was a decade which can be interpreted as a swirling kaleidoscope of contrasting takes on women: Mrs Tchaikovsky (Glenda Jackson) coming to a rolling boil in *The Music Lovers* (1970), the abused Olive (Anna Karen) in *Holiday on the Buses* (1974), Fontaine (Joan Collins) wantonly astride in *The Stud* (1978), the refined and sensual Rosy (Sarah Miles) in *Ryan's Daughter* (1970), the cannibalistic mother (Sheila Keith) with her bloody parcel in *Frightmare* (1974). This kaleidoscope seems, on the face of it, to lack those patterns or overall coherence that characterised other periods. How can we account for this?

The 1970s had been preceded by a period when British film-makers had enjoyed great American largesse. Dollars poured into the British industry during the 1960s, and they were withdrawn with indecent haste at the end of the decade when the American Government changed their fiscal regulations. The ensuing crisis meant that British film-makers had to get their funds in other ways. We can isolate eight different sources:

1   They could get financial co-operation from European sources and make co-productions such as *The Day of the Jackal* (1973). These had to display a degree of cosmopolitanism, and often had European settings.
2   They could try the EMI conglomerate, parts of which were organised in a fairly relaxed way, allowing it to support (for example) *The Man Who Fell to Earth* (1976). Some films which were quite high profile were made for it in the early part of the decade (*The Go-Between* in 1970). When Nat Cohen took over EMI, he persuaded Lord Brabourne to talk Agatha Christie into allowing adaptations of *Murder on the Orient Express* (1974) and *Death on the Nile* (1978).

3 Prospective film-makers could access funds from the music industry, which would finance films about popular culture. That was one of the sources of *That'll Be the Day* (1973) and *Stardust* (1974). The financial input of music impresario Robert Stigwood made it possible to produce *Tommy* (1975) and *Jesus Christ Superstar* (1973). Hand Made Films was formed by Beatle George Harrison, and was responsible for many films such as *Monty Python's Life of Brian* (1979).

4 Film-makers could try to get co-funding from the British Government (the National Film Finance Corporation), which had very limited resources. The NFFC vetted scripts, budgets and schedules.

5 They could get funding from television companies. Thames Television's Euston Films provides many examples of crossover, and it financed films of remakes of TV programmes such as *The Sweeney* films in 1977 and 1978. What such TV adaptations do is to replicate the aesthetic and the emotional range of their parent medium.

6 They could call on American funding for big-budget costume films such as *Mary Queen of Scots* (1972) which have a specific take on the past. Films like *Anne of the Thousand Days* (1970) purvey a warning message about unchecked power in the Old World.

7 They could call up personal collateral. Ken Russell mortgaged his own house to finance *Savage Messiah* (1972), and this meant that he had considerable freedom.

8 They could set up one-film companies between the director and producer. These companies often raised funds privately from those who knew little about films. Derek Jarman, for example, had financial input from David Hockney, the Marquis of Dufferin and Ava, and Lord Kenilworth in order to make *Sebastiene* (1976) (*Daily Express*, 3 February 1976).

Can these new economic structures account for the extreme variety of images of women in British cinema at this time? To a certain extent, yes. It is possible to argue that women in the European co-productions were smooth and impassive, and that the heroines of the American histories – Genevieve Bujold and the rest – all symbolised a residual European culture that was too venal for the modern world. We could also propose a modified auteurist approach. Some directors had managed, either through cheek or clout, to control the films in which they had invested (or persuaded their friends to). Certainly the way women function in Ken Russell's films can be ascribed to him. The women are heavy with the weight of sexual desire, and are the bearers of history, in that their bodies and demeanour display the burdens of the past. Georgina Hale in *Mahler* (1974), Vanessa Redgrave in *The Devils* (1971), Glenda Jackson in *Women in Love* (1969) are not exactly victims, but they are all an exquisitely soft tissue which holds the impression of male action and culture. And the way sexual difference is arranged in *Ryan's Daughter* (1970) can be entirely attributed to David Lean. His style of direction had changed utterly from his earlier work. In this film '[h]e stood between them and gazed into their eyes, each in turn. Then he took them aside separately, his hand on one shoulder, placed his mouth an inch from the actor's ear, and whispered some private thought' (press book of *Ryan's Daughter*, held in the BFI library). The sheer intimacy of this suggests that the real landscape of the film is that of romantic love, and indeed Lean instructed cameraman Freddie Francis to 'wring the emotions out of the people' (Brownlow 1996: 565). Accordingly the tremulous, impassioned Rosy *is* Lean, or a version of him. A similar argument about images of women can be proposed for the films of Stanley Kubrick, whose zeal to control all aspects of production – such as composition, design and costume – was legendary. Other, less experienced directors such as John Boorman or Nicolas Roeg could not aspire in this period to major auteur status, and also could not raise as much collateral as the others could, and so we cannot account for images of women in their films in the same way.

But that is as far as it goes. We cannot categorise the vast majority of 1970s films according to their funding sources. The women in the Agatha Christie blockbusters express neither the novelist's view of gender difference, nor indeed Nat Cohen's or Lord Brabourne's (even if we knew what these were). There is no pattern to the gender symbolism in films supported by the NFFC – unless there are similarities that I have missed between the heroines of *Up Pompeii* (1971), *Riddle of the Sands* (1979) or *Bugsy Malone* (1976). There is no consistent symbolic value carried by the females in the TV-based Euston Films or in films financed by the music industry. So a Marxist explanatory model, which proposes that the economic base determines the cultural superstructure, will not really answer the case of 1970s British cinema.

What about other determinants and constraints? The modus operandi of the British Board of Film Censors certainly had some effect on the way women functioned in films of the period. In general, the Board's policies were increasingly liberal as the decade progressed, although they, in a measured way, were preoccupied with the issue of violence and extreme sexual behaviour. But what marks the Scenario Reports throughout the whole decade is an extreme anxiety about the representation of female pleasure. The report on *Get Carter* (1971) demands that the film:

> reduce to an absolute minimum the scene in which a girl caresses herself as she writhes about on the bed as Jack talks to her on the telephone. In particular remove shots of the bottom of the bed showing her legs open and shots thus of her caressing her breasts and her thighs.
>
> (BBFC Scenario Reports, *Get Carter*, Examiners' Report, 30 October 1970)

Indeed, female genitalia are viewed as deeply troubling, especially when combined with hints of menstruation. One hapless examiner complained that in *Come Play With Me* (1977) 'we see either her vagina or a tampax string. Yes, folks, and that was just after breakfast' (BBFC Examiner's Report, 15 December 1976). Examiners were generally mild on *The Outer Touch* (1979), a film about alien females seducing earthmen (and originally entitled *Sexual Encounters of a*

Close Kind), and were loath to intervene. But they balked at the idea that the females might have aggressive sexual manners. They object that: 'The girls proceed to familiarise themselves with the men under the assumption that the process of making love … is a form of unarmed combat' (BBFC Examiner's Report, 2 April 1979). The BBFC were especially vigilant on lesbian scenes, showing on occasion a touching naiveté. With *The Vampire Lovers* (1970): 'Camilla bares Emma's breasts, kisses her face and her head travels down her body. We see a close-up of Emma's face with a very strange sensual expression. We do not think we can possibly accept this sequence' (BBFC Examiner's Report, 15 June 1970). The lovemaking and orgasm scene in *The Killing of Sister George* (1969) was completely removed by the Board's chief film censor, John Trevelyan (who was normally very accommodating) and it was only reinstated when an uncut version was shown without certification and seen by 400,000 people in four weeks (BBFC Scenario Report, *The Killing of Sister George* [whole file]). And although the examiners accepted the extensive rape scene in *Emmanuelle* (1974), they insisted on cuts in the lesbian lovemaking, and objected to the close-up of a girl skilfully smoking a cigar in her vagina (*Emmanuelle*, BBFC Exemption Form, 26 July 1976). By contrast, examiners felt quite at ease with the giant penis in *Liztomania* (1975), and engaged in much banter about 'when is a cock not a cock', ending with the suggestion that the object in question was so large that it should be termed at least 'un bijou de famille' (*Liztomania*, BBFC Examiner's Report, 30 September 1975). The BBFC, so enlightened in its other judgements in the period, was clearly not even-handed on gender matters in the 1970s. We can use the Board's material as an index of establishment attitudes to the female body and its regulation. It helps us to account for how women could *not* appear in film, but not for how they *could*.

Let us turn, therefore, to a more speculative level of discussion, which undoubtedly runs more risks but which might help us to say something else about the issue at hand. I want to work with notions of *mood*, *tone* and *shared notions of signification*, which might administer a smart tap to the 1970s kaleidoscope and allow some patterns to fall into place. In my view, the chaos in funding, and the profound changes in managerial structures, shook loose a whole set of certainties in the British film industry, and encouraged film-makers to fashion new symbolic and metaphorical systems. We can see that many film-makers focus on one object, and invest it with an unbearable heaviness of being – the crystal in *Zardoz* (1974), the red petticoat in *Ryan's Daughter*, the wedding rings in *The Man Who Fell to Earth* and (most telling of all) the silver spheres in *Tommy*. Very many films of the period play with the idea that material objects can be polysemic – everything and nothing at the same time. I want to argue that this polysemy often extends to the material of the female body. For many 1970s film-makers, it promises to tell all, while they fear that it tells nothing.

On every level – soft porn, horror films, Christie blockbusters, avant-garde experimentation, auteurist films – British cinema of the 1970s displays an extreme self-consciousness. This common mood and tone privileges irony, ambiguity and a sense of play. In a sense, the whole cinema plays a complex fort/da game:

everything is permitted, but nothing is important. Cultural symbols can be resonant with meaning, but they can be cast aside with ease. Something can be absolute one minute, and contingent the next. In British cinema of the 1970s, very many films exhibit *chronic disavowal* in their manner, and I want to suggest that this mood of disavowal is a consequence of two things. First, of the transformation of the industry from hidebound practices into more speculative endeavours. And second, from the cultural transformation engendered by developments within Modernism. The knowingness and jokiness of much 1970s British cinema is not a million miles away from the nihilist, agonised punning and self-awareness of Post-Modernism. It is a sort of early herald of it.

This has profound implications for the ways women appear and function in films of the 1970s. In film after film – and this is not a pattern repeated in other periods – the female protagonists are the site of unresolved contradictions. In John Berger's *Ways of Seeing*, the spectacle of the nude female body evokes a profound *relief*: 'She is a women like any other' (Berger 1972: 59). But in the sex films of the period, the display of the female body – breasts, vulvae – evokes *panic*, and subsequently a sort of awkward irony. David Sullivan, the producer of the Harrison Marks film *Come Play With Me* (1977), argued that the film 'will make Linda Lovelace look like Noddy. They show the lot. Nothing is simulated' (*Telegraph*, 15 November 1976).[1] But whether the penetration is simulated or not, the heroine seems to have been directed so as to appear simultaneously empty and full, and no hint is given as to her motivation or sensations. It is clear from her manner that what she is giving is a *performance* whose probity cannot be trusted. This is the case with the heroines of other sex films. The problem of interpreting female desire is exacerbated when older women want to get in on the sexual act. Robin Asquith, the hero of *Confessions of a Driving Instructor* (1976) is appalled when his client Miss Slenderparts turns out to be Irene Handl, and Roy Kinnear, the jailed pornographer in *Eskimo Nell* (1974) bewails the fact that his new film must contain the menopausal wife of the prison governor: 'Nice woman: terrible tits.' The comedy films of the period, too, deploy heroines whose manner is simultaneously incredulous and self-mocking: consider June (Jacki Piper) in *Carry On Up the Jungle* (1970), or Augusta Prodworthy (June Whitfield) in *Carry On Girls* (1973). Both elevate the smirk into an art-form.

But if we turn to other, more serious films of the decade, we see this 'doubling' effect in female protagonists there too. In *Zardoz* (1974), the heroine Consuela (Charlotte Rampling) is politically powerful and carries the film's whole message about elite cultures (Boorman 2003: 203). Yet she is remarkably bland in her manner. The final sequence shows her in orgasm speaking her lover's name, and then, via a swift cut, shows her repeating his name in the throes of childbirth. A series of dissolves shows the passage of the years – from maturity to death – without a change of expression. Consuela is transformed from individual to icon, but without giving any clues about how the process *feels*. Or consider the female leads in *The Wicker Man* (1974) – Willow (Britt

Ekland), the librarian (Ingrid Pitt) and the schoolteacher (Diane Cilento). All of them deploy a *functional* manner, even when engaging in things which challenge orthodoxy to an outrageous extent – the seduction of the virgin policeman, the teaching of phallic worship, the naked leap over the fire. This functionality of manner evokes the world of common sense, while simultaneously undercutting that in a profoundly radical way. Or consider the actresses in *Don't Look Now* (1973). Heroine Julie Christie displays, in demanding circumstances, a remarkable sang-froid – in losing her child, in coitus or in kissing the bishop's ring. She gives very little away, and there is a gap between how we know she *should* feel, and her self-sufficient manner. The medium (Hilary Mason) is perhaps more interesting, and is the secret centre of the film. Elderly and blind, her opaque eyes see the real truth, which is concealed from us. In a key scene, she 'sees' Christie's dead child. But in this moment of acute spiritual insight, she rubs her breasts rhythmically and moans in pleasure. This seeming contradiction between the erotic and the spiritual is never explained, and it works away at the heart of the film.

Now, these are all performances by actresses who are competent at the very least. This blankness of expression, this perceptible gap between the performance and the subjective, obtains across a range of genres, directors and actresses. If we now turn to specific actresses' style in the period, we can study the phenomenon in more detail. Let us look briefly at three who have quite different cultural resonances, ages and skills – Beryl Reid, Joan Collins and Glenda Jackson.

Case-studies

Beryl Reid (1920–96) had had a successful career in radio and film comedy in the 1950s and 1960s. Her most popular caricatures were the appalling schoolgirl Monica and the adenoidal Brummie Marlene, and in both she was expressive and exuberant. The fluid situation in late 1970s cinema suited Reid well, and she made a range of films in which her performances had a similar mask-like quality, although the raw material of her features was mobile and dimpled. She had been verbally and physically expressive in *The Killing of Sister George* (1969), but in the 1970s her acting style changed. In *Entertaining Mr Sloane* (1970), Reid deployed her version of Method acting:

> To get under the skin of each character that I play, I start by considering the feet. I always start with the shoes. I think she would wear stilettos, because a man once said to her 'your legs look marvellous in those,' and she's had very few compliments in her time, and this was one she hung on to.
> (ABC Film Review, February 1970: 7)[2]

Her Kath, in spite of the stilettos and the transparent frock, has an ironical distance in her delivery, which goes way beyond Orton's original script. This has to do with her intonation, which is simultaneously monotonal and intense, and is accompanied by an unfocused sideways glance. Her performances in

Dr Phibes Rises Again (1972) and *No Sex, Please – We're British* (1973) have the same quality – of appearing to believe and disbelieve in the character. But it is in *The Beast in the Cellar* (1970), *Psychomania* (1973) and *Joseph Andrews* (1977) that Reid turns in her most remarkable performances, and they are all the same, in spite of having directors of different style and ability (James Kelly, Don Sharp and Tony Richardson respectively). In *Beast*, she plays a mentally frail sister who walls up her brother alive for 40 years. This was a subject that might have unleashed an expressive performance, but instead Reid produces an impassive one which answers no questions (Reid, 1984: 162). In *Psychomania*, she plays a medium who is turned into a frog, which would be a severe test of anyone's sang-froid: but she manages to convey an immovable poise. And in *Joseph Andrews*, she allows the make-up to do most of the acting. The terror implicit in the spectacle of menopausal desire is defused by the comic edge which Reid provides.

Reid's 1970s performances evoke the sense of disavowal I alluded to earlier. The same could be said of the work of Joan Collins in this decade. Collins (1933–), though obviously an actress of less depth, exhibits similar performance traits of distance and irony. Collins appeared in some artistically undistinguished but popular films in the decade, and in the famously self-mocking Cinzano advertisements. In overblown film vehicles, all her performances are surprisingly deadpan. In *I Don't Want To Be Born* (1975), she plays an ex-stripper belaboured by her enormous baby, begotten by a curse from a malevolent dwarf. Collins' manner hints at the absurdity of the material: with one slightly raised eyebrow, she delivers bon mots without any attempt at sincerity. It is the same in *Tales From the Crypt* (1972) and *Tales That Witness Madness* (1973); her manner suggests that no-one in their right mind could take this seriously. *Alfie Darling* (1975) and *The Big Sleep* (1978) are both remakes of famous films, and Collins gives a nod in the direction of the original by her gestures and intonation, while at the same time implying the worthlessness of the imitation. But it is with *The Stud* (1978) and *The Bitch* (1979) that Collins excels in irony. As the rapacious Fontaine, she uses sex like a flail to lay waste the world of men. What is important is that she treats it as if it were nothing, and commented later: 'The character I played did to men what men have been doing to women for thousands of years' (Levine 1985: 85). It is the sheer *insouciance* of her sexual slash-and-burn technique which is notable. It is after all quite difficult to engage in copulation on a swing over deep water, but Collins carries it off with aplomb, and the overall effect is to make the viewer feel ashamed for expecting to understand her motivation. She combines robustness with an ironic patina in a way that would have been impossible for an actress in an earlier period.

Collins' 1970s performances, though powerful, were not subtle. The same cannot be said for the work of Glenda Jackson in the decade, but there are similarities. Jackson (1936–) is an actress whose specialism is to permit just so much audience identification and no more. Her performances in the Ken Russell films *Women in Love* (1969) and *The Music Lovers* (1970) put a sort of constraint on the exuberance of the material. Consider the manner in which she takes off her nightdress for Oliver Reed in *Women in Love*. It is the reverse of erotic; there is something resigned and commonsensical about it. Or consider the tone of her question to him: 'Do you love me? I must *ask*.' It is irritated and interlocutionary, as if she is going through the motions of something she is supposed to feel but does not. That is where the similarity lies with Reid and Collins: all three actresses construct a distance between themselves and their roles. That is how Jackson gets through the exigencies of *The Music Lovers* without looking silly. Of course, in films based on plays, such as *The Maids* (1974), *Hedda* (1975) or *Stevie* (1978), Jackson appears more at ease, because the relationship between stage actors and audiences is not so intimate.

Several of Jackson's films are about the predicaments of modern women in a sexually liberated society. *Sunday Bloody Sunday* (1971) and *The Triple Echo* (1972) are acutely about sexual choice, and Jackson chose to make them because she thought something serious could be said about women.[3] In both, her performance foregrounds the womanly rather than the feminine. Jackson had worked well with Russell and Schlesinger because they offered her sufficient interpretative space, and she thought that Losey would be a rewarding director when she was offered the lead in *The Romantic Englishwoman* (1975). But she and Losey were at odds because he would not permit that latitude, and so Jackson's performance is rife with tension. She was forced to try and identify with someone following their heart, and was unable to import her customary ironic dryness into the role. Losey thought that 'she didn't use herself deeply enough ... an actress has to be careful not to make herself invulnerable' (Woodward 1985: 109). He thought she was only able to identify with the heroine's feelings for her child, rather than her impetuous behaviour with her poet lover (Joseph Losey Papers, BFI Library, letter from Losey to Tom Stoppard, 21 August 1974).

I want to argue that these three actresses came, via their heightened awareness of feminism, and the unsettling instabilities in the patriarchal and industrial order, to a new kind of performance style. Sir Peter Hall commented recently that the professional actor does not merely imitate a character, but reveals him or herself in the performance of that role (BBC TV, *Any Questions*, 2 May 2008). The ambiguities, distance and irony in our actresses' performances are probably a testament to their uncertainties about themselves in society, as well as about the dramatic roles they were required to play. Of course, other actresses might well have adopted the same techniques (and possibly male actors too) and that is a project for another day.

Speculative conclusion

From the evidence presented in this chapter, it is possible to argue that images of women in the period before the 1970s were straightforwardly related to industrial cycles and to hegemonic circumstances which only altered very gradually. I propose, however, that a fault-line developed in the patriarchal order in the 1970s. This gave rise to extreme images of women without being able to resolve the contradictions which these invoked. I suggest that established ways of seeing fractured under a range of pressures in the 1970s – through the challenges of feminism, political unrest, economic instability and cultural transformations. When contingency seems omnipresent, the chain of cultural meanings can become broken, and irony and extreme self-consciousness can attempt to replace a fixed order. This has profound implications for the construction of a female subject in film. Were there any substantial material available about female film response, we would be in a position to make a link between the films' protagonists and the female audiences' feelings. But at the present we are not.

In addition to these broader ideological circumstances referred to above, structural changes in the film industry meant that there was an increased distance between those who *spent* the money in production, and those who *provided* it. This distance shook loose a set of hitherto firm alliances in both narrative and characterisation practices, and gave rise to a set of female stereotypes in film which were unprecedented in their lack of anchorage. The 1970s was a cinema which privileged déraciné characters, and it specialised in heroes who were peripatetic or picaresque. But the heroines are even more unfixed. They are bolters or drifters, who are powerful but whose motivation is forever opaque. Hence the persistence of the ambiguity motif. Women in 1970s British cinema mark a substantial break with former practices, where attempts were made to present women as authentic (though imprisoned) inhabitants of a coherent social order. In the 1970s, women are the puzzling fulcrum of the new order; they cannot know themselves, but they symbolise the new kind of knowledge on everyone's horizon.

Acknowledgement

The research for this chapter was carried out under the aegis of the University of Portsmouth project on 1970s British cinema, supported by the Arts and Humanities Research Council.

Notes

1 According to the *Guardian*, 9 August 1980, the film was a smash hit for three years and was a running mate with *Emmanuelle Meets the Wife Swappers*.
2 For an elaboration of the shoe discussion, see *Films and Filming*, April 1974: 18. See *TV Times* (22 September 1984: 82) for Reid's discussion of the shoe issue in *The Killing of Sister George*. For an interesting take on the way Reid's acting style was presented to audiences, see the script of a radio programme called *Film Time*, which was transmitted on 31 October 1970 (held in the BBC Archives, Caversham).
3 Interview with the author, November 2007.

Bibliography

Berger, J. (1972) *Ways of Seeing*, London: BBC & Penguin.
Boorman, J. (2003) *Adventures of a Suburban Boy*, London: Faber & Faber.
Brownlow, K. (1996) *David Lean*, London: Faber & Faber.

Glancy, M. (2009), *Hollywood and the Americanisation of Britain from the 1930s to the Present*, London: I.B. Tauris.

Harper, S. (2000) *Women in British Cinema: Mad, Bad and Dangerous to Know*, London: Continuum.

Harper, S. and Porter, V. (2003) *British Cinema of the 1950s: the Decline of Deference*, Oxford: Oxford University Press.

James, R. (2009) *A Round of Cheap Diversions? Working-Class Taste in Britain 1930–3*, Manchester: Manchester University Press.

Kuhn, A. (2002) *An Everyday Magic: Cinema and Cultural Memory*, London: I.B. Tauris.

Levine, R. (1985) *Joan Collins Superstar: A Biography*, London: Weidenfeld & Nicolson.

Reid, B. (1984) *So Much Love: an Autobiography*, London: Hutchinson.

Woodward, I. (1985) *Glenda Jackson: a Study in Fire and Ice*, London: Weidenfeld & Nicolson.

10 'The Hollywood formula has been infected'

The post-punk female meets the woman's film – *Breaking Glass*

Claire Monk

Of all the films considered in this volume, *Breaking Glass* (1980) may be the one that conforms most awkwardly, even questionably, to accepted definitions of the 'woman's picture' and women's genres. I want to propose, however, two things. First, that there is a connection between *Breaking Glass*'s awkward-nesses and contradictions – which it exhibits in relation to feminist *or* post-feminist expectations of a female-centred film as much as the 'woman's picture' – and the late-1970s British context (cinematic/industrial, social and popular-cultural) from which it emerged. Second, that this female-centred film – which works within popular and genre conventions, but would not claim to be a 'woman's picture', and is dominated by a distinctive female protagonist, but never references gender-consciousness or feminism – and its contexts are, despite this, an illuminating example to consider in this book. In particular, for the insights it offers into the gender politics – and the more particular, but less-investigated, punk-inflected *gender-neutral* politics – of the late 1970s, and the transitional (and hence uneven) shifts in female representation taking place in British films (and indeed the wider culture) at that time. These shifts in the spheres of representation and consciousness were, of course, taking place against an equally shifting industrial and political backdrop, as the UK film industry emerged from crisis towards its early-1980s revival, and the May 1979 election brought to power a new, radically ideologically reorientated, Con-servative Government under Margaret Thatcher as Britain's first woman Prime Minister.

As Sue Harper notes in her astute study *Women in British Cinema*, Britain in the 1970s saw a range of 'radical improvements to the everyday lives of women', as well as 'many theoretical advances in feminism and a broad shift in consciousness about what this might entail' (2000: 127). The decade also, of course, saw the beginnings of feminist film theory and a theorised feminist film practice – although the latter, by its nature and by choice, remained ghettoised within the independent/co-op sector. However, as Harper notes, 'the British film industry of the 1970s was in no condition to respond to [such] changes' (ibid.). On the contrary, in a context of industry crisis coupled with patriarchal panic, the dominant tropes of mainstream female representation, particularly in the most prolific 1970s British genres – low comedy, sex films, horror and their

hybrid permutations – showed a regression into sexual objectification and misogyny, while cinema exhibitors focused significantly on the predominantly male
audiences who could be lured by the promise of X-certificate gratifications
unavailable (in the pre-VHS era) at home.

This was not a climate in which female audiences were a priority for the mainstream industry. As a search of the standard reference sources (such as Goble
1999 and Gifford 1986) attests, the 1970s on the whole presented thin pickings
for anyone seeking 'women's genres' in British cinema. Harper argues that even
many of the 1970s British films made within genres with a traditional female
appeal, such as the costume film, either 'locked' women 'into rigid caricatures'
or 'foregrounded masculine sensibilities, even when the subject matter seemed
to require the reverse' (2000: 129). 'Female' genres and female-centred narratives flourished instead on 1970s British television – from soap opera to a great
variety of period dramas, the latter ranging from the 'quality' Classic Serial via
popular formats to the expressly feminist (notably *Shoulder to Shoulder*, BBC
TV's remarkable 1974 mini-series on the Suffragette movement) – albeit alongside
the persistence of overt sexism elsewhere in the schedules.[1]

Despite the stasis associated with the decade, the late-1970s moment which
spawned *Breaking Glass* is identifiable as a dynamic, optimistic and iconoclastic
time, both for British film production and for the cultural projection and participation of women: the latter notably stimulated by the impacts of the British
punk and post-punk cultural scene (to which this chapter will return). The more
negative legacies of the 1970s nevertheless need to be weighed against this dyna-
mism when evaluating *Breaking Glass*'s achievements and limitations as a female-
centred popular-cinema text born of a transitional moment. On the one hand,
the late 1970s/early 1980s saw advances in British films in the representation of
women and the address of female pleasures, concerns and audiences – via both
the gradual mainstreaming of feminist consciousness in popular cinema, and
newly engaging work from feminist filmmakers in the independent sector,
notably Sally Potter (whose breakthrough 16mm short, *Thriller*, came in 1979,
followed in 1983 by her ambitious, if less well-received, first feature *The Gold
Diggers*, made with an all-female cast and crew). The emergence of complex
and newly politicised female characters was also evident in some of the nascent
black British filmmaking of the period, most notably Menelik Shabazz's *Burning
An Illusion* (1981).

On the other hand, the mainstream female-centred films of the period which
broke the sexist mould present no clear blueprint for the cycle of post-1980
'contemporary British woman's films' which Justine King (now Justine Ashby)
would subsequently identify in her 1996 paper 'Crossing thresholds' (revisited
and updated in her chapter for this book). In support of this, it is significant
that King argued the case for such a cycle beginning, in her 1996 account, with
Educating Rita (1983) 'with the benefit of hindsight' (1996: 217). Indeed, she
was stimulated to do so by the much more recent successes of Potter's breakthrough mainstream feature *Orlando* (1992) and Gurinder Chadha's female-
ensemble film *Bhaji on the Beach* (1993): both demonstrating that 'the feminist

cultural politics of the woman's film have finally found a place in mainstream British cinema in the 1990s' (King 1996: 216) – a place, by implication, not fully available to them in the 1980s.

Breaking Glass resists categorisation in relation to such frameworks precisely because its ethos of gender representation – and the politics expressed by its female protagonist – are inflected centrally by 1970s British punk, with traces (in its song lyrics particularly) of anarcho- and eco-feminism, rather than the conventions of the 'woman's picture' or 1970s (non-punk) feminist cultural politics and practice. In view of this, the remainder of this chapter situates *Breaking Glass* in relation to the wider corpus of late-1970s British punk films, the active place of women within late-1970s punk and post-punk culture, and the particular gender and sexual politics of punk – and also institutionally, as an ambitiously conceived, distinctively British youth film – before returning to the questions surrounding its female-centred narrative and treatment of its female protagonist in the light of these contexts. As a film dominated by a forceful post-punk female protagonist and drawing on a mainstream 'feminine' genre narrative model (the 'a star is born' backstage musical), but lacking clear female point-of-view and eschewing a gendered audience address or a focus on 'the traditional realms of women's experience' as defined by Maria LaPlace (1987: 139), *Breaking Glass* also invites a broader critical reflection on the parameters of the 'woman's picture' itself and its presumed relationship to feminist politics.

British punk rock, punk films and punk women

Reactive against both the self-indulgence of mainstream 1970s rock and the lingering grey, Establishment conformity and economic meltdown of 1970s Britain, British punk rock was defined by its hard-edged, raw musical style and lyrics that were anti-establishment, political and/or designed to shock. Its eruption from late 1975 (when the first punk bands appeared in London) to 1979 – followed by its musical successors loosely bracketed as 'post-punk' or 'new wave' – was captured raw in documentary footage shot by observers/participants, alongside its sensationalist coverage by the mainstream British media. British punk also provided inspiration or subject-matter for two documentary feature films – *Punk in London* (shot by Munich film student Wolfgang Büld, 1977), and *The Punk Rock Movie* (filmed in 1977–8 by Don Letts) – and, from Derek Jarman's *Jubilee* (1978) onwards, a number of narrative British features, although these varied greatly in form.[2]

The liberating impact of punk rock for young women, their high visibility on the late-1970s British punk scene and their powerful creative contributions across many areas of punk and post-punk culture have been widely acknowledged. As Michael O'Pray has noted, 'the role of women in punk was more forceful and provocative than in any previous pop music movement' (1996: 96). Given the limited and often abject roles to which women had been consigned by the male-dominated rock industry over the preceding 20 years, however (as female singers of men's lyrics, girl groups shaped and controlled by male managers and producers, groupies, singers and journalists treated as groupies, secretaries),[3] the factors – or consciousness – that enabled 1970s punk women to so boldly transcend, trash or ignore these precedents are of some interest.

In their book *Art Into Pop* (1987: 155), Simon Frith and Howard Horne argued that punk 'from the start raised questions about sexual codes', opening up an expressive space which women felt able to enter on their own terms, unconstrained by narrow norms of femininity or 'acceptable' sexuality, a trend which continued as punk segued into post-punk/new wave. It is clear, however, that women's participation in punk in so many capacities was also facilitated by punk's DIY, anti-professional ethos (in reaction against the professionalisation and masculinism of late-1970s conventional rock) and the levelling effects of this in practice. As Paul Marko of the punk history website www.punk77.co.uk, explains it:

> Punk did something very special ... One: You didn't have to pay your dues or even know how to play. Two: You had a ready-made audience who may hate you but would listen and Three: You could say what you wanted. The rules were the same for men and women. Neither of you knew how to play ... Check out the lyrics: they sure weren't about love. In fact, a lot of them were about women's changing role in society and their view of that society and their place in it, i.e. more equal and more a force to be reckoned with.
>
> (Marko, no date)

The participation of women in 1970s British punk bands spanned all-female groups (the Slits being the best known), lead vocalists/lyricists with a range of individual styles and concerns – from Poly Styrene of X-Ray Spex to Siouxsie Sioux of the Banshees – and female instrumentalists. But women were also involved in such diverse non-musical areas as the management of punk bands, as fanzine writers/publishers and journalists for the rock press, graphic design/art (hence contributing to a key aspect of the punk aesthetic: see Monk 2008) and fashion.

By contrast with a catalogue of female punk achievement that ranged from Sophie Richmond's management role for the Sex Pistols, via Vivienne Westwood's notorious contributions to punk fashion, to the graphic art of Helen Wellington Lloyd (originator of the Pistols' blackmail-note typography) or Linder/Linder Sterling (still famed for her iconic artwork for the Buzzcocks' 1977 single *Orgasm Addict*), women were surprisingly marginal, or marginalised, in most of the key British punk-related films. Two useful distinctions can be drawn here. First, between Büld's and Letts' early observational documentaries – both of which featured ample footage of the all-female or female-led bands, but barely commented on this female participation and presence – and the narrative punk and post-punk feature films. Second, within the latter, between the two belated 1980 feature vehicles for Britain's highest-profile male punk bands, the Clash drama-documentary *Rude Boy* (1980) and the more hybrid posthumous Sex Pistols feature *The Great Rock 'N' Roll Swindle* (1980) – both of which addressed a broadly masculine audience – and the two wholly invented punk or post-punk features *Jubilee* and *Breaking Glass* – the only two British punk-related films to centre on female protagonists.[4]

Breaking Glass as 'inauthentic' post-punk product

Breaking Glass is set apart from all the above films, however, by its status as a popular-cinema text with a questionable relationship to punk – particularly to notions of punk 'authenticity'. It was filmed in 1979 and released in London cinemas – on the heels of *Rude Boy* and *Swindle* – for August Bank Holiday weekend 1980. But unlike these delayed punk films *Breaking Glass* was unambiguously a product of the post-punk period, and unambivalently mainstream in its production impetus and origins. Accordingly, it has generally been dismissed as inauthentic.

Critical accounts of British punk films either ignore *Breaking Glass* or exclude it from the category, and it is not difficult to appreciate why. Its star, 24-year-old songwriter-performer Hazel O'Connor – 'discovered' for the film by music-industry consultants – was a strong personality with a colourful, marketable personal history (as recounted to Badger 1980: 19)[5] but not a 'real' punk. It lacked the participation of real (extra-diegetically existent) bands onscreen or on the soundtrack; and it was made by figures with no affinity with the punk or post-punk scene. Indeed, the film's production notes suggest some unease with the punk milieu, describing *Breaking Glass* as 'a dramatic street-level look at modern youth' 'inspired by the current volatile and explosive trend in rock music'. Brian Gibson, its 35-year-old screenwriter-director, came from quality television (where his credits for the BBC's Play for Today included Dennis Potter's BAFTA-award-winning *Blue Remembered Hills* (1979)). Its soundtrack and tie-in album (on the major label A&M records) were produced by the high-profile Brooklyn-born industry veteran Tony Visconti. Viewed from a film-critical and punk perspective alike, *Breaking Glass* operated within very well-worn narrative and genre conventions; stylistically, it aimed for a conventional realism rather than exploring how a punk or post-punk aesthetic might be expressed through film. For Kevin J. Donnelly, it was merely 'a highly conventional backstage musical story ... dressed up ... in punk apparel' (1998: 110).

Breaking Glass is nevertheless of interest, and merits re-examination, for (I propose) three main reasons. First, as a commercially ambitious youth-orientated production of late-1970s British cinema which was widely well-received at the time, but which, in contrast with its near-contemporaries – notably the mod-revival musical *Quadrophenia* (1979), with which *Breaking Glass* shared a headline star, Phil Daniels, and some other cast members – posterity has forgotten or dismissed rather than elevated. Second, as one of only two feature films – and the only *mainstream* film – inspired by 1970s British punk or post-punk culture to centre on a female protagonist – and, moreover, a *sympathetic* female protagonist in contrast with *Jubilee*'s nihilistically violent, overtly transgressive female gang. Third – and intriguingly in relation to questions of 'authenticity', female agency and authorship – for the internal split it exhibits between a stock genre narrative and the more emotionally powerful, political – and memorable – parallel discourse presented by O'Connor's songs (as lyrics and in performance).

In stark contrast with *Jubilee*'s underground sensibility, ultra-low budget and darkly Swiftean vision, *Breaking Glass* was an unapologetically mainstream backstage musical tracing the rise, exploitation and crash of a spikily idealistic young female singer-songwriter, Kate. O'Connor, who played her, also wrote the 12 songs at the core of the soundtrack, and enjoyed a period of significant stardom and chart success via the film's tie-in album (which spent 37 weeks in the charts, peaking at number 5) and spin-off hit singles ('Eighth Day', 'Will You', and the less successful 'Give Me An Inch'). Indeed, *Breaking Glass* was one of the biggest-budget British feature productions of 1979, filmed in widescreen Panavision, Technicolor and Dolby Stereo (Bilbow 1980) on a budget of £1–£1.5 million.[6] Most startlingly, a further £300,000 was pumped into its promotion two weeks into its release when it failed to make the expected impact in West End cinemas (Anon., *Evening News* 1980).

Breaking Glass was further set apart from the 'authentic' British punk features – and from *Quadrophenia* – in that it was consciously conceived for a more innocent, non-X-certificate young audience. The punk features were all X-certificate films, and were permeated in a variety of ways by the exploitation/porn connections endemic in the 1970s British film industry.[7] In contrast with such 'adult' excesses, *Breaking Glass* offered a tentative, sweetly chaste, romance between O'Connor and Phil Daniels as Danny a young record 'promoter' (paid to bulk-buy singles to help fix the charts) who volunteers himself as Kate's manager and becomes her boyfriend, to be frozen out by record-company sharks when her career takes off. While the film's narrative took in a range of topical concerns (police violence, harassment of squatters, the death of a young fan in violent clashes between the National Front and Anti-Nazi League), its visual handling of these showed a delicacy about detail. This was sometimes at the cost of narrative clarity, but in other cases achieved with subtlety: notably in a much-praised performance from Jonathan Pryce, cast in his first significant film role as Kate's gentle deaf saxophonist who becomes addicted to heroin.

Production background

Some brief consideration of *Breaking Glass*'s production genesis is helpful in clarifying the background to its packaging as a youth movie, its ethos of non-explicitness and its approach to gendered representation and address. The film had been developed by producers Davina Belling and Clive Parsons with financial backing from Goldcrest's Jake Eberts – initially for United Artists, but passing to Dodi Fayed's newly formed company Allied Stars before shooting began (Hodges 1979: 17; Murphy 1985: 51). Belling and Parsons had been hands-on

1317A - PHIL DANIELS as he appears in the role of Danny, an
ambitious young pop manager, in BREAKING GLASS a
contemporary musical drama. HAZEL O'CONNOR as Kate the
energetic lead singer in the group. A film from GTO Films.

Figure 10.1 A chaste romance coupled with topical concerns packaged for a youth audience: Kate (Hazel O'Connor) with Danny (Phil Daniels), her self-appointed
manager and later boyfriend, in *Breaking Glass*, directed by Brian Gibson
(1980).
Source: The Steve Chibnall Collection.

producers on Alan Clarke's *Scum* (1979), the commercially successful big-screen
version of Roy Minton's banned TV borstal drama backed by maverick producer
Don Boyd. The publicity generated during *Breaking Glass*'s autumn 1979 shoot
was able to trade on *Scum*'s concurrent UK box-office success, while positioning both films as part of a wider 1979 'revival of the "youth movie"' (Hodges
1979: 17) in the wake of *Quadrophenia* and *That Summer!* (1979), the latter
produced by Belling and Parsons and re-casting Ray Winstone from *Scum*.

While *Scum*'s main selling point was the opportunity to see controversial and
extremely brutal 'banned' material on the big screen, *Breaking Glass*'s funder
Goldcrest (about to become the key player in the British film renaissance of the
early 1980s) had, by contrast, been formed with the express goal of developing
'good-quality feature films for adult and family entertainment which do not
depend on explicit sex or violence for their audience appeal' (cited by Murphy
1985: 51). The latter approach brought Belling and Parsons' more significant
success in their next effort as producers, Bill Forsyth's 1981 hit Scottish school-
age comedy *Gregory's Girl* – which, like *Breaking Glass*, featured an unorthodox

female (gifted, enigmatic footballer Dorothy, played by Dee Hepburn) making an impact in a male-dominated milieu.

Peculiarly, however, *Breaking Glass*'s origins as reported by *Screen International* suggest that it began life rather differently, as a film with a female ensemble cast at its centre: 'as the movie of Howard Schuman's *Rock Follies* television series', with Schuman spending a year working on a script with Gibson as director. But 'all attempts to settle on a final version ... came to nothing', leading Gibson to start afresh (Hodges 1979: 17). Belling and Gibson explained this change of plan by citing a desire to make a film that was 'more gritty and based in realism', viable 'for today's market': a notion at odds with Schuman's 'theatrical, almost cartoon' style of writing (ibid.). The oddity of these statements is that *Rock Follies* (Thames Television, 1976) and its sequel *Rock Follies of 77* – both following the adventures of an all-female rock-music trio with contrasting personalities and backgrounds (played by Rula Lenska, Julie Covington and Charlotte Cornwell) – were comedy-dramas, renowned for their flamboyance and larger-than-life characters and dialogue. They owed more to a camp, glam-rock sensibility than to the established traditions of British TV drama, and it is hard to believe that anyone involved in *Breaking Glass* ever thought that Schuman would deliver a 'gritty' realist script.

For reasons not recorded, *Breaking Glass* also emerged in Gibson's new script as a film centred around a lone female protagonist, rather than the potential female-ensemble text implied by its *Rock Follies* origins – with consequences I will explore shortly.

Punk attitude: the gender-neutral ethos

The comments of Paul Marko, quoted earlier, symptomatise and highlight a further, crucial, determinant of *Breaking Glass*'s gender politics, namely what I will term punk's *gender-neutral* ethos. The 1970s punk scene conceived of itself as a milieu in which women could simply *be there*: ostensibly on the same terms as men, defined (however problematically) as (in Marko's words) *already* 'equal' and 'a force to be reckoned with'. This gender-neutral stance is equally evident – in a form more clearly inflected by feminism – in the way many of the women active as punk lyricists and performers articulated their *own* position. It therefore has important ramifications for understanding and interpreting the self-presentation and self-representation of punk women and – by extension – the representation of the 1970s–80s punk and post-punk female in film, and specifically in *Breaking Glass*.

A common theme in interviews with key punk women is an assertion of their own independence and resistance to misogyny and sexist manipulation, coupled with a self-distancing from notions of collectivist feminist politics and female victimhood. As Siouxsie of the Banshees stated in a 1977 interview: 'I don't want to appear as some kind of women's libber 'cos I'm not, but neither am I someone who lets herself be pushed around and manipulated – I've got a mind of my own.'[8] Or, as Viv Albertine of the Slits explained to Caroline Coon:

'We're just not interested in questions about women's liberation ... You either think chauvinism is shit or you don't. We think it's shit' (Coon 1977: 4).[9]

Curiously, the gender-neutral – yet still, logically, feminist – stance expressed here has dropped out of fashion in discourses and debate around feminism, gender and female identity today – perhaps because it is easily dismissed as outmoded from the perspective of contemporary feminisms, post-feminisms and femininities predicated on self-conscious sexual difference. The latter contrast sharply with the overtly androgynous self-presentation which characterised Albertine and most of the Slits, and key 1970s US punk figures such as Patti Smith. Yet there was clearly both a practical logic and a utopian potential in the gender-neutral stance which contributed to the sense of empowerment of so many punk women: if the hurdles of gender difference and acceptable feminin-ity can be overcome by just ignoring them at will, women can do anything. On the other hand, the individualism of this strategy, while inspiring and liberating, also presents evident limitations. But in the mood of 1977, Caroline Coon was able to write that:

> the Slits are highly defined examples of an ideal type that is becoming more attractive to women all the time. What they represent is a revolutionary and basic shift of female ego from one which is biologically defined to one which is made strong by an assertive, mainstream role in society. Thus they are far more 'threatening' than the male musicians they are touring with.
>
> (Coon 1977: 3)

Gender-neutrality, punk politics and the post-punk female in *Breaking Glass*

Punk's gender-neutral ethos and its contradictions can be seen in both the character and narrative positioning of Kate in *Breaking Glass*, but in a dilute form expunged of either threatening androgyny or overt sexuality. The script, O'Connor's forceful performance and the concerns expressed in her songs all establish Kate as an independent-minded, socially aware and spirited character. The politics of O'Connor's lyrics span opposition to nuclear weapons and their escalation ('Who Needs It?'), police brutality, racism and unemployment; but the unifying theme is a (hyperbolic) doom-laden vision of an authoritarian state controlling the depersonalised masses (replacing them, by the film's climactic song 'Eighth Day', with robots), aided by a faceless bureaucratic Establishment and brutal police. This is most explicit in the songs 'Monsters in Disguise' ('Today you went out to inspect your servants/I saw you wave and rave from my TV') and 'Big Brother' ('They'll tear out your heart, throw it neatly in a cart/'Cause that's what they do with the scum like me and you'). However, Kate's off-stage persona (and dialogue) are characterised by a less focused sullen dissent on these matters – and never by an articulation of gender or sexual politics. While she projects a powerful presence – indignant onstage, sceptical off – the film also stresses her vulnerability: revealed first through her necessary resilience as female frontwoman to a fledgling band performing in hostile situations, then later (and less credibly) through her sudden emotional breakdown and volte-face into compliance once she starts to be manipulated and exploited by the major-label record business and her Svengali-esque new manager Woods (played without conviction by Jon Finch, the film's token 'major' star).

While O'Connor's dominating presence is crucial to the film's highly efficient manipulation of audience emotion, Kate's vulnerability and gawky modesty ('I think they liked us', she understates after one triumphant gig) render her sympathetic to young audiences, while undercutting the 'unfeminine' punk qualities that might alienate older male critics, from what Peter Ackroyd (1980) called Kate's 'radiant uncouthness' to her hard-edged appearance (a frizzed peroxide bob and hard, clown-like, almost monochrome make-up). As critic Tom Hutchinson (1980) noted, 'she dominates with an assurance and vitality [but] can communicate waif-like tenderness as well as bawling ferocity'. It should be added that the film's costume designers Monica Howe and Lorna Hillyard, and make-up artist Patricia Hay, excel in providing Kate with a succession of on- and off-stage looks which draw credibly on new wave trends (from Gary Numan to Blondie) while expressing her transformation to glossy product and, finally – in the brilliantly expressionistic 'Eighth Day' finale – to drugged up, depersonalised profit machine, in a spandex bodysuit which, under ultraviolet light, reveals Kate as nothing but a skeleton made of computer circuitry.

However, the film's treatment of Kate simultaneously reflects punk's gender-neutral politics and places her in strange isolation at the centre of a narrative otherwise populated almost entirely by men, leaving unchallenged the clichés of both the backstage musical and the music business itself as milieux dominated by male cynics exploiting female victims. O'Connor is, almost literally, the only female cast member apart from a one-scene appearance by Janine Duvitski as Kate's colleague (and apparent friend) in a pre-success day-job as a petrol-pump attendant – never referred to again – and a non-speaking (and, by definition, female) record-company secretary.

Despite Kate's centrality – as female protagonist and lyricist, composer and leader of an otherwise male band – none of the dialogue or characters directly refer to her gender, and the narrative account of her rise and fall only occasionally foregrounds the particular hazards of sexist harassment and condescension she must face as a female performer in the post-punk scene (as when an audience member at an early gig forces himself on her as her 'groupie'). If there is a gendered dimension to the larger music-industry structures that drive her exploitation, Gibson appears to accept this uncritically as natural – and so too do Kate and her band. While Kate (via O'Connor) demonstrates (at least for the film's first hour) that she is 'a force to be reckoned with' on the same terms as men, she is shown to do so in an environment where there are effectively *no other women* (except among her audience) – nor, therefore, any prospect of female friendship and support or the possibility of bringing other women into the band.

As already noted, O'Connor's lyrics do not encompass gender issues, and mostly address the listener from a genderless position, as in the love song 'Will

You?' (used narratively to signal Kate's growing feelings for Danny). The oppressive state, Establishment and police railed against in the more politicised songs (such as 'Big Brother') are, however, decisively projected as male, while the film's striking opening song, 'Writing on the Wall' disdainfully addresses a conservative male commuter ('I say sir, get your nose out of the paper/Take a good look at what's going down') as a sullen Kate sings her way through a succession of London Underground carriages to the driver's cab, plastering stickers and graffiti along the way. In an intriguing nod to eco-feminism, the climactic set-piece 'Eighth Day' posits 'man' as the destroyer of the planet, lording it over his victim/slave 'machine'. But the costume design, narrative context and performance of this moment – a blockbuster light-and-smoke show for which Kate has been forced onstage drugged, and from which she escapes in (presumably) a final career walk-out in full costume down the Tube at Finsbury Park – also position Kate herself as the 'machine', controlled by the aptly named Overlord Records.

The film itself addresses (as it sought) a cross-gender audience defined mainly by youth. The hostility, spitting and heckling Kate endures from her early pub audiences is shown to come from men; but as her career builds, the duration and editing of audience reaction shots show that she is acquiring both female and male fans, who are given equal weighting. By the film's close, Kate is shown to have attracted a distinct female following; but – in an unwitting analogy for the (post-)punk female's individualistic allergy to collectivist feminisms – they serve as expressionistic symptoms of her mental crisis and loss of identity. She becomes agitated during a radio phone-in when girl fans express disappointment at the changes in her music; and in her final (hallucinatory) escape down the Tube she recoils from the concerned, silent gaze of girls who have cloned her trademark look.

Kate's unconvincing, undermotivated slide downhill in the film's last 40 minutes highlights a final ambiguity around the question of female agency. While Kate, and O'Connor, indisputably provide the film with its core and impact, the over-familiar 'a star is born and falls' narrative which *Breaking Glass* foists on its post-punk female is advanced by the male figures around her – first Danny, with his insistence on securing Kate a record deal when she only wants 'decent gigs', then Overlord Records and Woods – not motivated by the desires of Kate herself. However, the permeation of punk politics into the film code this non-desire as positive, given the opprobrium attached to signing up and 'selling out' among committed punks. As the *Morning Star*'s critic Virginia Dignam pointed out: 'Kate, with her social awareness ... has no ambitions to become a recording star' anyway (Dignam 1980). She is driven instead 'by her belief that society is wrong and she has the answers' (Hughes 1980), and by her desire for her voice (however naïve) on political issues to be heard. It can thus be argued that the intrusion of punk (or post-punk) ideals transforms Gibson's generically 'tragic' ending, with its 'sheen of false piety' (as Hutchinson 1980 complained) – if accidentally – into something more ambiguous and potentially even optimistic.

BREAKING GLASS AA
Starring HAZEL O'CONNOR

This copyright advertising material is licensed and not sold and is the property of National Screen Service Ltd. and upon completion of the exhibition for which it has been licensed it should be returned to National Screen Service Ltd. Printed in Great Britain.

Figure 10.2 A hallucinatory expression of 'the (post-)punk female's allergy to collective feminisms': Kate (Hazel O'Connor) recoils from her female fans. *Breaking Glass*, directed by Brian Gibson (1980).
Source: The Steve Chibnall Collection.

Conclusion: 'the best female role in British film in years': *Breaking Glass* as reluctant woman's film?

Peter Ackroyd, who found *Breaking Glass* 'absurdly compelling', argued that the too-familiar plot was its least important aspect:

> Something foreign has got into the works, and manufactured an original and strange celluloid object. The Hollywood formula has been infected ... As though it had touched something sticky and viscous and cannot now break free. There's an ingenuousness, an energy and a kind of grittiness which lend the film a distinctive flavour.
>
> (Ackroyd 1980)

Ackroyd thought that the 'foreign' infectant was Englishness; but a strong case can be made that it was also the utopian energy of punk and the post-punk female. Contrary to Winston Wheeler Dixon's (2006: 224) claim that *Breaking Glass* 'was not kindly reviewed by British critics', it in fact received considerable critical support as an ambitious British production, and was greeted cynically by relatively few. Many critics cited recent US musical films for purposes of comparison or cultural contrast – particularly the recent *The Rose* (1979), starring Bette Midler as a self-destructive rock star modelled on Janis Joplin (marketed with the tagline: 'She gave and gave, until she had nothing left to give'); and they often did so in order to define or praise *Breaking Glass*'s authenticity and distinctive 'British' qualities.

Most critics expressed striking support for O'Connor as a new star regardless of their evaluation of the wider film. For the *Daily Mail*'s Margaret Hinxman (1980), *Breaking Glass* was 'invigorating proof of life and vitality' in the 'parched' British film industry, and 'presents us with a home-made superstar' who 'explodes as vibrantly as Bette Midler in *The Rose*' in 'the best female role in British films for years'. David Hughes (1980) of *The Sunday Times* declared O'Connor 'a find ... gawky, funny and sullen ... Neasden's own Judy Garland' (even though her actual birthplace was Coventry).

Equally striking were the high commercial expectations for *Breaking Glass* expressed by the trade press ('Simo.' 1980 in *Variety* and Bilbow 1980 in *Screen International*) and the (surely unrealistic) expectation that it would compete in British cinemas on the same terms as its Hollywood counterparts. Thus *Screen International* judged that *Breaking Glass* had had a 'disappointing first week in its seven London cinemas, with total takings of £18,102';[10] whereas the £17,194 taken by a competing musical, Bob Fosse's *All That Jazz* (1979) – released the same week – on one prestige West End screen, was judged 'outstanding'. By the second week of release, the London *Evening News* reported that 'Hazel lacks pulling power up West' (Anon. 1980). Interestingly, the explanation for this from *Breaking Glass*'s distributor GTO was that 'it is a kid's film, and many of them can't afford West End prices. We expect the film will really take off in the suburbs and provinces' (ibid.). (On a personal note, I can confirm that as a teenager I was not strongly aware of the film until it reached the London suburbs.)

However, some details of *Breaking Glass*'s £300,000 promotional rescue package – a female-authored mass-market paperback novelisation and a 'Guess Kate's mood' competition for local newspapers (supplied as camera-ready artwork in the film's pressbook), alongside a 'massive' TV, radio, Tube and billboard advertising campaign, a nationwide tour by O'Connor and 'disco competitions' (ibid.) – suggest that its publicists had also belatedly realised the film's female appeal. Thus the 'Guess Kate's mood' artwork features a range of her looks from the film, while appealing to new wave proto-girl-power sensibilities by suggesting that she may be 'thoughtful', 'confident' or 'aggressive' as well as 'happy', 'sultry' or 'apprehensive'. The pressbook plot synopsis is also less ambivalent than the finished film in orientating *Breaking Glass* as *Kate*'s story – 'the story of one girl's rise to stardom from the rock clubs of London to Bowie-style status' – and telling it from her point of view ('[Danny] offers his services as a manager – which Kate finds a bit of a joke as he looks like he couldn't organise a p...-up in a brewery').

Despite its initial box-office underperformance and chequered origins, *Breaking Glass* was not quite the big-budget (by 1970s British standards) flop it might sound. As Robert Murphy explains, 'the package was sufficiently commercial to attract enough pre-sales to cover its costs', and Goldcrest were satisfied enough with the return on their investment to collaborate again with Fayed on *Chariots of Fire* (Hugh Hudson, 1981) (1985: 51). But it is as (in Ackroyd's words) a 'strange celluloid object' – an almost accidental expression of the significant shifts in the cultural place and representation of women taking place in the late 1970s, and an oblique, reluctant precursor of 1980s developments in the British woman's film – that it remains of continuing interest. An emotionally powerful female-centred narrative, operating within 'woman's' genre conventions, yet insistently gender-neutral in its ethos of representation and audience address, *Breaking Glass* today seems oddly hesitant about the female appeal of its story and star, and its potential as a young-woman's film rather than an ostensibly genderless 'youth movie'. While this reluctance is both a symptom and salutary reminder of a utopian but now-marginalised moment in gender politics, it seems equally symptomatic of the marginalised position of women's cinema within British film culture and its historiography.

Notes

1 From the early 1980s, soaps of course became a key focus of the pioneering work theorising women's genres and 'feminine' spectatorship (notably Brunsdon 1981 and Kuhn 1984).
2 For a more detailed overview of British punk films, including their aesthetic and institutional differences, with a particular focus on *Jubilee*, see Monk 2008.
3 For first-hand testimonies on such experiences, see Steward and Garratt (1984).
4 As well as starring in *Jubilee*, punk icon Jordan (born Pamela Rooke), initially an assistant at Vivienne Westwood's boutique Sex, also brokered Adam Ant's role in the film more than two years before his 1980s pop-chart success. *Jubilee* also cast Wellington Lloyd (credited as 'Helen of Troy') as Elizabeth I's dwarf lady-in-waiting.
5 Since 1999, O'Connor has performed a musical show based on her life story, *Beyond Breaking Glass*, annually at the Edinburgh Festival Fringe and on tour, alongside a continuing musical career.
6 The London *Evening News* (Anon. 1980) reported the film's budget as £1million; the *Daily Mail* (Foster 1979) £1.5million.
7 For a more detailed discussion, see Monk 2008.
8 Quoted at www.punk77.co.uk/groups/womeninpunkintheirownwordspart2.htm (accessed 20 June 2008). Marko credits the quotation to an interview by Kris Needs in *Zigzag* magazine, October 1977.
9 Interview on 16 June 1977, published in Coon 1977; reprinted at www.punk77.co.uk/groups/slitscaroline1.htm (accessed 20 June 2008). Page numbers cited refer to pagination used on www.punk77.co.uk.
10 West End box-office report, 30 August 1980: 2.

Bibliography

Ackroyd, Peter (1980) 'This England' (*Breaking Glass* review), *Spectator*, 30 August.*
Anon. (1980) 'Hazel lacks pulling power up West', London *Evening News*, 4 September.*
Badger, Dave (1980) 'A triple first for Hazel' (production report), *Film Review*, 30.4, April: 18–19.

Bilbow, Marjorie (1980) 'The new films' (*Breaking Glass* review), *Screen International*, 23 August: 14.

Brunsdon, Charlotte (1981) '*Crossroads*: notes on soap opera', *Screen*, 22.4: 32–7.

Coon, Caroline (1977) *1988: The New Wave Punk Rock Explosion*, London: Omnibus. Slits interview, 16 June 1977 and published in the book, accessed at www.punk77.co.uk/groups/slitscaroline1.htm (20 June 2008)

Dignam, Virginia (1980) Untitled *Breaking Glass* review, *Morning Star*, 22 August.*

Dixon, Winston Wheeler (2006) 'Brian Gibson', in Robert Murphy (ed.), *Directors in British and Irish Cinema: A Reference Companion*, London: BFI: 224.

Donnelly, Kevin J. (1998) 'British punk films: rebellion into money, nihilism into innovation', *Journal of Popular British Cinema*, 1: 101–14.

Foster, Howard (1979) 'Leading lady is a punk', *Daily Mail*, 31 October.*

Frith, Simon and Horne, Howard (1987) *Art into Pop*, London: Methuen.

Gifford, Denis (1986) *The British Film Catalogue, 1895–1985: A Reference Guide*, Newton Abbot: David & Charles.

Goble, Alan (ed.) (1999) *The Complete Index to British Sound Film Since 1928*, East Grinstead: Bowker-Saur.

Harper, S. (2000) *Women in British Cinema, Mad, Bad and Dangerous to Know*, London: Continuum.

Hinxman, Margaret (1980) Untitled *Breaking Glass* review, *Daily Mail*, 22 August.*

Hodges, Adrian (1979) '*Breaking Glass* set to shatter images' (production report), *Screen International*, 22 December: 17.

Hughes, David (1980) 'Once upon a time in Neasden' (*Breaking Glass* review), *The Sunday Times*, 24 August.*

Hutchinson, Tom (1980) 'Raw talent unleashed as the band strikes up for Hazel' (*Breaking Glass* review), *Now*, 22 August.*

King, Justine (1996) 'Crossing thresholds: the contemporary British woman's film', in Andrew Higson (ed.), *Dissolving Views: Key Writings on British Cinema*, London: Cassell: 216–31.

Kuhn, Annette (1984) 'Women's genres: melodrama, soap opera and theory', *Screen*, 25.1: 18–28.

LaPlace, Maria (1987) 'Producing and consuming the woman's film: discursive struggle in *Now, Voyager*', in Christine Gledhill (ed.), *Home is Where the Heart is: Studies in Melodrama and the Woman's Film*, London: BFI: 138–66.

Marko, Paul (no date) (website owner, no other authors stated), 'Women in rock part 2', Punk 77 website: www.punk77.co.uk/groups/womeninrockpart2.htm

Monk, Claire (2008) '"Now, what are we going to call you? Scum! ... Scum! That's commercial! It's all they deserve!": *Jubilee*, punk and British film in the late 1970s', in Robert Shail (ed.), *Seventies British Cinema*, London: BFI/Palgrave: 81–93.

Murphy, Robert (1985) 'Three companies: Boyd's Co., Handmade and Goldcrest', in Martyn Auty and Nick Roddick (eds), *British Cinema Now*, London: BFI: 43–56.

O'Pray, Michael (1996) *Derek Jarman: Dreams of England*, London: BFI.

'Simo.' (1980) '*Breaking Glass*' (review), *Variety*, 28 May: 42–3.

Steward, Sue and Garratt, Sheryl (1984) *Signed, Sealed and Delivered: True-Life Stories of Women in Pop*, London: Pluto.

* Accessed on microfiche at the British Film Institute Library; page numbers not recorded.

11 'It's been emotional'

Reassessing the contemporary British woman's film

Justine Ashby

What follows is an abridged version of a chapter I wrote in 1996, 'Crossing Thresholds: The Contemporary British Woman's Film' (for the full version of this chapter see Ashby 1996), in which I argued that feminist cultural politics had begun to make a palpable impression on British Cinema. In particular, a cycle of woman's films made during the 1980s had offered some politically progressive narratives which arguably help pave the way for a more feminist British woman's film in the 1990s. Since writing 'Crossing Thresholds', however, the genre – and, of course, British cinema more generally – has continued to reinvent itself and diversify, and to operate within and respond to new cultural and industrial contexts. As such, it certainly seems to me to be high time we revisit the genre to reassess its current viability. Following on from my original discussion, then, I will look at some more recent films which draw upon and rework the thematic and narrative paradigms developed by the 1980s cycle, to gauge the continued cinematic and cultural currency of what, for the time being at least, I want to persist in describing as 'the contemporary British woman's film'.

Crossing thresholds

The so-called 'renaissance' of British cinema in the 1980s yielded scant opportunities for women film-makers to break into mainstream feature film production. Yet despite the continuing marginalization of 'women's cinema' (that is, films made *by* women) in this country, it was, perhaps somewhat paradoxically, a period marked by the emergence of a series of memorable and innovative British woman's films (that is, films made *for* women). Although these films were, with only one exception, the products of all-male scriptwriting and directing collaborations, they nonetheless occupied much of the terrain traditionally held by 'women's cinema'. Thus they tackled head-on the conflicts and vicissitudes of contemporary gender relations; they foregrounded charismatic and transgressive female protagonists; and they offered what were, within the context of mainstream cinema at least, refreshingly radical resolutions to the conflicts they portrayed.

The series of movies I have in mind comprises David Goldschmidt's *She'll be Wearing Pink Pyjamas* (1985) from a script by Eva Hardy (for my discussion of the film, see Ashby 1996: 220–1), Chris Bernard's *Letter to Brezhnev* (1985),

David Leland's *Wish You Were Here* (1987) and Lewis Gilbert's two screen adaptations of Willy Russell's stage plays, *Educating Rita* (1983) and *Shirley Valentine* (1989). As woman's films, they follow convention in portraying their heroines railing against the constraints of their roles as wives, mothers, daughters and lovers within a rigidly confining patriarchal order. But their status as British films often signals this confinement as specifically symptomatic of a still hopelessly class-bound and politically polarized British culture (which, as with these films, so often in practice becomes reductively subsumed within terms of what is considered representative of *English* culture).

In *Wish You Were Here*, it is not only Lynda's (Emily Lloyd) hostile Oedipal relationship with her dogmatic widowed father which drives her to transgress at every turn (hence, on one level, the title of the film, which refers to the dead mother); it is also the suffocating, petit-bourgeois morality of a 'Little England' scandalized by a bike on a bowling green (the film is set in a seaside town in the early 1950s). Similarly, in *Educating Rita*, it is not only the persistent demands of her husband and father that Rita (Julie Walters) should fulfil her class and gender *raison d'être* and have a baby (considered well overdue at the age of twenty-six) which prompts Rita to turn to education; it is also her belief that education will empower her to defy the petty moral and social strictures of her working-class positioning. Thus, there is undoubtedly an intersection of discourses in these films which attempts to codify conflicts of class and gender as corollary to one another in English culture. However, it seems to me that these discourses may not always be so conveniently and seamlessly elided, either politically or aesthetically, and that the critique of gender conflict in these films may be superseded or compromised by an overarching project to interrogate wider issues of class and national identity.

There is, though, another more insidious problem attendant upon any discussion of the British woman's film. As Richard Dyer has perceptively pointed out, the 'official' characterization of British cinema almost precludes the recognition of its propensity for melodramatic emotionality (Dyer 1994). The conceptualization of the 'typically English film' constantly seems to attract the ideologically loaded epithet 'restrained' (which reflects not only a middle-class bias but, I would argue, a masculinist bias too) whereby demonstrative displays of 'excessive' emotionality – worst of all, tears – are regarded as inappropriate, both on and off screen. It is, then, an easy enough matter to see why the woman's film might be regarded as something of an unwelcome cuckoo-in-the-nest here. For, despite twenty years or more of sustained critical attention which has repeatedly demonstrated the aesthetic and ideological complexities of the genre, the woman's film still carries the taint of triviality, emotional excessiveness and brash Hollywood populism. In short, it might well be considered as rather 'un-British'.

One could speculate at length as to the various motivations underpinning such a conceptualization, but, whatever the case, it is, as Dyer also notes, a peculiarly skewed and selective characterization which fails to take account of British cinema's sustained investment in melodramatic emotionality. It is of course possible to trace a legacy of films such as *Millions Like Us* (1943) and *Two Thousand Women* (1944), *A Taste of Honey* (1961) and *The L-Shaped Room* (1962), *Jane Eyre* (1970) and *A Room with a View* (1985), which all adhere to the fundamental tenets of the woman's film, but which are swept under the umbrella of other film movements or genres (the wartime morale film, the New Wave film, the 'quality' literary adaptation) in order to fit them, however reductively, into a dominant scheme of national cinema. The same generic eclipse seems to have overtaken *Shirley Valentine*, *Educating Rita*, *Wish You Were Here*, *Letter to Brezhnev* and *Pink Pyjamas* (all of which were predominantly promoted and apparently received as comedies), for it certainly strikes me as curious – not to say negligent – that these films have been explicitly discussed neither within their generic context as woman's films nor in juxtaposition to one another as a cycle of real significance to 1980s British cinema.

What, then, at a thematic level, constitutes this group of films as a distinctive cycle? As I have already suggested, these films concern themselves with the representation of transgressive women who circumvent the prescribed norms of their cultural and sexual positioning, but this hardly distinguishes them from their numerous British and American generic counterparts. What unifies and distinguishes these films as a coherent cycle is, above all else, the all-pervasive and recurring motif of escape. This escape takes a variety of narrative forms: a foreign holiday in *Shirley Valentine*, a ticket to the USSR in *Letter to Brezhnev*, an all-women adventure holiday in *Pink Pyjamas*, the removal from the patriarchal home in *Wish You Were Here*, an Open University course in *Educating Rita*. But the function of escape is consistent: all five films allow their respective female protagonists to resist the generically conventional drive towards a reinscriptive and punitive ideological and narrative closure.

The motif of escape is perhaps best understood here in terms of a movement through a *liminal* space, a realm of possibility. Once this threshold has been crossed, once she enters this realm of possibility, the female protagonist is able to remove herself from her initial narrative (and cultural) situation, distance herself from the demands and entrapment of everyday life, and undergo a redefining and re-empowering transformation of identity or rite of passage. In *Shirley Valentine*, *Pink Pyjamas* and *Letter to Brezhnev*, this liminality is explicitly located as a topographical space (Greece, the Lake District, the USSR) which the female protagonist journeys to or through. In *Educating Rita* and *Wish You Were Here*, liminality is not a concrete, physical space, but a symbolic trajectory. For both Rita and Lynda, the liminal threshold is located within the rites of passage through which they pass (the educational process for Rita, sexual initiation and motherhood for Lynda) in order to redefine their initial narrative positioning.

For much of the narrative *Wish You Were Here* oscillates between the possibilities of escape and entrapment, as Lynda's exuberant, rebellious outbursts (the bike on the bowling green, mooning at the neighbours, the striptease in the bus depot) are juxtaposed with the recurring image of Lynda seated at her bedroom window staring out to the space beyond the patriarchal home.

Towards the end of the film, the narrative seems to move inexorably towards a closure that will mete out a predictable come-uppance. There is what appears to be Lynda's final outrageous outburst of carnivalesque rebellion, as she jumps on a table and proclaims to the assembled company of the sedate seaside tearoom where she works that she is pregnant. This is followed by an anti-climactic scene in which Lynda's aunt admonishes her for causing her father so much grief and humiliation and she is given money to go off quietly and have an abortion (which Lynda appears to do, as the following scene shows her poised to enter the house of a backstreet abortionist). Thus Lynda's final entrapment by a culture whose rules can only be broken at great expense seems unavoidable at the close of the film.

But this is not quite the end of the film. As if by magic, we next see Lynda disembarking from a bus in the depot where she once worked, dressed in vibrant, conspicuous, unapologetic yellow, defiantly meeting the half-lecherous, half-censorious gazes of the men with whom she once worked. She walks along the same bowling green where once she rode her bike to the consternation of the club members, only this time she proudly promenades with the pram bearing her illegitimate child. Here, the liminality which provides the female protagonist's escape route is not so much a trajectory as an ellipsis which magically rescues her from what seemed the inevitability of a reinscriptive and punitive

Figure 11.1 Entrapment in a sedate seaside tearoom: Lynda (Emily Lloyd) serving customers in *Wish You Were Here*, directed by David Leland (1987).
Source: The Steve Chibnall Collection.

closure. The final shot of the film shows Lynda standing outside the patriarchal home smiling delightedly at the baby she proudly holds aloft, waiting for her father to open the door. We are left to speculate as to whether her reception will be hostile or reconciliatory, for the film positively refuses to gesture beyond this final moment of apparent wish fulfilment.

In *Educating Rita*, liminality is not so much a space as a process. At the beginning of the film, Rita is characterized as brash, disarmingly outspoken and apparently assertive. She is the kind of stereotype of working-class femininity (vulgar, sexy, funny) that would not look amiss in *Coronation Street*. But, at the age of twenty-six, Rita's life is closing in around her. Having left school without qualifications and married young, Rita is desperate to broaden her horizons. She undertakes an Open University course and changes her name from Susan to Rita to emphasize the change of her identity she intends to affect. Her weekly tutorials with Frank (Michael Caine) increasingly become the central focus of her life; they represent a kind of liminal space where she can shape and assert her new identity.

Rita's escape route is thus secured. She moves out of the marital home, shares a flat with a neurotic bohemian, goes to summer school and begins to socialize with the 'proper students' she once found so intimidating. By the end of the movie, Rita has been empowered to resist the pattern of stifling domesticity and motherhood that, at the outset, seemed to beckon inexorably. However, it is difficult to ignore the ironic undertones of her apparent triumph. While Rita aspires to join the ranks of the 'educated classes' because she believes them to be free from the petty constraints of her own class, the text continually belies such a prospect, most obviously by juxtaposing Rita's wide-eyed enthusiasm and unrestrained honesty with Frank's cynicism, apathy and worsening alcoholism. As such, the positive aspects of Rita's escape must be tempered by the fact that the world she escapes into is one of repression and pretension.

As in *Wish You Were Here,* which finally fixes the rebellious Lynda within the role of mother, it becomes difficult to avoid the conclusion that Rita's rite of passage renders her a rather less transgressive female figure than when the film began (she gives up smoking, stops dyeing her hair, wears muted casual clothes and is generally a good deal more restrained). But I would argue nonetheless that, in some important ways, Rita's transformation is still a predominantly positive one. Perhaps this is where the rift between the text's concurrent discourses of class and gender begins to make its presence felt. While Rita's entrance into the educated middle classes is portrayed as merely trading one form of entrapment for another, reading the film as a woman's film (and therefore privileging the significance of its gender discourse over that of class), it is clear that Rita's escape from her socially and sexually prescribed roles remains a radical one. The closure resists reinscribing Rita within the all too convenient heterosexual coupling that has been threatening to take place throughout the narrative (a disgraced Frank goes off to Australia to find his own liminality alone), and instead leaves us with the positive image of a single woman who has some real choices available to her.

The distinction between escape and escapism is central to the construction of liminality in *Letter to Brezhnev*. The first half of the narrative, which recounts Elaine (Alexandra Pigg) and Teresa's (Margi Clarke) night on the town, maps out a narrative liminality which seems to be confined to the prospect of an escapist adventure. Elaine's yearning to escape the monotony and hardship of her life as an unemployed Kirkby girl for more romantic climes is explicitly signalled at the very beginning of the movie when she tells her friend Tracy, 'I'm sick of the men up here, they've got no romance in them. ... I wish I was in Casablanca or somewhere'. The comment clearly locates Elaine's narrative goal within the terrain of the woman's film with its reference to one of the most memorable romantic weepies of them all.

Casablanca being out of the question, Elaine limits her sights on the prospect of 'getting away for a few hours'. Having stolen a bulging wallet from two lecherous Greek Cypriots who have tried to buy a dance (demonstrating that not all foreign men fit the bill of the romantic hero), Elaine and Teresa embark upon a no-holds-barred night to remember. As Teresa quite literally lets her hair down, transforming herself in the toilets from factory worker to vamp, Elaine first spies Peter (Peter Firth), a Russian sailor on shore leave for one night only (a necessary narrative device to heighten the sense that their encounter must be an intense one-night stand).

When Peter sets off for home the following day, the narrative moves on to another stage in which Elaine attempts to transform the temporary escapism of their one-night stand into a more permanent form of escape. Here, *Letter to Brezhnev*'s ironic mobilization of the romance formula (with its anticipation of the heterosexual union as closure) and its commitment to delivering a stinging critique of a recession-hit 1980s English culture no longer seem to fit together so easily. Elaine's rite of passage becomes dependent upon the outcome of her relationship with Peter. Her journey to the USSR is one which takes her *towards* her sexually allotted roles (as she tells the pompous Home Office official who attempts to deter her from her politically embarrassing plans, she *wants* to be a wife and mother).

The positive aspects of her escape must therefore be limited to the fact that she has secured her removal from her social positioning as a working-class (though out of work) girl in a down-on-its-luck Northern city, rather than opening up any prospects beyond the traditional expectations of her gender. In this way, it seems to me that *Letter to Brezhnev* ultimately utilizes the motif of escape in order to privilege a social critique over that of gender; its primary polemical drive is to deliver an indictment of a class-bound Northern English culture polarized and demoralized by Thatcherism.

It is impossible to deal with the motif of escape in *Letter to Brezhnev* without paying some attention to the secondary narrative that revolves around Teresa. Of the two women, she is by far the more subversive (her characterization again trading upon the codes of transgressive femininity set out in *Educating Rita* and *Wish You Were Here*). But for Teresa there is little prospect of any permanent escape; her life is a vicious circle whereby she continues to do a job

Figure 11.2 Yearning for romantic escape: Alexandra Pigg and Peter Firth in *Letter to Brezhnev*, directed by Chris Bernard (1985).
Source: The Steve Chibnall Collection.

she loathes in order to earn enough money to enjoy herself, and spends her nights desperately chasing a good time to make the prospect of another day in the chicken factory tolerable. Like Elaine, she fantasizes about the possibility of foreign travel. She boasts to an uncomprehending Sergei (Alfred Molina) of a fantasy jet-set job in which she 'gets to travel everywhere: Paris, New York, Amsterdam, the moon'.

Despite its adherence to the romance formula, the expected closure – that of Peter and Elaine's (re)union – is never realized on screen. Instead, the film closes as the two women say their goodbyes (surely confirming that their strong, mutually supportive friendship is the privileged pairing of the text). The final image, then, is one of passive entrapment as Teresa watches her friend walk towards the boarding gate (perhaps another ironic reference to *Casablanca*?) and we learn, way too late, that Teresa has entertained the same romantic fantasies of escaping to join Sergei, but has reconciled herself to the fact that their encounter can only ever be another short-lived moment of escapist fun.

If the liminal trajectory in *Letter to Brezhnev* can be aligned to that of a rite of passage which takes its female protagonist towards a life as a wife and mother, then precisely the reverse process is in operation in *Shirley Valentine*. Shirley's (Pauline Collins) escape to an idyllic Greek island enables her to cross back over the threshold of her passage into adult femininity and the attendant constraints and disappointments that it has imposed. As the opening song clearly informs us, Shirley's narrative goal is to rediscover the freedom and courage she once took for granted, to become once again, 'the girl who used to be me, the girl who could fly, she was free'. For, at the age of forty-two, Shirley is consigned to a life of shopping, cooking and talking to the wall, which has long since proved to be a more animated listener than her husband Joe (Bernard Hill). She dreams of escape, of foreign travel, of 'drinking wine in the country where the grape is grown', and keeps a poster of her intended place of escape on the back of the larder door. The motif of liminality, then, is constructed in terms of two polar realms of containment and freedom: the dull, regulated and claustrophobic monotony of Shirley's drab suburban home and fading marriage, and the bright, expansive, adventurous world she discovers on her Greek island where inhibitions dissolve and anything seems possible.

Shirley Valentine's parodic treatment of the conventions of the romantic woman's film does not necessarily imply an attempt to undermine the viability of the genre. On the contrary, it seems to me that, of all the films of the 1980s cycle, *Shirley Valentine* makes the fewest compromises and concessions as a mainstream British woman's film. Coming as it does, at the end of the cycle, its closure is perhaps the most positive and radical of all. As in *Letter to Brezhnev*, its liminal trajectory is codified as a journey to a foreign country. But unlike *Letter to Brezhnev*, the valorization of this foreign space seems less bound to a specific critique of English culture and more concerned with providing a space where the imperatives of Shirley's life as a middle-aged mother and wife may be suspended and a new identity asserted. Moreover, this new identity is one which explicitly rejects the prescribed roles of femininity. Whereas both *Letter to Brezhnev* and *Wish You Were Here* affect a rite of passage which simply trades one familial role (as daughters) with those of adult femininity (as wives and/or mothers), Shirley's transformation resists such reinscription. At the end of the movie, as a repentant Joe, who has come to Greece to 'reclaim' his absent wife, fails to recognize the new (or rather the 'old') Shirley, it is explicitly stated that her redefinition renders her identity independent of such conventional roles. As she finally tells Joe, 'I used to be the mother, I used to be the wife. But now I'm Shirley Valentine again'.

Something old, something new: the British's woman's film now

I concluded 'Crossing Thresholds' with what now appears to me to be a rather upbeat assessment of the legacy of the 1980s cycle and the extent to which it helped render a mainstream feminist British cinema more viable and visible. Pointing to films such as Mike Newell's *Enchanted April* (1991) and Gurinder Chadha's *Bhaji on the Beach* (1993), it seemed possible to trace the paradigms of liminality and female camaraderie in films of the new decade. But as the 1990s wore on, the potential to make popular woman's films with clear feminist content appeared to diminish as British cinema increasingly focused upon politically ambivalent interrogations of masculinity. Thus, many of the landmark successes of British cinema in the second half of the 1990s, such as *Trainspotting* (1995), *Brassed Off* (1996), *The Full Monty* (1997) and *Lock, Stock and Two Smoking Barrels* (1998), were preoccupied with homosocial relationships, peripherizing or – in the case of *Lock, Stock*, entirely eschewing – female characters and often colluding with a 'laddish' culture that pervaded other media forms in Britain in the late 1990s. When, at the end of *Lock, Stock*, Big Chris (Vinnie Jones) sums up the preceding catalogue of violence with the line, 'it's been emotional', it seemed to me that his words resonated with an even bleaker sense of irony than was explicitly intended; they appeared to epitomize the increasing scarcity of the kind of emotional engagement and pleasure that, as I discussed earlier, Dyer had celebrated as such a rich vein in British cinema history, and which had been so fundamental to the woman's films of the 1980s.

On the strength of this argument, one might assume that a once viable space to make mainstream films for and about women was closing down by the end of the 1990s as British cinema turned its attention to male genres and male stars. But British cinema seldom fits so conveniently into such polarized political and production patterns. Indeed, it may be possible to argue that the cultural pervasiveness of the 'chick flick' and 'rom-com' labels after the watershed success of *Four Weddings and a Funeral* (1994) also did much to eclipse and subsume how the British woman's film was produced, marketed and received. However, a look below these surface trends reveals the contours of far more complex generic renegotiations and cross-fertilization. I do not have the space here to explore what is potentially a broad raft of British woman's films made during the past fifteen years or so, though historical films such as *Charlotte Gray* (2001), or comedies such as *High Heels and Low Lifes* (2001), to name a couple, variously draw upon the paradigms I discussed in 'Crossing Thresholds'. For now, I will look in more detail at three films: David Leland's *The Land Girls* (1998), Gurinder Chadha's *Bend it like Beckham* (2002) and Lynne Ramsey's *Morvern Callar* (2002). Each film takes up the theme of liminality and explores relationships between women, but they do so in such contrasting ways that they surely represent three very different departure points for the genre. Moreover, the fact that two of these key films were directed by women perhaps suggests that the terms of the woman's film and women's cinema have begun to converge more productively as opportunities for female film-makers have incrementally opened up since the 1980s.

At the time of its release in 1998, one could not fail to notice the extent to which *The Land Girls* was unapologetically marketed to appeal to women. As Amy Taubin suggests, it is 'a modern version of the woman's picture' (Taubin 1998: 154). In more specific terms, I would argue that it makes sense to read *The Land Girls* as an explicit return to the formula of the 1980s British woman's film (perhaps unsurprising since, like *Wish You Were Here*, it is primarily a vehicle for Leland as director and scriptwriter). It chronicles the experiences of three young women, the middle-class Stella (Catherine Mac-Cormack), the gauche public schoolgirl Ag (Rachel Weisz) and the free-spirited and vulgar working-class Prue (Anna Friel), as they are pitched into a new life as agricultural workers on the Lawrence family's West Country farm in the early years of World War Two. Like its 1980s forerunners, it affords its heroines the opportunity to escape their old lives and the predictable futures mapped out for them. The farm and indeed, the war itself, therefore become a liminal space of experimentation and empowerment where each of the women undergoes a transformation and forges close and enduring bonds of friendship.

Prue is undoubtedly initially marked as the most transgressive of the three women, her attitude to life perhaps best summed up by the line she sings from 'Lambeth Walk', 'do as you damn well pleasy'. In this way, her characterization is closely reminiscent of the working-class heroines featured in the 1980s cycle: like Rita or the young Shirley we encounter in flashback, like Elaine and Teresa

Figure 11.3 Close and enduring bonds of friendship: Anna Friel, Catherine MacCormack and Rachel Weisz in *The Land Girls*, directed by David Leland (1998).
Source: The Steve Chibnall Collection.

in *Letter to Brezhnev* or Lynda in *Wish You Were Here*, Prue exemplifies a resilient, exuberant and non-conformist version of working-class femininity that challenges the ideals of feminine modesty and restraint. But unlike her 1980s counterparts who escape the censure of punitive closures, Prue is ultimately made to suffer. In the spirit of 'live-for-today', she marries an RAF pilot who, predictably enough, is soon killed in action. Broken by grief, she retreats to the familiar security of her Manchester home, with not a hint of the 'good-time girl' appearing to remain. As such, Prue's narrative is reframed as a cautionary tale, a significant departure from both Angela Huth's best-selling novel from which the film is adapted and the 1980s cycle which characteristically resisted the conventional narrative (and cultural) drive to punish its wayward heroines.

Despite stressing the interdependency of the three women and their respective stories, *The Land Girls* ultimately prioritizes Stella's narrative and her growing feelings for farmer's son, Joe (Stephen Mackintosh), even though she is engaged to the more socially appropriate naval officer, Philip (Paul Bettany). Within the liminal space of the farm, Stella and Joe make plans for their future together, but the outside world eventually intrudes as Philip is horrifically wounded in action and, conceding that it is her duty to marry him, Stella leaves the farm, and Joe, forever.

The Land Girls closes as the three women gather together once more after the war for the christening of Prue's baby. Prue has married again, only this time for money rather than love: while this once promiscuous, unconventional woman is finally fixed within the socially respectable roles of wife and mother, her former vivacity and vulgarity is at least partially restored. Likewise, this postscript also reinflects Stella's narrative as she reveals she is divorcing Philip for adultery. She has set up in business as a travel agent and, as she tells Joe, she is free to travel when and where she wishes. Stella's new mobility is in stark contrast to Joe's claustrophobic life on the farm which, without Stella, he can never escape. Thus, Stella's independence is sustained as the liminal space of the farm is refigured as a space of containment. Stella's exile – initially signalled in terms of sacrifice, duty and curtailment – ultimately becomes another form of escape which indefinitely prolongs her mobility and freedom.

Whatever the subtleties of the closure, it would be difficult to argue that *The Land Girls* is more politically radical than its 1980s forerunners. Indeed, at the film's premiere, one of its stars, Anna Friel, insisted, 'This is not a feminist film, it's a good old-fashioned tale about three wonderful women' (Cooper 1998: 5). Friel's rather breezy denial of the film's feminist credentials perhaps signals an intention to depoliticize its content – or at least the way that content might be perceived by some of the film's potential audiences. However, within the context of a British cinema in the late 1990s increasingly prioritizing themes of masculinity, the very act of producing such an uncompromisingly female-centred film, celebrating female heroism and camaraderie, may well be understood as a politically forthright gesture in itself.

Like *The Land Girls*, *Bend it like Beckham* might also be best understood as 'a modern version of the woman's picture', though it was almost uniformly marketed as a 'girl power' comedy. It was also undoubtedly one of the most critically and commercially successful British films of the early 2000s, perhaps suggesting that the woman's film's viability might be strengthened by extending its address to younger audiences. Elsewhere I have discussed *Bend it like Beckham* as reacting to, and largely endorsing, a Blairite vision of a modernized Britain where the rhetoric of 'girl power' and multiculturalism can sweep aside the intransigent social and gender problems that were so central to the 1980s cycle of woman's films and the politically polarized Britain in which they were set (see Ashby 2005). Here, I want to focus specifically on the ways in which the film shifts the key generic themes of female friendship and liminality into a post-feminist idiom.

From the outset, the staple generic tension between constraint and escape is both foregrounded and problematized in *Bend it like Beckham*. Jess (Parminder Nagra) attempts to juggle the competing expectations of her traditional Sikh background with her own less orthodox aspiration to succeed as a footballer and the pressure to conform to the ideals of studiousness, domesticity and physical modesty which are increasing as she approaches adulthood. Significantly, the family home is situated under a flight path near Heathrow Airport; as the jets soar noisily over Jess's head, they function as a constant reminder of another world beyond the claustrophobia of her suburban home. For Jess, football, and the social and physical freedom it affords her, constitutes a temporary release from the stultifying world of study and duty that awaits her at home and, perhaps as importantly, initially offers her the means by which she attempts to hold adulthood – and its attendant restrictions – at bay.

Joining a local women's football team, Jess forges a close (though competitive) bond with team mate, Jules (Keira Knightley). They vie for the romantic attentions of their coach, Joe (Jonathan Rhys Meyers) – a rivalry which initially proves divisive – but Jules also acts as a kind of coach for Jess, initiating her pursuit of a footballing career and offering emotional support along the way. At the beginning of the film, we are encouraged to expect that the hurdles Jess will need to clear are the coterminous (if culturally disparate) problems of her restrictive Sikh background, personified and implemented by her father as head of the family, and the entrenched sexism of a male-dominated sport hostile to female participation. As the narrative draws to a close, however, it becomes increasingly clear that it is ultimately neither her father nor football which constitutes the greatest source of chauvinism: it is, in fact, Jess's mother who consigns Jess to the kitchen and insists that she learns to prepare a full Indian meal (and thus, in doing so, prepare herself for an early marriage). While she justifies her objections to Jess's behaviour because it transgresses Sikh precepts, the fact that Jules's mother also attempts to divert her daughter from football (assuming that it 'is making her a lesbian') and embarks on a misguided mission to 'feminize' her (buying her an inflatable bra), draws clear parallels between the two mothers and reframes the issue around femininity. In the end, the film suggests that not only are these pre-feminist mothers *more* sexist than any of the men in the film, but that they simply do not understand their post-feminist daughters.

In contrast, the fathers of both girls help facilitate their ambitions to become professional footballers. Jules's father practices with his daughter, while Jess's father overcomes his initial misgivings and, shedding any semblance of the stern father figure, passionately implores his daughter to try out for a scholarship. Having been debarred from a cricket team, he declares to his entire family that Jess will not suffer the same racist exclusion: 'I don't want her to make the same mistakes her father made. I want her to fight. I want her to win.' Once again, the discourses about race and gender become inter-dependent and muddled. In 'Crossing Thresholds', I noted that films such as *Educating Rita* and *Letter to Brezhnev* dovetailed discourses of gender and class conflict in ways which often obscured or compromised the more radical possibilities of their generic status as woman's films. In *Bend it like Beckham*, the relationship between issues of racial and gender identity is further complicated: to banish the spectre of racism in favour of a newly forged multiculturalism, the film needs recourse to the optimistic and largely depoliticized rhetoric of post-feminism. As a consequence, it would be impossible for the narrative to tackle the full force of chauvinism in sport (and culture) since, in a kind of ideological

Figure 11.4 Departing for a new liminal space: Jess (Parminder Nagra) and Jules (Keira Knightley) say their farewells at the airport in *Bend it like Beckham*, directed by Gurinder Chadha (2002).

sleight-of-hand, the film's logic insists that, if 'girl power' can render traditional sexism all but obsolete for a new generation of women, it can also conquer another old problem – racism.

In a politically nuanced closure, the girls finally depart for the USA where they will take up football scholarships. As they say their farewells to their assembled families, they leave behind a unified community (the final shot of the film sees Joe and the two fathers playing cricket as a jumbo jet soars overhead). However, like *The Land Girls* and *Letter to Brezhnev*, the closure reconfirms the primacy of the relationship between the girls: despite Jess's romantic involvement with Joe, it is Jules with whom she strides confidently through the departure gates to board a plane that will take her across that familiar flight path to a new, more sustained, liminal space beyond the family home.

In the late 1990s, two gritty films by women directors making their feature film debuts seemed to take the contemporary British woman's film in a markedly different direction. Coky Giedroyc's *Stella Does Tricks* (1998) and Carine Adler's *Under the Skin* (1998) were uncompromising explorations of dysfunction and dystopia which, as Charlotte Brunsdon points out, offered little opportunity for their young heroines to escape their solipsistic and abusive lives (Brunsdon 2000). More recently, this trend has been extended by films such as *Hold Back the Night* (2002), *Morvern Callar* and *My Summer of Love* (2004), all of which centre upon psychologically brittle girls who undergo painful, emotionally ambivalent rites of passage. If films such as *Wish You Were Here*, *Letter to Brezhnev* or *Bend it like Beckham* depict young women railing against the confines of domesticity and their roles as daughters, in contrast, the girls in these later films are typically motherless, cast adrift in a confusing and alienating world. Of these films, it is perhaps Ramsay's critically acclaimed *Morvern Callar* which reinflects – or even distorts – the motifs of liminality and female friendship in the most innovative ways and thus it seems a fitting point to conclude any reassessment of the genre.

The first shots of the film, which intermittently fade from darkness to close-ups of Morvern's (Samantha Morton) face bathed in a red light, do much to disorientate and obstruct our initial understanding of the central female protagonist, a distancing device which recurs throughout the subsequent narrative. One of the defining characteristics of the other contemporary woman's films I have discussed is the extent to which they invite a sustained, and often quite intense, level of emotional engagement with the central female protagonist. We engage because we understand and (in a preferred reading at least) share her point of view. In *Morvern Callar*, these generic dynamics are continually problematized or denied. On a formal level, a number of shots obscure Morvern's face at key emotional moments. At other points (for example, when Morvern is in the bath), she appears to stare into the camera, but this is not a collusive direct address, as we find in *Shirley Valentine*, for example; it is, at best, an uncommunicative blank stare.

It gradually emerges that Morvern has just discovered the body of her boyfriend after he has committed suicide and she is lying with his corpse under the

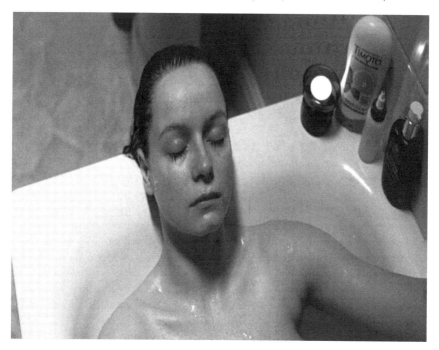

Figure 11.5 Uncommunicative and blank: Samantha Morton in the title role in *Morvern Callar*, directed by Lynne Ramsay (2002).

flickering Christmas tree lights. She finds a suicide note telling her to be brave and that he has left a computer disk containing his recently completed novel, a list of publishers to whom she should send it and enough money to pay for his funeral. Morvern doesn't report his death, but instead vamps up and embarks on an alcohol and ecstasy-fuelled night of partying with her best friend, Lanna (Kathleen McDermott). The night that unravels into aimless, escapist incoherency makes for an interesting comparison with *Letter to Brezhnev* in which the young friends find genuine, if temporary, fun and freedom on their night on the town. In *Morvern Callar*, the night merely marks the first of Morvern's fruitless attempts to find some form of liminal escape that will take her, quite literally, out of herself.

Having failed to report her boyfriend's death, Morvern deletes his name from the manuscript and replaces it with her own and, dispatching it to the first publishing house on the list, she uses the funeral money to buy tickets for herself and Lanna for a two week holiday in a Spanish resort. But, far from discovering a more sustained liminal space, Morvern finds herself in a built-up resort which resembles little more than a concrete warren inhabited by permanently wasted young British tourists. Thus, Morvern escapes once again and hires a taxi to take her – and a less than enthusiastic Lanna – to 'somewhere beautiful'. Stranded in the mountains, the girls quarrel and Morvern continues her journey alone, temporarily changing her name to Jackie, reinventing her outward appearance and presenting herself as the author of her boyfriend's novel to the commissioning editors who fly out to secure a deal for the book. As such, Morvern's identity is certainly rendered increasingly unstable while she inhabits the liminal space of Spain, but in contrast to *Shirley Valentine*, for example, it is hard to see how the various transformations that Morvern undergoes are either authentic or liberating.

Morvern never stops trying to escape, but her liminal journey simply renders her yet more rootless. Returning from Spain, she collects the royalty cheque and asks Lanna to leave Scotland permanently and escape to London with her. Despite being signalled as self-obsessed and unadventurous, Lanna's final words to Morvern have a dreadful ring of truth: 'I'm happy here. There's nothing wrong with here. It's the same crap as everywhere so stop dreaming', a judgement which seems to gather a further level of irony and poignancy when it is understood in the broader context of all those British woman's films which set their heroines free at the end of their respective narratives. Here, the final shots see Morvern in a nightclub, presumably in London. The strobe lights sporadically and unsatisfactorily illuminate her face, lost in the crowd; the obvious formal symmetry with the film's opening shots suggests that, for all her travels, Morvern has gone nowhere.

I am of course aware that it makes little sense to claim that films as thematically and aesthetically diverse as *The Land Girls*, *Bend it like Beckham* and *Morvern Callar* can or should be understood as part of a coherent cycle in the same way as *Educating Rita*, *Wish you Were Here*, *Letter to Brezhnev* and *Shirley Valentine* can be. Rather my aim here has been to trace some of the often subtle ways in which the contemporary British woman's film has mutated and diversified in a changing commercial and cultural climate. In the effort to hybridize and reinvent, it is probably fair to concede that there has inevitably been some dilution of the genre, both in terms of its staple themes and the cultural politics they express. As such, I would certainly hesitate to describe any of the three more recent films I have discussed here as more overtly 'feminist' than their 1980s predecessors: they are simply too politically opaque to be identified in this way. What is clear is that, as it jostled for position among male-centred dramas and comedies, 'rom-coms' and 'chick flicks', the genre has been tugged in a variety of different ways which has tested its formal and political elasticity. However, it seems to me that, if aesthetic diversity and emotional and thematic complexity are signs of a healthy continued existence, then 'the contemporary British woman's film' still demarcates a viable and distinctive form in British cinema.

Bibliography

Ashby, J. (1996), writing as J. King, 'Crossing Thresholds: the contemporary British woman's film', in A. Higson (ed.), *Dissolving Views: Key Writings on British Cinema*, London: Cassell, 216–31.

——(2005) 'Postfeminism in the British frame', in D. Negra and Y. Tasker (eds), 'In Focus: Postfeminism and Contemporary Media Studies', *Cinema Journal*, 44.2: 127–33.

Brunsdon, C. (2000) 'Not having it all: women and British cinema of the 1990s', in R. Murphy (ed.), *British Cinema in the 90s*, London: BFI, 167–77.

Cooper, T. (1998) 'Wartime girl power tale marks Friel's move to the movies', *Evening Standard*, 3 September.

Dyer, R. (1994) 'Feeling English', *Sight and Sound*, 4.3: 17–19.

Taubin, A. (1998) 'Career Girls', *Village Voice*, 16 June, 43: 124.

12 Not to be looked at

Older women in recent British cinema

Imelda Whelehan

Feminist excursions into the concept of femininity posit the ageing female body as lack, so that the older woman, unrepresented in mainstream culture, might be seen as liberated from the prison-house of normative femininity. From another perspective, she might simply be rendered invisible – not purely to the desiring male gaze, but also to the eye of the feminist critic. Indeed one can argue that feminism has itself remained orientated around youth, despite the fact that some of its most notable exponents have written at length about ageing (De Beauvoir 1972; Greer 1991; Friedan 1993). Feminist scholarship has thoroughly analysed our era's obsession with the nubile youthful female body and the tendency to portray women only in relation to men; it has explored less frequently aspects of female experience across the ages. Ageing is too often associated with a diminishing of powers, or loss of material resources, friends, health, and there is scant analysis of the radical possibilities that invisibility brings to women over forty, who may be perfectly placed to challenge what femininity means. Those contemporary commentators who have concerned themselves with age note in particular the discrepancies between the images and descriptive terms available to men and women: 'it is difficult to find masculine counterparts to terms such as *crone*, *witch*, and *hag*, each of which has the ability to call forth strong visual images of maliciousness and degeneracy' (Stoddard 1983: 3). It is women in contemporary western culture who are socialised to acutely fear age and 'among older people, women suffer most from both ageism and sexism' (Paloetti 1998: 2). The popular cultural messages fed back to them confirm that women must remain at war with the visible effects of age, or fear the consequences.

Film is just one medium that has traditionally favoured the youthful woman, not least because men generally control the creative and financial processes in film. Numerous actors and commentators have, over the years, lamented the paucity of meaty film roles for older women. Regularly available parts offer few demands to those who have in the past enjoyed star billing; roles such as mother, grandmother, domestic servant, spinster, infirm person are narrative function more often than narrative fulcrum. There appears to be little engagement with representations of women who are beyond childbearing years, even less so beyond menopause. In *All About Eve* (1950) Margo Channing's (Bette

Davis) fate as an ageing actress most evocatively summarises the tensions within a woman's identity:

> Funny business a woman's career. The things you drop on your way up the ladder – so that you can move faster – you forget you'll need them again when you go back to being a woman. That's one career all females have in common whether we like it or not. Being a woman. Sooner or later we've got to work at it, no matter what other careers we've had or wanted. And in the last analysis nothing is any good unless you can look up just before dinner – or turn around in bed – and there he is. Without that, you're not a woman. You're something with a French provincial office – or a book full of clippings. But you're not a woman. Slow curtain. The End.

An older Davis starred with Joan Crawford in *Whatever Happened to Baby Jane?* (1962) further emphasising that the ageing movie star is at best an object of sympathy, but at worst nothing but a grotesque; the Dorian Gray to her own enduring youthfulness in the films. In one sense their bravura performances add weight to a view that these women are actually at the height of their powers once they are no longer bankable starlets; yet ironically they can only play a role which emphasises the impossibility of the older woman being anything but a representation of the 'abject' in Kristevan terms. These films, in common with Wilder's *Sunset Boulevard* (1950), acknowledge the obliteration of ageing women from the silver screen even as they reanimate these legendary creatures; the satirical edge only reinforcing the inexplicable fear of representing the older woman in a positive fashion. As Sally Chivers notes, 'Contemporary mass media love to prey on cultural fears of aging … There is always someone further along the age continuum to mock and consider vulnerable' (2003: x) and the notion of what each age can mean is so firmly socially constructed that it further preys upon people's fears of decline and decrepitude.

We live in a gerontophobic society. More than ever before we have become expert in analysing the age of women in the public sphere: indeed a popular British reality TV show, *10 Years Younger*, makes a virtue of these skills at the same time as introducing dental veneers, tummy tucks and botox as the high street solution to decline. High profile celebrity women such as Madonna have reached fifty and are still fit to be looked at. Her recent video of the single *Four Minutes* draws attention to a body which seems to be undergoing a reverse trajectory from the softer curves of her early years in the music business to the toned muscular definition which speaks of intense self-discipline. Dressed in lingerie that tantalisingly recalls her own skin tone and therefore plays with nakedness, cross-cut camera work focuses not just on the breasts and face but on the hot spots for the middle-aged woman: the upper arms, thighs and neck. Madonna might be seen as radical, challenging the association of middle age with decline, but she also demonstrates the deferral of the conventional signs of ageing and the rebranding of middle age in the new millennium to 'middle youth'.

However, as the birthrate among the white middle classes in the western world dips and the population ages there may be increased toleration for older females on screen and the possibility for greater degrees of variation in the images we find, as a legion of ageing women consume films and want to see themselves reflected there. As the producer of *Ladies in Lavender* (2004) Nik Powell discovered, 'older audiences actually wanted to see films in the cinema. They hadn't got out of the cinema-going habit, had cash flow and plenty of time on their hands'; this is in addition to the already identified consumer group of younger women filmgoers. As Clark Woods from MGM has noted, 'In the competition for entertainment dollars we're seeing males being more interested in Xboxes and cable television, whereas younger females are continuing to be strong moviegoers' (both quoted in Solomons 2007: 7). Recent notable British films such as *The Queen* (2006) and *Notes on a Scandal* (2006) foreground older women actors in key roles which have depth and complexity and this mirrors recent Hollywood successes such as *The Devil Wears Prada* (2006), where Meryl Streep's fashion magazine editor Miranda Priestly again suggests that more serious acting opportunities were becoming available for older women. The 2007 Academy Award for 'Best Actress in a Leading Role' nominations included Judi Dench and Meryl Streep from the aforementioned films and was won by Mirren in *The Queen*, meaning that three of the five nominees in this category were over fifty.

In this chapter I shall look at the representation of the ageing woman in three recent British films: *Calendar Girls* (2003), *The Mother* (2003) and *Vera Drake* (2004). Naturally there are older women in numerous films of the period, but I chose three where they are at the narrative's core (and I will make briefer mention of *Ladies in Lavender*, discussed in detail elsewhere in this volume). In each film these women destabilise deeply held preconceptions about the social place and function of the ageing woman as mother, wife and widow. In *Calendar Girls* and *The Mother* the battle against age is played out by appropriating the kind of 'visibility' normally reserved for the younger woman; whereas in *Vera Drake* women's caring impulses are problematised, as nurturance is seen from the outside as destructive or perverse. Just as there is relatively little cultural criticism on the representation of ageing women in general, not surprisingly there is little material on the representation of older women in film – much less on recent British film specifically. But these films have provoked media attention for their unusual or otherwise striking depiction of women.

The publicity for *Calendar Girls* capitalised on the fact that this story had some basis in truth and was peculiarly English: a number of members of the Rylstone branch of the Women's Institute decide to pose nude for a calendar to raise funds for Leukaemia Research. This story had been particularly newsworthy because the calendar itself became a bestseller, subverting Pirelli-style camera shoots by having mature women photographed nude while doing crafts in domestic settings. The sunflower motif on each photograph is intended as a symbol of hope, in memory of John Baker, whose illness and death prompted the making of the calendar. The unexpectedly high level of media attention for this event had a number of unpredictable side effects, one being a substantial volume of correspondence from older women appreciative of images which better equated to their sense of their older selves reflected back.

After such attention a dramatisation seemed inevitable and Suzanne Mackie of Harbour Pictures wanted to film the story because it 'really pushes all the buttons for me as a woman. It makes me laugh and feel very triumphant for them' (Simpson *et al.* 2004: 62). For a while 'real' women were in demand and these 'calendar girls' modelled clothes ranges for magazines, becoming instant celebrities in a culture that embraces and fetishises 'reality', especially on TV. This mixture of laughter and triumphalism is what the film of *Calendar Girls* attempts to capture; the central characters are presented laughing at the absurdities of the Women's Institute in the opening scenes of the film and later they are laughing at themselves and the anachronisms of their own naked bodies. There is good reason to draw attention to the portrayal of ageing in the mass media and good reason to find a positive spin on the drama replayed in *Calendar Girls* because the ageing body on display is fundamentally a women's issue in our culture. The messages become ever more mixed, as in the past decade the increased availability of cosmetic surgery and the advocacy of regular fitness and dieting regimes offers more older women on display, but just as few 'real' ageing bodies. *Calendar Girls* is not immune to these mixed messages, and the reawakening or sudden empowerment of key characters is achieved through the 'liberation' of undressing and then becoming draped again, but this time in the garb of the sexualised woman.

Unlike the glamorous celebrities in music videos or those being 'exposed', usually unflatteringly, in the proliferating celebrity-focused publications such as *Heat* magazine, *Calendar Girls* draws on women in the domestic setting and seeming essential qualities of femininity are reinforced by the Women's Institute context of family, community and country. In the film portrayal of the community the milieu is middle aged. With children teenaged or grown up, these women live in a world where they need to fill their own days and have more time for female friendship. In a way, they are starting a new chapter in their lives and their communal Tai Chi sessions suggest a continuation of activity and good health rather than decline and increasing idleness. However, it might be argued that film (and television) is still not good at presenting female diversity, and none of the women featured, even though they represent 'variety' in the terms of the film, have 'let themselves go' or are shown resisting the allure of body culture.

The dreary predictability of Women's Institute events as portrayed in the film reinforces a common assumption about the emptiness of older women's lives caused by 'empty nest syndrome', or widowhood. The use of the WI church hall premises as establishing shot, alongside the rolling Yorkshire Dales, affirms the quintessential Englishness of the film and despite the assurance that the WI 'isn't just Jam and Jerusalem' the focus on rural life, domesticity and tradition evokes a nostalgic construction of women as custodians of the past. In contrast to British films where regional (especially 'northern') accents connote class – for example Clayton's *Room at the Top* (1959) where the casting of Simone Signoret as the seductive older woman is further exoticised by her Frenchness – in *Calendar Girls* they connote nothing more than quirky regional Englishness. The trope of *Jerusalem*, sung at every WI meeting, also recalls heritage film classic *Chariots of Fire* (1981). Beginning with a series of vignettes showing WI meetings over the first few months of the year, events merge into each other and guest speakers become more tedious until finally even the Chair is momentarily caught out napping.

The camera focuses on Chris (Helen Mirren) and Annie (Julie Walters) as they share sniggering and subversive secrets near the back row at each meeting. Chris proves the most subversive of all as she provides a shop-bought Victoria sponge for a competition. She claims to have joined the Women's Institute to please her mother but what she clearly derives from her membership are her closest friends and her social life. Despite attempts by the real Women's Institute to play down its elderly, conservative image (the strapline on their website boasts 'All kinds of opportunities for all kinds of women') the women of the fictional Knapely are at least middle aged, with only Chris standing out a little with her bleached blonde hair, striking figure and bright clothes. Regardless of the fact that the WI became momentarily newsworthy and potentially subversive for subjecting Tony Blair to a slow handclap after he tried to turn their AGM into a political platform in 2000, the film's WI is a safe institution which can eventually incorporate and desexualise the famous calendar. This film simultaneously is and isn't an extension of the media love affair with the story of a handful of middle-aged post-menopausal women who position themselves, ironically, as objects of desire. The calendar, started as a tribute to a much-loved husband and member of a small community, becomes an acute comment on the fate of the ageing female in contemporary culture, but ultimately the film retreats from social comment back into the story of two friends who discard their fetching black outfits and retreat, giggling, to the back of the WI meetings.

The focus on the WI gives the lie (or maybe the truth?) that this Yorkshire village is peopled largely by the old and by women. This is a film centrally about female homosociality, where age-old gender apartheid has maintained its sway, so that when the women are having their photos taken, intercut scenes show an increasing number of anxious men sitting silently together in the pub, until Laurence (Philip Glennister) announces 'it's a calendar', summoning ancient filmic images of men waiting for news of the birth of a child. The setting of the Yorkshire Dales emphasises the closeness of nature and community, just as the holistic group outdoor Tai Chi sessions emphasise the women's location in this community and the strength of their friendship bonds. Chris's idea to raise money for the hospital where Annie's husband died destabilises this steady rhythm, and this instability is indirectly associated with the women's age. As Chris's son's friend tells him comfortingly, 'It's a difficult age', suggesting that the menopause might be affecting her judgement and contributing to the belief that women of a certain age go slightly mad. Stripping off for the camera, the film suggests, allows other layers to be discarded: some women admit to never showing their nude bodies even to their husbands, even in their most intimate moments. Caught in the act of rehearsing their poses by Chris's son, he is further convinced of his mother's incipient lesbianism, and ageing female sexuality is positioned as dangerous and destabilising (and lesbianism is played for laughs).

The negative reception to the calendar by the WI hierarchy bonds the group and is in some ways a healing process; another effect of stripping away the layers. The photo shoot allows them to all see that they share imperfect bodies, but that the camera can make them beautiful as objects too. Annie's early distinction that 'it's not naked, it's nude', emphasises the distinction between life and art, and the images act as a counterpoint to the big bosoms in the soft porn magazine Chris finds under her son's bed. The act of posing is itself seen as empowering, and yet Chris's new power is tellingly portrayed as extreme and distorting. Her PR and marketing prowess are directly responsible for the national and international success of the calendar, but this deskills her as a wife, mother and co-worker. On the cusp of their success Chris's son is arrested for suspected drug possession and her husband is hoodwinked into giving an 'exclusive' to a tabloid journalist; yet much to Annie's displeasure Chris joins the rest of the 'girls' in Hollywood, with Annie's criticism of Chris's abandonment of her family allowing her to give expression to her own deep sense of loss.

There is a conflict here that can't safely be unpacked: the calendar girls in their ironised imaging of the female body are offering a revision of the calendar nude who is traditionally youthful and latterly airbrushed to perfection. On one hand it is a celebration of the ageing female body as beautiful, tantalisingly arranged behind or around household objects and domestic crafts, and by extension the 'craftiness' of the Women's Institute is momentarily sexualised. Yet there is no space for the sexualised older woman's body in the home: Ruth (Penelope Wilton) has been displaced by her husband's mistress; Chris's husband has admitted to the tabloids that he hasn't had sex for months. Nonetheless these women's sudden fame and, most significantly, their transatlantic trip, signifies them as re-commodified for sexual consumption. The women don their signature black outfits and sunflower pins; the camera lingers over fragmented parts of the body showing a tight bodice with a black lacy bra underneath; Ruth slowly pulls sheer black stockings over her peerless legs, Celia (Celia Imrie) applies bright red lipstick, and the emphasis is on the manufactured glamour that accords much more easily with the acceptable face of feminine attractiveness, concealing their mature age in the iconography of the 'sexy' draped body. When they are asked to strip for a soap powder commercial, it is clear even to Chris that they are little better than professional nudes: being naked is no longer a statement of empowerment but rather denotes a low point of their fame, as they shuffle in embarrassment behind a clothes line with items of clothing intended to shield the most compromising parts of their bodies. Once back in the United Kingdom, they re-enter the Church Hall to the strains of Jerusalem which arguably re-positions the WI *as* just Jam and Jerusalem, and normality is restored in their return to their all-female community away from the objectifying gaze of men. Chris and Annie resume their friendship

Figure 12.1 Older women re-commodified for sexual consumption in *Calendar Girls*, directed by Nigel Cole (2003).

unhampered by the conflict generated by the calendar: in a penultimate scene they're seen walking out of shot together, giggling once again.

The positive image of enduring female friendship and commonality is one feature this film shares with others such as *Ladies in Lavender* (indeed the trope of two female compatriots walking out of shot together is repeated near the end of this film) and to a lesser extent *Vera Drake*. Yet the two laughing friends at the end of *Calendar Girls* remind us of its title, as if to 'girl' these women and to hold up their experiences to be shared and laughed with (as opposed to directly laughed *at*) suggests that with female maturity comes regression. If femininity can only be measured by the stages of menarche, pregnancy and motherhood, then the menopause is womanhood's end. Just as extreme old age has been traditionally cast in terms of a return to childhood, here the woman becomes a 'girl':

> Redefining age in these discourses seems to rely exclusively on the 'girling' of older women; attributing glamour to older bodies is linked to rejuvenating them. It seems too obvious to state, but younger women are not encouraged in these discourses to 'aspire' to age. To put this slightly differently, if chronological boundaries are indeed blurring, this only happens in one direction.

(Wearing 2007: 294)

As Sadie Wearing argues in her essay on popular reality TV makeover shows, masquerade conceals one's age and the idea of ageing 'naturally' becomes increasingly problematic when the only dignified way for a woman to age is beginning to be associated with cosmetic and surgical intervention. In the contemporary popular cultural frame, to age visibly is to indulge in 'excess', just as recent makeover and lifestyle programmes take an overtly judgemental view of people who are overweight or who smoke. As Wearing continues, 'not only is "youth" procured by patterns of consumption, but also the possibility of escaping the necessity to conform to its "girlish" precepts is fast eroding' (2007: 294).

Another side effect of the focus on Chris in *Calendar Girls* is that her capabilities as a mother are found wanting. Her laissez-faire attitude to her son's porn use is misinterpreted by him, and her omission to explain the nude posing or the reason for it, leads to his acute embarrassment: in an attempt to heal the damage done, he throws over a rocky precipice all the newspapers which contain the report on the calendar he is supposed to deliver. Chris becomes threatening and uncontainable because she leaves her family to pursue her PR campaign in the USA; further, she symbolically emasculates her husband, visually summarised by the tabloid journalist's photo of him holding a bunch of flowers. In trying to combine a glamorous role with motherhood Chris commits the cardinal sin. As E. Ann Kaplan notes:

> to suggest that women can be *something* after being young and desirable to men, after childbearing and motherhood, or to suggest that one need not be chronologically young to be desirable or to have children – is to suggest that women can play a role that does not *per se* depend upon men, or in particular their voyeuristic gaze. It is in the interest of patriarchal culture to keep alive the myth that, after menopause, women have no particular function and therefore can be passed over for young women who still depend on men.
>
> (Kaplan 1999: 190)

Roger Michell's *The Mother* plays on this notion that women after menopause have no particular function by presenting May, after the death of her husband, in just such a predicament. *The Mother* starts in silence showing May (Anne Reid) staring at herself in a mirror while in bed with her husband Toots. The silence continues as she gets Toots ready for their journey to their son's house in London, with the film's focus fixed on May. As they wait by the front door May kneels at her husband's feet to do up his shoelaces and these unthinking 'maternal' gestures characterise her behaviour in the first part of the film. In their son's London home, conversely, all is noise and chaos. The unruly children barely seem to know them and their son and daughter-in-law evince no interest in them.

In the background of this scene lurks the builder, Darren (Daniel Craig), an old friend of May's son and her daughter's lover. Paula, May's daughter, doesn't have the visible wealth of her brother, but the commonality between them is represented by their indifference to and buried resentment of May after

Toots dies suddenly. Their utter self-absorption is only matched by May's efface-ment of self onto her husband and then her family. Hanif Kureshi's powerful and challenging script offers a sympathetic voice to May who is simply baffled by her children's lives and their problems. Paula teaches creative writing, has a failed marriage, a small child and is in therapy (May asks why she can't talk to her hairdresser like everyone else). The inference is that she is a damaged child; when May reads her own account of the distressing nullity of her experience of mothering, Paula refuses to hear, feels affronted and demands attention to her own needs.

At the beginning of the film May is classically invisible. It is Toots who comes to life when they arrive in London, dancing with his daughter-in-law and chatting about cricket to Darren while May lurks in the garden. Toots articulates a longing for the (mis)memory of the happy family as he wistfully toasts to long life over dinner in Paula's little basement flat. When he dies later that night what is left is the children's inability to communicate with or understand their parents. The children palpably express their dislike of their mother, but when she is taken home and is confronted with Toots's slippers as if 'waiting for him' she feels that to return home is to quietly wait for death (which is what her children expect her to do). Her son brings her back to London, to the chagrin of his wife and Paula, where she is quickly deployed as babysitter and cook. Left alone all day, she becomes friends with Darren, who is able to talk to her across the age barrier on equal terms. Her view of him is conflicted, however, as she witnesses him exploiting the devotion of her daughter who abnegates herself to him in desperation for his love as he leaves her to return to his wife and child after their lovemaking. As voyeur on her daughter's relationship we feel the depth of May's disappointment and witness, as well, how Paula steers every conversation with her mother back to her own peculiar narrative of pain.

As May watches Darren working, stripped to the waist, the look migrates from one of maternal concern (or bafflement) to the desiring gaze and here, as in Ursula's desire for Andrea in *Ladies in Lavender*, the jolt for the audience is in recognition that such an infatuation does not sit easily with expectations about what is proper for a woman of such an age, and because desire is expressed via a perverse mixture of the maternal and the courting lover. The more Darren befriends May and they share food the more her nurturing maternal gestures become fused with sexual desire. She wants a physical relationship with him and her need for his touch is required as an affirmation that she is alive. It is she who kisses him and who invites him to the spare room where they make love. In the sexual act she is rendered visible, the taboo more shocking as she has literally stolen this man from her daughter. Clothes mark this move to the visible, and the anorak and the muted beiges of the elderly are replaced by colours and younger fabrics such as denim, accessorised with bright scarves. Her skirts become more fluid, the blouses emphasise her figure and her hair frames her face. Physical love, it is implied, gives life, and she marvels at the gift of touch, articulating her fear that the next person to touch her would be the undertaker.

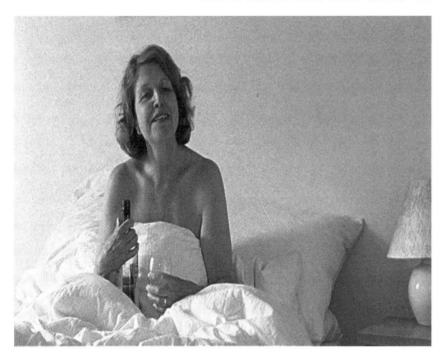

Figure 12.2 The older woman made visible by the sexual act: May (Anne Reid) in *The Mother*, directed by Roger Michell (2003).

As she gains visibility and dominance, other norms are reversed so that she is placed in direct competition with her daughter, for example her bravura performance at Paula's creative writing course where her account of hating her children and having to leave them to cry themselves to sleep is greeted with astonished silence. Her guilt is articulated here and inferred later, but the affair gives her life and soon, despite her fears of being naked with Darren and 'a shapeless old lump', she begins to occupy the subject position of her daughter, quietly desperate to maintain his affection, giving him gifts, serving him and offering him money. As she says, 'I'm not ready for old age' and her husband's death allows her to turn against the past, to replace self-abnegation with self love, but at a highly destructive cost as her children wish her to return to the state of suspended animation she had previously occupied. Of course there is a backdrop of grief at her loss, and another explanation for her actions is a complex response to this, but what seems more evident is that Toots's death is her liberation. Every day she grows in confidence and regains a self long buried under the role of 'mother', symbolised by her return to sketching. Unimpeded by the classic romance narratives where the romance heroine's 'independence and career aspirations are downgraded in favour of the pursuit of "personal" happiness, understood in relation to men' (Garrett 2007: 94), older women's lives potentially offer new forms of feminist engagement with social constructions of femininity, questioning this association with youth. The more May finds herself, the more lost her children seem: in response to her asking her son, 'when did you get so cold?' he ripostes 'when did you get so hot?' The drama of her transgression (not just in terms of betraying her daughter but of the expectations of age) sets up a series of crises as Darren demands money and laments his bondage to work and the numerous women who desire him. At the same time, May's son finds himself in financial difficulties, and Paula burns her writing, blaming her mother (she has found May's erotic drawings of Darren). The final scenes tease us with the promise of a closed cycle: May, back in her house, wakes up in her own bed and catches sight of herself in the mirror, just as we watch and fail to be able to read her self-appraisal in this same position at the film's opening. This foreshadowing of her gloomy sinking into ageing and death is immediately contrasted with a scene showing her packing her 'young clothes' as once again she is transformed into an active agent of her destiny. The return home, it seems, has merely been a temporary stopping-off point, as May packs sketch books and passport on a journey no longer to be experienced vicariously through the younger generation. As she leaves we see her framed by her comfortable semi, but the final opposing shot from inside her living room window shows her from behind, walking out of shot and out of suburbia.

The film avoids stark shock value by its focus on May; the title reinforces the notion that the role of 'mother' is one of cultural norms and children's expectations. The film is not just about *sexual* reawakening, as her positive encounter with Darren is set against a tawdry scene with Bruce, a man her age who screws her without heeding her objections to penetration and her manifest lack of pleasure in the act in sharp contrast to the exploratory touching and mutuality of her and Darren's lovemaking. Darren has more in common with May, the film suggests; he shares her sense of entrapment, of not being known for himself. Even though Paula accuses May of being a 'snob' for her early disapproval of Darren the film makes clear that there are no clashes of class here. The class divide, if there is one, is an effect of generational gain in prosperity. The relationship with Darren only becomes discordant when he calls her 'Mother' and later, in anger, Paula, as if her name is unnecessary to him. Oedipal threads are playfully suggested only to be discarded; rather the film focuses on the rightness of her need for individuation and love, even if it repulses her children.

What makes the film so refreshing is that May does not return to domestic quietude, and the question of whether she was actually a 'bad' mother (as per her own testimony) is left open. Age in May's terms shifts from inevitable decline to self-discovery and freedom, the journey acting as metaphor for growth and development. Reid's performance (she had to turn down a part in *Calendar Girls* because she signed up for this film) is remarkable for how she physically enacts the transition from bowed and anoraked carapace of age to a person of grace and visibility. Mark Kermode, reviewing this film notes that 'While audiences embrace the spectacle of septuagenarian men romancing actresses half their age, any woman older than Mrs Robinson promptly becomes Miss Daisy – amusing but asexual' (Kermode 2003) but *The Mother* clearly rejects the Miss Daisy model and Zoe Brennan's '"Miss Havisham" figure who lives in the past and cannot cope with the present, much less the idea of the future' (Brennan 2005: 2), for a woman liberated by widowhood and the attentions of a much younger man.

A more politicised engagement with the mother and the post-menopausal woman is offered in Mike Leigh's *Vera Drake*, whose harsh realist representation of the working-class mother during the early 1950s offers another view of ageing. Vera (Imelda Staunton) is depicted in terms of her surroundings and role, to the point that she is both dwarfed and effaced by the tenements around her. The opening scene shows her helping out a neighbour, inviting a young man to have a meal, then coming home and putting the kettle on while preparing tea. Devoid of makeup and most often portrayed in the overall she puts on for all domestic work, Vera is portrayed as open, kind and smiling, as honest as she is virtuous. She isn't just invisible from the desiring gaze of men, she effaces the self from all gazes: she cleans in the home of one of her prosperous employers and melts in the background as far as that lavishly dressed woman is concerned. Class in this depiction is seen as a permanent and unbridgeable location, even though Joyce, her sister-in-law, is attempting class mobility by moving to a semi and acquiring the trappings of middle-class existence, such as a washing machine, car and television. Vera and her family quiescently accept their social placing and support their peers with generosity.

This film's social realism is given a more poignant edge by Mike Leigh's signature directorial style, where actors develop the characters through understanding their past and through improvisation, and do not encounter each other until the point in the narrative where they are to meet (as he says himself, 'the film is the screenplay'). Unlike the patriarchal shape of some of the working class films of the 60s, such as *Saturday Night and Sunday Morning* (1960) or the anxiety of lost masculinity in *The Full Monty* (1997), *Vera Drake* celebrates 'feminine' virtues of care, emotional empathy and self-sacrifice, only to confront the audience with the shock of Vera's other life as a local abortionist. Vera's husband, while clearly shocked by these revelations, unwaveringly supports her as someone who only likes to help people out. In this she is contrasted with her aspirational sister-in-law, who attempts to distance herself from the Drakes and is simply an acquirer of 'things' that Vera philosophically resigns herself to never being able to afford. Unlike the films about working class life in the 90s, figuring 'a male working-class that is pictured as struggling to cope with economic superfluousness along with the perceived irrelevance and anachronism of its masculinist cultural and political traditions' (Dave 2006: 61), *Vera Drake* shows her husband Stan (Phil Davis) as a gentle loving man whose affection for Vera has settled into comfortable contentment (as we see them cuddling and chatting in bed). Sid, her son, is angry and disgusted by what she does and we have a historical reflection of the Second World War generation whose masculinity is secure and uninterrogated set against the 'angry young men' of the next generation. Equally, Leigh's cast of largely supportive and empathetic men (even the arresting police officer is visibly moved by her endearing honesty), offers a 'post-feminist' vision of gender.

Roberta Garrett's *Postmodern Chick Flicks* (2007) analyses the self-conscious allusiveness of the women's film in the 70s, 80s and 90s and evaluates the 'fifties-ness' of contemporary rom-coms such as *Down with Love* (2003), which replays the Doris Day single girl drama. The 'fiftiesness' of *Vera Drake*, however, lies in its stark comparison of the lives of working-class women embodied in those Vera 'helps out', set against the daughter of one of her wealthy employers who is 'assessed' by a psychiatrist before relatively easily obtaining a safe medically administered abortion. This scene of the young woman who falls pregnant after she is raped by her date is counterpoised by one where Vera operates on a young Jamaican girl: these juxtaposed scenes emphasise the shared experiences of women even while they demarcate the material differences in their experiences as a result of their social status. Vera, imprisoned for administering illegal abortions, is depicted talking to two other women serving time for the same offence, except that their 'girls' died. Vera's naïve shock at this is palpable, just as one of the most touching scenes in the film is when she discovers that one of the girls she 'helped' nearly died from the procedure. Yet despite her separation from these more worldly wise women, we're offered an insight into a community of female experience; of women administering to others beyond the law when the alternative is more unwanted children, poverty and want.

Garrett, commenting on the 'post modern' chick flick notes that 'it is clear that female audiences prefer desperate women to successful ones' (2007: 204); the women in these films are themselves desperate for different reasons as they encounter the vacuum of age and are cowed by expectations, restrictions and loss. As Woodward notes, age 'is the one difference we are all likely to live into' (1999: x), yet the repression or attempted prevention of visible ageing 'characterizes our culture as a whole' (1999: x–xi). What some feminist commentaries on film and popular culture show is that, perhaps unconsciously, ageism is entrenched within feminism itself. Post-feminism, with all its many inflections, can signify that feminism has ceased to maintain its impact; and the emergence of Third Wave feminism raises again the spectre of generational conflict – the old not understanding the young. Third Wave feminism, for all its verve and potential has its theoretical grounding in youth (remembering that its forebear, Second Wave feminism, was primarily a youthful movement), even in a society with an ageing population. Post-menopausal women are assumed to disappear into a dismal, neutered future, or else the kind of femininity available with age remains unutterable in contemporary popular culture. Yet in a technologically sophisticated environment where this is no bar to childbearing or continued sexual activity, the ideology of traditional femininity lags behind. As Kaplan notes:

> The shocked reaction to the postmenopausal women in their fifties and sixties in England, Italy, and the United States who, with the aid of in vitro

fertilization, recently gave birth to children, exemplifies the public and medical establishment's underlying disgust of the aging female body, a disgust that women internalize growing up in western cultures.

(1999: 175)

Gradually more films may come to represent ageing women in a more nuanced challenging way, not least because a generation of actors, producers and directors who are women might refuse to 'act their age' and because 'all women are, indeed, aging women (regardless of chronological age)' (Stoddard 1983: 153).

Bibliography

Brennan, Z. (2005) *The Older Woman in Recent Fiction*, Jefferson, NC: McFarland & Company.

Chivers, S. (2003) *From Old Woman to Older Women: Contemporary Culture and Women's Narratives*, Columbus: The Ohio State University Press.

Dave, P. (2006) *Visions of England: Class and Culture in Contemporary Cinema*, Oxford: Berg.

De Beauvoir, S. (1972) *The Coming of Age*, New York: G. P. Putnam.

Friedan, B. (1993) *The Fountain of Age*, London: Simon and Schuster.

Garrett, R. (2007) *Postmodern Chick Flicks: The Return of the Woman's Film*, Basingstoke: Palgrave.

Greer, G. (1991) *The Change: Women, Ageing and the Menopause*, London: Hamish Hamilton.

Kaplan, E. A. (1999) 'Trauma and aging: Marlene Dietrich, Melanie Klein and Marguerite Duras', in K. Woodward (ed.), *Figuring Age: Women, Bodies, Generations*, Bloomington: Indiana University Press.

Kermode, M. (2003) 'Passion on a pension', *Observer*, 16 November, no page number.

Paloetti, I. (1998) *Being an Older Woman: A Study in the Social Production of Identity*, Mahwah, NJ: Lawrence Erlbaum Associates.

Simpson, J. and 'the real calendar girls' (2004) *The Calendar Girls Story*, Skipton, N. Yorks: Dalesman Publishing Company.

Solomons, J. (2007) 'Hollywood's new first ladies', *Observer*, 14 January, no page number.

Stoddard, K. M. (1983) *Saints and Shrews: Women and Aging in American Popular Film*, Westport, CT: Greenwood Press.

Wearing, S. (2007) 'Subjects of rejuvenation: aging in postfeminist culture', in Y. Tasker and D. Negra (eds), *Interrogating Postfeminism: Gender and the Politics of Popular Culture*, Durham, NC: Duke University Press.

Woodward, K. (ed.) (1999) *Figuring Age: Women, Bodies, Generations*, Bloomington: Indiana University Press.

Selective filmography

Melanie Bell and Melanie Williams

Abbreviations used: m (running time in minutes); ft (feet; indicating length when a running time is unavailable); bw (black and white); col (colour); *pc* (production company); *d* (director); *prod* (producer); *sc* (author of screenplay); *orig story* (original story by); *cast* (four leading players).

Angus, Thongs and Perfect Snogging

2008 100m col
pc Goldcrest Pictures/ Nickelodeon Movies/ Paramount Pictures
d prod Gurinder Chadha
sc Gurinder Chadha, Paul Mayeda Berges, Will McRobb, Chris Viscardi
orig novel Louise Rennison
cast Georgia Groome, Eleanor Tomlinson, Aaron Johnson, Alan Davies

Anita and Me

2002 92m col
pc Portman Productions/Film Council/BBC Films/East Midlands Media Initiative/ Icon Film Distribution/Starfield Productions/Take 3 TV Partnership/Chest Wig & Flares Productions/European Regional Development Fund/UK Film Council New Cinema Fund/Baker Street Media
d Metin Hüseyin
prod Paul Raphael
sc, orig novel Meera Syal
cast Chandeep Uppal, Sanjeev Bhaskar, Anna Brewster, Kathy Burke

Anne of a Thousand Days

1969 145m col
pc Hal Wallis Productions
d Charles Jarrott
prod Hal Wallis
sc Bridget Boland, John Hale, Richard Sokolove

orig play Maxwell Anderson
cast Richard Burton, Genevieve Bujold, Irene Papas, Anthony Quayle

The Belles of St Trinian's

1954 91m bw
pc British Lion Film Corporation/London Film Productions
d Frank Launder
prod Frank Launder, Sidney Gilliat
sc Frank Launder, Sidney Gilliat, Val Valentine
cast Alastair Sim, Joyce Grenfell, George Cole, Hermione Baddeley

Bend it like Beckham

2002 112m col
pc Kintop Pictures/Bend It Films/Road Movies Filmproduktion GmbH/Roc Media/Film Council/FilmFörderung Hamburg/British Sky Broadcasting/British Screen/Helkon SK/Works International/Future Film Financing/National Lottery through the Film Council
d Gurinder Chadha
prod Deepak Nayar, Gurinder Chadha
sc Paul Mayeda Burges, Guljit Bindra, Gurinder Chadha
cast Parminder Nagra, Keira Knightley, Jonathan Rhys Myers, Anupam Kher

Bhaji on the Beach

1993 101m col
pc Umbi Films
d Gurinder Chadha
prod Nadine Marsh-Edwards
sc Meera Syal, Gurinder Chadha
cast Ginder Kim Vithana, Sarita Khajuria, Lalita Ahmed, Zohra Segal

Black Narcissus

1947 100m col
pc Independent Producers/Archers Film Productions
d, prod, sc Michael Powell, Emeric Pressburger
orig story Rumer Godden
cast Deborah Kerr, Jean Simmons, David Farrar, Kathleen Byron

Blue Murder at St Trinian's

1957 86m bw
pc John Harvel Productions/British Lion Films

d Frank Launder
prod Frank Launder, Sidney Gilliat
sc Frank Launder, Sidney Gilliat, Val Valentine
cast Terry-Thomas, Alastair Sim, Joyce Grenfell, George Cole

Breaking Glass

1980 104m col
pc Sprint N.V./Film & General Productions/Allied Stars
d Brian Gibson
prod Davina Belling, Clive Parsons
sc Brian Gibson
cast Hazel O'Connor, Phil Daniels, Jon Finch, Jonathan Pryce

Brick Lane

2007 102m col
pc FilmFour
d Sarah Gavron
prod Chris Collins, Alison Owen
sc Laura Jones, Abi Morgan
orig novel Monica Ali
cast Tannishtha Chatterjee, Satish Kaushik, Christopher Simpson, Naeema Begum

Bride and Prejudice

2004 111m col
pc Bend It Films/ Bride Productions/ Inside Track Films/ Media/ Kintop Pictures/ Pathé Pictures International/ UK Film Council
d Gurinder Chadha
prod Gurinder Chadha, Deepak Nayar
sc Gurinder Chadha, Paul Mayeda Berges
cast Aishwarya Rai, Martin Henderson, Nadira Babbar, Naveen Andrews

Bridget Jones's Diary

2001 92m col
pc Universal Studios/StudioCanal/Miramax Film Corp./Working Title Films/ Universal Pictures
d Sharon Maguire
prod Tim Bevan, Eric Fellner, Jonathan Cavendish
sc Helen Fielding, Andrew Davies, Richard Curtis
orig story Helen Fielding
cast Renée Zellweger, Colin Firth, Hugh Grant, Jim Broadbent

Bridget Jones: The Edge of Reason

2004 106m col
pc Universal Studios/StudioCanal/Miramax Film Corp./Working Title Films/
Little Bird Company Limited
d Beeban Kidron
prod Tim Bevan, Eric Fellner, Jonathan Cavendish
sc Helen Fielding, Andrew Davies, Richard Curtis, Adam Brooks
orig story Helen Fielding
cast Renée Zellweger, Colin Firth, Hugh Grant, Jim Broadbent

Brief Encounter

1945 86m bw
pc Cineguild/Independent Producers
d David Lean
prod Nöel Coward
sc Nöel Coward, David Lean, Anthony Havelock-Allan, Ronald Neame
orig play Nöel Coward
cast Celia Johnson, Trevor Howard, Stanley Holloway, Cyril Raymond

Calendar Girls

2003 108m col
pc Buena Vista International/Touchstone Pictures/Harbour Pictures
d Nigel Cole
prod Nick Barton, Susan Mackie
sc Juliet Towhidi, Tim Firth
cast Helen Mirren, Julie Walters, Annette Crosbie, Celia Imrie

Caravan

1946 122m bw
pc Gainsborough
d Arthur Crabtree
prod Harold Huth
sc Roland Pertwee
orig story Lady Eleanor Smith
cast Stewart Granger, Jean Kent, Ann Crawford, Robert Helpmann

Career Girls

1997 87m col
pc Channel Four Films

d sc Mike Leigh
prod Simon Channing Williams
cast Katrin Cartlidge, Lynda Steadman, Kate Byers, Mark Benton

Carve Her Name With Pride

1958 119m bw
pc Rank/Keyboard
d Lewis Gilbert
prod Daniel M. Angel
sc Vernon Harris, Lewis Gilbert
orig story R. J. Minney
cast Virginia McKenna, Paul Scofield, Jack Warner, Sydney Tafler

Charlotte Gray

2001 121m col
pc Senator Film Produktion GmbH/Ecosse Films/Pod Films
d Gillian Armstrong
prod Sarah Curtis, Douglas Rae
sc Jeremy Brock
orig story Sebastian Faulks
cast Cate Blanchett, Billy Crudup, Michael Gambon, Rupert Penry-Jones

The Constant Nymph

1928 10,600ft bw
pc Gainsborough
d Adrian Brunel
prod Basil Dean
sc Margaret Kennedy, Basil Dean, Alma Reville
orig story Margaret Kennedy, Basil Dean
cast Ivor Novello, Mabel Poulton, Frances Doble, Mary Clare

The Courtneys of Curzon Street

1947 120m bw
pc Imperadio
d, prod Herbert Wilcox
sc Nicholas Phipps
orig story Florence Tranter
cast Anna Neagle, Michael Wilding, Gladys Young, Coral Browne

Crush

2001 112m col
pc Film Four Limited/Film Council/Senator Film Produktion GmbH/Industry
Entertainment/Pipedream Pictures/National Lottery through the Film Council/
Film Four International
d sc John McKay
prod Lee Thomas
cast Andie MacDowell, Imelda Staunton, Anna Chancellor, Kenny Doughty

Dance with a Stranger

1985 102m col
pc Channel Four Films
d Mike Newell
prod Roger Randall-Cutler
sc Shelagh Delaney
cast Miranda Richardson, Rupert Everett, Ian Holm, Stratford Johns

Darling

1965 127m bw
pc Anglo-Amalgamated/Vic/Appia
d John Schlesinger
prod Joseph Janni, Victor Lyndon
sc Frederic Raphael
cast Julie Christie, Dirk Bogarde, Laurence Harvey, Roland Curram

The Edge of Love

2008 110m col
pc BBC Films/ Capitol Films/ Prescience Film Fund/ Rainy Day Films/ Sarah
Radclyffe Productions Limited/ Wales Creative IP Fund
d John Maybury
prod Rebeckah Gilbertson, Sarah Radclyffe
sc Sharman MacDonald
cast Keira Knightley, Sienna Miller, Matthew Rhys, Cillian Murphy

Educating Rita

1983 110m col
pc Rank/Acorn
d, prod Lewis Gilbert
sc Willy Russell
orig story Willy Russell
cast Julie Walters, Michael Caine, Michael Williams, Maureen Lipman

Elizabeth

1998 124m col
pc Polygram Filmed Entertainment/ Working Title Films/ Channel Four Films
d Shekhar Kapur
prod Tim Bevan, Eric Fellner, Alison Owen
sc Michael Hirst
cast Cate Blanchett, Joseph Fiennes, Geoffrey Rush, Christopher Eccleston

Emma

1996 121m col
pc Miramax
d sc Douglas McGrath
prod Patrick Casavetti, Steve Haft
orig novel Jane Austen
cast Gwyneth Paltrow, Toni Collette, Jeremy Northam, Alan Cumming

Enchanted April

1991 99m col
pc Curzon/ Miramax/ BBC/Greenpoint
d Mike Newell
prod Ann Scott
sc Peter Barnes
orig story Elizabeth von Arnim
cast Miranda Richardson, Josie Lawrence, Polly Walker, Joan Plowright

The Experiment

1922 4900ft bw
pc Stoll Film Company
d Sinclair Hill
sc Ethel M. Dell, William J. Elliott
cast Evelyn Brent, Clive Brook, Templar Powell, Norma Whalley

Fanny by Gaslight (US title *Man of Evil*)

1944 108m bw
pc Gainsborough
d Anthony Asquith
prod Edward Black
sc Doreen Montgomery, Aimée Stuart
orig story Michael Sadleir
cast Phyllis Calvert, James Mason, Stewart Granger, Wilfred Lawson

First a Girl

1935 94m bw
pc Gaumont
d Victor Saville
prod Michael Balcon
sc Marjorie Gaffney
orig story Reinhold Schunzel
cast Jessie Matthews, Sonnie Hale, Griffith Jones, Anna Lee

The Flesh is Weak

1957 88m bw
pc Eros
d Don Chaffey
prod Raymond Stross
sc Leigh Vance
cast Milly Vitale, John Derek, Freda Jackson, William Franklyn

The Gentle Sex

1943 93m bw
pc Rank/Two Cities/Concanen
d Leslie Howard, Maurice Elvey
prod Leslie Howard, Derrick de Marney
sc Moie Charles, Aimée Stuart, Phyllis rose, Roland Pertwee
cast Joan Greenwood, Rosamund John, Joan Gates, Lilli Palmer

Georgy Girl

1966 100m bw
pc Columbia/Everglades
d Silvio Narizzano
prod Otto Plaschkes, Robert A. Golston
sc Margaret Foster, Peter Nichols
orig story Margaret Foster
cast James Mason, Lynn Redgrave, Charlotte Rampling, Alan Bates

Girl with Green Eyes

1963 91m bw
pc UA/Woodfall
d Desmond Davis
prod Oscar Lewenstein
sc Edna O'Brien

orig story Edna O'Brien
cast Rita Tushingham, Peter Finch, Lynn Redgrave, Marie Kean

Girl's Night

1998 102m col
pc Granada Film Productions/Showtime Entertainment
d Nick Hurran
prod Bill Boyes
sc Kay Mellor
cast Brenda Blethyn, Julie Walters, Sue Cleaver, Meera Syal

Good Time Girl

1948 93m bw
pc Triton/Rank
d David MacDonald
prod Sydney Box
sc Muriel Box, Sydney Box, Ted Willis
orig story Arthur La Bern
cast Jean Kent, Dennis Price, Flora Robson, Griffith Jones

The Governess

1998 115m col
pc Arts Council of England/ BBC/ British Screen Productions/ Pandora Cinema/
Parallax Pictures
d sc Sandra Goldbacher
prod Sarah Curtis
cast Minnie Driver, Tom Wilkinson, Harriet Walter, Florence Hoath

Great Day

1945 79m bw
pc RKO British
d Lance Comfort
prod Victor Hanbury
sc Wolfgang Wilhelm, John Davenport
orig story Lesley Storm
cast Flora Robson, Eric Portman, Sheila Sim, Isabel Jeans

Greatheart

1921 5551ft bw
pc Stoll Picture Productions

d George Ridgwell
sc Ethel M. Dell, Sidney Broome
cast Cecil Humphreys, Madge Stuart, Ernest Benham, Olive Sloane

The Heart of Me

2002 96m col
pc Martin Pope Productions/Arch Enterprises Limited/ BBC Films/ Isle of Man
Film Commission/ Pandora/Take 3 Partnership
d Thaddeus O'Sullivan
prod Martin Pope
sc Lucinda Coxon
orig novel Rosamund Lehmann
cast Helena Bonham Carter, Olivia Williams, Paul Bettany, Eleanor Bron

Heat and Dust

1983 133m col
pc Merchant Ivory Productions
d James Ivory
prod Ismail Merchant
sc Ruth Prawer Jhabvala
cast Julie Christie, Greta Scacchi, Shashi Kapoor, Christopher Cazanove

Hideous Kinky

1998 98m col
pc AMLF/Arts Council of England/BBC Films/ Film Consortium/Greenpoint
Films/
L Films
d Gillies MacKinnon
prod Ann Scott
sc Billy MacKinnon
orig novel Bella Freud
cast Kate Winslet, Said Taghmaoui, Bella Riza, Carrie Mullan

High Heels and Low Lifes

2001 86m col
pc Buena Vista International/Fragile Films
d Mel Smith
prod Uri Fruchtmann, Barnaby Thompson
sc Kim Fuller, Georgia Pritchett
cast Minnie Driver, Mary McCormack, Kevin McNally, Mark Williams

Hindle Wakes

1918 5250ft bw
pc Samuelson Film Manufacturing Company
d Maurice Elvey
cast Norman McKinnel, Edward O'Neil, Ada King, Colette O'Niel

Hindle Wakes

1927 8800ft bw
pc Gaumont-British Picture Corporation
d Maurice Elvey
prod Maurice Elvey, Victor Saville
sc Victor Saville
orig play Stanley Houghton
cast Estelle Brody, Norman McKinnel, Humberstone Wright, Maria Ault

Hold Back the Night

1999 104m col
pc UIP/Film Consortium/Film 4/Arts Council/BIM/Wave/Parallax
d Phil Davis
prod Sally Hibbin
sc Steve Chambers
cast Christine Tremarco, Stuart Sinclair Blyth, Sheila Hancock, Richard Platt

Howards End

1992 140m col
pc Merchant Ivory Productions
d James Ivory
prod Ismail Merchant
sc Ruth Prawer Jhabvala
orig novel E. M. Forster
cast Anthony Hopkins, Emma Thompson, Helena Bonham Carter, Vanessa Redgrave

The Hundredth Chance

1920 5255ft bw
pc Stoll Picture Productions
d Maurice Elvey
sc Ethel M. Dell, Sinclair Hill
cast Ellie Norwood, Mary Glynn, Sydney Seaward, Dennis Neilson-Terry

I Capture the Castle

2003 113m col
pc BBC Films/Trademark Films/Distant Horizon
d Tim Fywell
prod David M. Thompson, David Parfitt, Anant Singh
sc Heidi Thomas
orig novel Dodie Smith
cast Romola Garai, Bill Nighy, Sinead Cusack, Rose Byrne

I Know Where I'm Going!

1945 91m bw
pc GFD/The Archers
d, prod, sc Michael Powell, Emeric Pressburger
cast Wendy Hiller, Roger Livesey, Pamela Brown, Nancy Price

I Live in Grosvenor Square

1945 113m bw
pc Associated British Pictures
d, prod Herbert Wilcox
sc Nicholas Phipps, Willaim D. Bayles, Maurice Cowan
cast Anna Neagle, Dean Jagger, Rex Harrison, Robert Morley

Illegal

1932 64m bw
pc Warner Brothers First National Productions
d William McGann
prod Irving Asher
sc John Hastings Turner, Roland Pertwee
orig story Roland Pertwee
cast Isabel Elsom, Margot Grahame, D. A. Clarke-Smith, Moria Lynd

Irene

1940 101m bw
pc RKO/Imperator
d, prod Herbert Wilcox
sc Alice Duer Miller
orig play James H. Montgomery
cast Anna Neagle, Ray Milland, Roland Young, Alan Marshal

Iris

2001 91m col
pc BBC Films/Mirage Enterprises/Intermedia/Miramax
d Richard Eyre
prod Robert Fox, Scott Rudin
sc Richard Eyre, Charles Wood
orig story John Bayley
cast Judi Dench, Jim Broadbent, Kate Winslet, Hugh Bonneville

It Always Rains on Sunday

1947 92m bw
pc Ealing
d Robert Hamer
prod Henry Cornelius
sc Angus MacPhail, Robert Hamer, Henry Cornelius
orig story Arthur La Bern
cast Googie Withers, John McCallum, Patricia Plunkett, Susan Shaw

It Started in Paradise

1952 94m col
pc British Film-Makers
d Compton Bennett
prod Sergei Nolbandov, Leslie Parkyn
sc Marghanita Laski
cast Jane Hylton, Ian Hunter, Terence Morgan, Muriel Pavlow

Jane Eyre

1970 110m col
pc British Lion/Omnibus/Sagittarius
d Delbert Mann
prod Frederick H. Brogger
sc Jack Pulman
orig story Charlotte Brontë
cast George C. Scott, Susannah York, Ian Bannen, Jack Hawkins

Jassy

1947 102m col
pc GFD/Gainsborough
d Bernard Knowles
prod Sydney Box

sc Dorothy and Campbell Christie, Geoffrey Kerr
orig story Norah Lofts
cast Margaret Lockwood, Patricia Roc, Basil Sydney, Denis Price

The Knack and How to Get It

1965 84m bw
pc UA/Woodfall
d Richard Lester
prod Oscar Lewenstein
sc Charles Wood
orig play Ann Jellicoe
cast Rita Tushingham, Michael Crawford, Ray Brooks, Donal Donnelly

The Knight Errant

1922 5290ft bw
pc Stoll Picture Productions
d George Ridgwell
sc Leslie Howard Gordon, Mrs Sydney Groome
orig play Ethel M. Dell
cast Olaf Hytten, Rex McDougall, Judd Green, Norma Whalley

Ladies in Lavender

2004 108m col
pc Take Partnerships/UK Film Council/Scala Productions/Baker Street Media/
Future Films/Paradigm Hyde Films/UK Film Council Premiere Fund/Lakeshore
International/Freeway CAM B.V.
d Charles Dance
prod Nicolas Brown, Elizabeth Karlsen, Nik Powell
sc Charles Dance
orig story William J. Locke
cast Judi Dench, Maggie Smith, Natascha McElhone, Miriam Margolyes

The Lamp in the Desert

1923 58m bw
pc Stoll Picture Productions
d F. Martin Thornton
sc Leslie Gordon Howard, Ethel M. Dell
orig story Ethel M. Dell
cast Gladys Jennings, Louis Willoughby, George K. Arthur, Joseph R. Tozer

The Land Girls

1998 111m col
pc Intermedia Land Girls Ltd/Caméra One/Aréna Films (Paris)/InterMedia Films/
Greenlight Fund/Channel 4 Films/Greenpoint Films/West Eleven Films/National
Lottery through the Arts Council of England
d David Leland
prod Simon Relph
sc David Leland, Keith Dewhurst
orig story Angela Huth
cast Catherine McCormack, Rachel Weisz, Anna Friel, Steven Mackintosh

Letter to Brezhnev

1985 95m col
pc Yeardream/Film Four International/Palace Productions
d Chris Bernard
prod Janet Goddard
sc Franke Clarke
cast Margi Clarke, Alexandra Pigg, Peter Firth, Alfred Molina

Love Story (US *A Lady Surrenders*)

1944 112m bw
pc GFD/Gainsborough
d Leslie Arliss
prod Harold Huth
sc Leslie Asrliss, Dorothy Montgomery, Rodney Ackland
orig story J. W. Drawbell
cast Margaret Lockwood, Patricia Roc, Stewart Granger, Tom Walls

The Loves of Joanna Godden

1947 89m bw
pc Ealing
d Charled Frend
prod Sidney Cole
sc H. E. Bates, Angus Macphail
orig story Sheila Kaye-Smith
cast Googie Withers, John McCallum, Jean Kent, Derek Bond

The L-Shaped Room

1962 142m bw
pc British Lion/Romulus

d Bryan Forbes
prod James Woolf, Richard Attenborough
sc Bryan Forbes
orig story Lynne Reid Banks
cast Leslie Caron, Tom Bell, Brock Peters, Cecily Courtniedge

Madonna of the Seven Moons

1944 110m bw
pc GFD/Gainsborough
d Arthur Crabtree
prod R. J. Minney
sc Roland Pertwee, Brock Williams
orig story Margery Lawrence
cast Phyllis Calvert, Patricia Roc, Stewart Granger, Jean Kent

The Magic Bow

1946 106m bw
pc GFD/Gainsborough
d Bernard Knowles
prod R. J. Minney
sc Norman Ginbury, Roland Pertwee
orig story Manuel Komroff
cast Jean Kent, Phyllis Calvert, Stewart Granger, Denis Price

The Man in Grey

1943 116m bw
pc GFD/Gainsborough
d Leslie Arliss
prod Edward Black
sc Margaret Kennedy, Leslie Arliss, Doreen Montgomery
orig story Lady Eleanor Smith
cast Margaret Lockwood, Phyllis Calvert, James Mason, Stewart Granger

Mandy (US The Crash of Silence)

1952 93m bw
pc Ealing
d Alexander Mackendrick
prod Leslie Norman
sc Nigel Balchin, Jack Whittingham
orig story 'This Day is Ours' by Hilda Lewis
cast Phyllis Calvert, Mandy Miller, Terence Morgan, Jack Hawkins

Mansfield Park

1999 112m col
pc BBC Films/ Miramax/HAL Films
d sc Patricia Rozema
prod Sarah Curtis
orig novel Jane Austen
cast Frances O'Connor, Jonny Lee Miller, Embeth Davidtz, Alessandro Nivola

Mary, Queen of Scots

1971 128m col
pc Universal Pictures
d Charles Jarrott
prod Hal Wallis
sc John Hale
cast Vanessa Redgrave, Glenda Jackson, Patrick McGoohan, Timothy Dalton

Maytime in Mayfair

1949 95m col
pc British Lion/Imperadio
d, prod Herbert Wilcox
sc Nicholas Phipps
cast Anna Neagle, Michael Wilding, Nicholas Phipps, Peter Graves

Me Without You

2001 108m col
pc Dokota Films/Momentum Pictures/Road Movies Filmproduktion GmbH/Isle of Man Film Commission/British Screen/British Sky Broadcasting/Finola Dwyer Productions/Wave Pictures UK Ltd/MEDIA/Capitol Films
d Sandra Goldbacher
prod Finola Dwyer
sc Sandra Goldbacher, Laurence Coriat
cast Anna Friel, Michelle Williams, Oliver Milburn, Trudie Styler

Millions Like Us

1943 103m bw
pc GFD/Gainsborough
d Frank Launder, Sidney Gilliat
prod Edward Black
sc Frank Launder, Sidney Gilliat
cast Patricia Roc, Eric Portman, Anne Crawford, Gordon Jackson

Miranda

1947 80m bw
pc GFD/Gainsborough/Sydney Box
d Ken Annakin
prod Betty Box
sc Peter Blackmore
orig play Peter Blackmore
cast Glynis Johns, Griffith Johns, Googie Withers, John McCallum

Morvern Callar

2002 97m col
pc Morvern Callar Productions Limited/Alliance Atlantis/BBC Films/Film Council/
Scottish Screen/Glasgow Film Fund/Company Pictures/BBC Scotland/National
Lottery through the Film Council/Alliance Atlantis/H20 Motion Pictures
d Lynne Ramsay
prod George Faber, Charles Pattinson, Robyn Slovo
sc Lynne Ramsay, Liana Dognini
orig story Alan Warner
cast Samantha Morton, Kathleen McDermott, Linda McGuire, Ruby Milton

The Mother

2003 112m col
pc BBC Films/Free Range Films/BBC Films/Renaissance Films/Renaissance Films
d Roger Michell
prod Kevin Loader
sc Hanif Kureishi
cast Anne Reid, Cathryn Bradshaw, Daniel Craig, Steven Mackintosh

Mrs Brown

1997 105m col
pc BBC Scotland/ Ecosse films/Irish screen/Mobile Masterpiece Theatre/WGBH
d John Madden
prod Sarah Curtis
sc Jeremy Brock
cast Judi Dench, Billy Connolly, Anthony Sher, Geoffrey Palmer

My Summer of Love

2004 86m col
pc Take Partnerships/Apocalypso Pictures/BBC Films/Film Consortium/Baker
Street Media/UK Film Council/Works International

d Pawel Pawlikowski
prod Tanya Seghatchian, Christopher Collins
sc Pawel Pawlikowski, Michael Wynne
orig story Helen Cross
cast Natalie Press, Emily Blunt, Paddy Considine, Dean Andrews

Nell Gwyn

1934 85m bw
pc B and D
d, prod Herbert Wilcox
sc Miles Malleson
cast Anna Neagle, Cedric Hardwicke, Jeanne de Casalis, Muriel George

No Time for Tears

1957 86m col
pc ABPC
d Cyril Frankel
prod W. A. Whittaker
sc Anne Burnaby
cast Sylvia Syms, Anna Neagle, Flora Robson, Anthony Quayle

Notes on a Scandal

2006 92m col
pc BBC Films/DNA Films
d Richard Eyre
prod Robert Fox, Scott Rudin
sc Patrick Marber
orig novel Zoe Heller
cast Judi Dench, Cate Blanchett, Bill Nighy, Andrew Simpson

Odette

1950 123m bw
pc Herbert Wilcox Productions
d, prod Herbert Wilcox
sc Warren Chetham Strode
orig story Jerrard Ticknell
cast Anna Neagle, Trevor Howard, Peter Ustinov, Marius Goring

Operation Bullshine

1959 84m col
pc ABPC
d Gilbert Gunn
prod Frank Godwin
sc Anne Burnaby, Rupert Lang, Gilbert Gunn
cast Barbara Murray, Carole Lesley, Dora Bryan, Donald Sinden

Orlando

1992 93m col
pc Electric/Adventure Pictures/Lenfilm/Mikado/Sigma/British Screen
d Sally Potter
prod Christopher Sheppard
sc Sally Potter
orig story Virginia Woolf
cast Tilda Swinton, Billy Zane, Quentin Crisp, Jimmy Somerville

A Passage to India

1984 163m col
pc EMI/ HBO
d sc David Lean
prod John Brabourne, Richard Goodwin
orig novel E. M. Forster
cast Judy Davis, Victor Banerjee, Peggy Ashcroft, James Fox

The Passionate Friends

1948 91m bw
pc GFD/Cineguild
d David Lean
prod Ronald Neame
sc Eric Ambler
orig story H. G. Wells
cast Ann Todd, Trevor Howard, Claude Rains, Betty Ann Davies

Peg of Old Drury

1935 76m bw
pc British and Dominions
d, prod Herbert Wilcox
sc Miles Malleson
orig play Masks and Faces by Charles Reade
cast Anna Neagle, Cedric Hardwicke, Jack Hawkins, Margaretta Scott

Petticoat Pirates

1961 87m col
pc Gordon L. T. Scott/ABPC
d David MacDonald
prod Gordon L. T. Scott
sc Lew Schwartz, Charlie Drake
cast Charlie Drake, Anne Heywood, Cecil Parker, Eleanor Summerfield

Piccadilly Incident

1946 102 m bw
pc ABP
d, prod Herbert Wilcox
sc Nicholas Phipps
cast Anna Neagle, Michael Wilding, Michael Laurence, Coral Browne

Pink String and Sealing Wax

1945 89m bw
pc Ealing
d Robert Hamer
prod Michael Balcon
sc Diana Morgan, Robert Hamer
orig play Roland Pertwee
cast Googie Withers, Mervyn Johns, Gordon Jackson, Sally Ann Howes

A Place of One's Own

1944 92m bw
pc GFD/Gainsborough
d Bernard Knowles
prod R. J. Minney
sc Brock Williams
orig story Osbert Sitwell
cast Margaret Lockwood, James Mason, Barbara Mullen, Denis Price

Poor Cow

1967 101m col
pc Fenchurch/The National Film Finance Corp/Vic Films Productions
d Ken Loach
prod Joseph Janni
sc Nell Dunn
cast Carol White, Terence Stamp, John Bindon, Queenie Watts

The Prey of the Dragon

1921 5305ft bw
pc Stoll Picture Productions
d F. Martin Thorton
sc Leslie Howard Gordon
orig story Ethel M. Dell
cast Harvey Braban, Gladys Jennings, Hal Martin, Victor McLaglen

Pride and Prejudice

2005 125m col
pc Focus Features/Universal Pictures/Studio Canal/Working Title/Scion Films
d Joe Wright
prod Tim Bevan, Eric Fellner, Paul Webster
sc Deborah Moggach
orig novel Jane Austen
cast Keira Knightley, Matthew Macfadyen, Rosamund Pike, Donald Sutherland

The Prime of Miss Jean Brodie

1969 116m col
pc Twentieth Century Fox
d Ronald Neame
prod Robert Fryer
sc Jay Presson Allen
orig novel Muriel Spark
cast Maggie Smith, Robert Stephens, Pamela Franklin, Gordon Jackson

The Pumpkin Eater

1964 118m bw
pc Romulus Films
d Jack Clayton
prod James Woolf
sc Harold Pinter
orig novel Penelope Mortimer
Cast Anne Bancroft, Peter Finch, James Mason, Janine Gray

The Queen

2006 97m col
pc BIM Distribuzione/Canal+/France 3 Cinéma/Future Films/Granada Film
Productions/Pathé Pictures International/Pathé Renn Productions/Scott Rudin
Productions

d Stephen Frears
prod Tracey Seaward, Christine Langan, Andy Harries
sc Peter Morgan
cast Helen Mirren, Michael Sheen, James Cromwell, Roger Allam

A Question of Trust

1920 4549ft bw
pc Stoll Film Company
d Maurice Elvey
sc Sinclair Hill
orig story Ethel M. Dell
cast C. H. Crocker-King, Teddy Arundell, Harvey Braban, Kitty Fielder

Red Road

2006 113m col
pc Advanced Party Scheme/BBC Films/Glasgow Film Office/Scottish Screen/Sigma
Films/UK Film Council/Verve Pictures/Zentropa Entertainments/Zoma Films Ltd
d, sc Andrea Arnold
prod Carrie Comerford
cast Kate Dickie, Tony Curran, Martin Compston, Nathalie Press

The Red Shoes

1948 133m col
pc The Archers, Independent Producers
d, prod, sc Michael Powell and Emeric Pressburger (based on fairy tale by Hans
Christian Andersen)
cast Moira Shearer, Anton Walbrook, Marius Goring, Leonide Massine

Rita, Sue and Bob Too

1987 95m col
pc Mainline/Umbrella/British Screen/Film Four
d Alan Clarke
prod Sandy Lieberson
sc Andrea Dunbar
orig play Andrea Dunbar
cast Michelle Holmes, Siobhan Finneran, George Costigan, Lesley Sharp

The Rocks of Valpre

1919 6272ft bw
pc Stoll Film Company

d Maurice Elvey
sc Ethel M. Dell
cast Peggy Carlisle, Cowley Wright, Winifred Sadler, Basil Gil

The Romantic Englishwoman

1975 116m col
pc Dial/Meric-Matalon
d Joseph Losey
prod Daniel M. Angel
sc Tom Stoppard, Thomas Wiseman
orig story Thomas Wiseman
cast Glenda Jackson, Michael Caine, Helmut Berger, Michael Lonsdale

A Room with a View

1985 115m col
pc Merchant Ivory/Goldcrest
d James Ivory
prod Ismail Merchant
sc Ruth Prawer Jahabvala
orig story E. M. Forster
cast Maggie Smith, Judi Dench, Helena Bonham Carter, Denhom Elliot

The Root of All Evil

1946 110m bw
pc Gainsborough
d Brock Williams
prod Harold Huth
sc Brock Williams
orig story J. S. Fletcher
cast Phyllis Calvert, Michael Rennie, John McCallum, Hazel Court

Ryan's Daughter

1970 206m col
pc MGM/Farraway
d David Lean
prod Anthony Havelock-Allan
sc Robert Bolt
cast Sarah Miles, Robert Mitchum, Christopher Jones, John Mills

Sense and Sensibility

1995 136m col
pc Columbia pictures/Mirage
d Ang Lee
prod Lindsay Doran
sc Emma Thompson
orig novel Jane Austen
cast Emma Thompson, Kate Winslet, Hugh Grant, Greg Wise

The Seventh Veil

1945 94m bw
pc Theatrecraft/Sydney Box/Ortus
d Compton Bennett
prod Sydney Box
sc Muriel Box, Sydney Box
cast Ann Todd, James Mason, Herbert Lom, Hugh McDermott

Shadowlands

1993 131m col
pc Price Entertainment/Shadowlands Productions/Spelling Films
d Richard Attenborough
prod Richard Attenborough, Terence A. Clegg, Brian Eastman, Diana Hawkins,
Alison Webb
sc William Nicholson
cast Anthony Hopkins, Debra Winger, Edward Hardwicke, Joseph Mazzello

She'll Be Wearing Pink Pyjamas

1985 90m col
pc Virgin/Pink Pyjamas/Film Four International
d John Goldschmidt
prod Tara Prem, John Goldschmidt
sc Eva Hardy
cast Julie Walters, Jane Evens, Janet Henfrey, Paula Jacobs

Shirley Valentine

1989 108m col
pc UIP/Paramount
d Lewis Gilbert
prod Lewis Gilbert
sc Willy Russell

orig story Willy Russell
cast Pauline Collins, Tom Conti, Julia McKenzie, Alison Steadman

Sixty Glorious Years

1938 95m col
pc Imperator
d, prod Herbert Wilcox
sc Robert Vansittart, Miles Malleson, Charles de Grandcourt
cast Anna Neagle, Anton Walbrook, C. Aubrey Smith, Walter Rilla

Smashing Time

1967 96m col
pc Partisan/Selmur/Paramount British Pictures
d Desmond Davis
prod Roy Millichip, Carlo Ponti
sc George Melly
cast Rita Tushingham, Lynn Redgrave, Michael York, Anna Quayle

Spring in Park Lane

1948 92m bw
pc Imperadio
d, prod Herbert Wilcox
sc Nicholas Phipps
orig play Alice Duer Miller
cast Anna Neagle, Michael Wilding, Tom Walls, Peter Graves

Stella Does Tricks

1996 99m col
pc British Film Institute Production/Channel Four/Compulsive Viewing/Sidewalk Productions/Scottish Arts Council Lottery Fund/Scottish Film Production Fund
d Coky Giedroyc
prod Adam Barker
sc Al Kennedy
cast Kelly MacDonald, James Bolan, Hans Matheson, Ewan Stewart

Stevie

1978 102m col
pc Bowden Productions/First Artists/Grand Metropolitan
d, prod Robert Enders

sc Hugh Whitemore
cast Glenda Jackson, Mona Washbourne, Alec McCowen,Trevor Howard

Street Corner

1953 94m bw
pc Rank/LIP/Sydney Box
d Muriel Box
prod William MacQuitty
sc Muriel Box
cast Rosamund John, Ann Crawford, Peggy Cummins, Eleanor Summerfield

Sunday Bloody Sunday

1971 110m col
pc UA/Vectia
d John Schlesinger
prod Joseph Janni
sc Penelope Gilliat
cast Peter Finch, Glenda Jackson, Murray Head, Peggy Ashcroft

A Taste of Honey

1961 100m bw
pc British Lion/Bryanston/Woodfall
d, prod Tony Richardson
sc Shelagh Delaney, Tony Richardson
orig play Shelagh Delaney
cast Rita Tushingham, Dora Bryan, Murray Melvin, Robert Stephens

That Hamilton Woman (aka *Lady Hamilton*)

1941 114m bw
pc Alexander Korda/London Films
d, prod Alexander Korda
sc Walter Reisch, R. C. Sherriff
cast Vivien Leigh, Laurence Olivier, Alan Mowbray, Sara Allgood

They Flew Alone

1941 103m bw
pc RKO/Imperator
d, prod Herbert Wilcox
sc Miles Malleson
cast Anna Neagle, Robert Newton, Nora Swinburne, Edward Chapman

They Were Sisters

1945 115m bw
pc GFD/Gainsborough
d Arthur Crabtree
prod Harold Huth
sc Roland Pertwee
orig story Dorothy Whipple
cast Phyllis Calvert, Dulcie Gray, James Mason, Anne Crawford

The Tidal Wave

1920 6226ft bw
pc Stoll Picture Productions
d Sinclair Hill
sc Sinclair Hill
orig story Ethel M. Dell
cast Poppy Wyndham, Sydney Seaward, Pardow Woodman, Annie Esmond

A Town Like Alice

1956 117m bw
pc Rank/Vic Films
d Jack Lee
prod Joseph Janni
sc W. P. Lipscomb, Richard Mason
orig story Nevil Shute
cast Virgina McKenna, Peter Finch, Nora Nicholson, Renee Houston

Truly Madly Deeply

1990 106m col
pc BBC/ Lionheart/Winston
d, sc Anthony Minghella
prod Robert Cooper
cast Juliet Stevenson, Alan Rickman, Michael Maloney, Bill Paterson

Turn the Key Softly

1953 81m bw
pc GFD/Chiltern
d Jack Lee
prod Maurice Cowan
sc Jack Lee, Maurice Cowan
orig story John Brophy
cast Yvonne Mitchell, Joan Collins, Kathleen Harrison, Terence Morgan

Two Thousand Women

1944 97m bw
pc GFD/Gainsborough
d Frank Launder
prod Edward Black
sc Frank Launder
cast Phyllis Calvert, Patricia Roc, Flora Robson, Renee Houston

Under the Skin

1997 83m col
pc BFI/Channel 4/Strange Dog/Rouge/MFP
d Carine Adler
prod Kate Ogborn
sc Carine Adler
cast Samantha Morton, Claire Rushbrook, Rita Tushingham, Christine Tremarco

Unrelated

2007 100m col
d sc Joanna Hogg
prod Barbara Stone
cast Kathryn Worth, Tom Hiddleston, Mary Roscoe, David Rintoul

Vera Drake

2004 124m col
pc Untitled 03 Limited/Films Alain Sarde/UK Film Council/Thin Man Films/
Films Alain Sarde/Inside Track 1 LLP/Inside Track/National Lottery through
UK Film Council/UK Film Council Premiere Fund/Fine Line Features/StudioCanal
d Mike Leigh
prod Simon Channing Williams, Alain Sarde
sc Mike Leigh
cast Imelda Staunton, Phil Davis, Peter Wight, Alex Kelly

Victoria the Great

1937 112m bw
pc British Lion/Imperator/Herbert Wilcox
d, prod Herbert Wilcox
sc Robert Vansittart, Miles Malleson
orig play Laurence Housman
cast Anna Neagle, Anton Walbrook, H. B. Warner, Walter Rilla

The Weak and the Wicked

1953 88m bw
pc ABPC/Marble Arch
d J. Lee Thompson
prod Victor Skutezky
sc J. Lee Thompson, Anne Burnaby
orig story Joan Henry
cast Glynis Johns, Diana Dors, Jane Hylton, Olive Sloane

The Wicked Lady

1945 104m bw
pc GFD/Gainsborough
d Leslie Arliss
prod R. J. Minney
sc Leslie Arliss
orig story Magdalen King-Hall
cast Margaret Lockwood, Patricia Roc, James Mason, Griffith Johns

Wish You Were Here

1987 92m col
pc Zenith/Film Four
d David Leland
prod Sarah Radclyffe
sc David Leland
cast Emily Lloyd, Tom Bell, Clare Clifford, Jesse Birdsall

Woman in a Dressing Gown

1957 94m bw
pc Godwin/Willis/J. Lee Thompson
d J. Lee Thompson
prod Frank Godwin, J. Lee Thompson
sc Ted Willis
orig play Ted Willis
cast Yvonne Mitchell, Sylvia Syms, Anthony Quayle, Andrew Ray

The Woman of his Dream

1921 4320ft bw
pc Stoll Picture Productions
d Harold M. Shaw
sc Leslie Howard Gordon

orig story Ethel M. Fell
cast Mary Dibley, Alec Fraser, Sydney Seaward, Fred Thatcher

Women Talking Dirty

1999 97m col
pc Jean Doumanian Productions/Petunia Productions/Rocket Pictures
d Coky Giedroyc
prod Jean Doumanian, David Furnish, Polly Steele
sc Isla Dewar
cast Helena Bonham Carter, Gina McKee, Eileen Atkins, Kenneth Cranham

Yanks

1979 141m col
pc CIP
d John Schlesinger
prod Joseph Janni, Lester Persky
sc Colin Welland
cast Richard Gere, Lisa Eichhorn, Vanessa Redgrave, William Devane

Yield to the Night (US *Blonde Sinner*)

1956 99m bw
pc Associated British Picture Corporation/Kenwood Films/Associated British Pathé
d J. Lee Thompson
prod Kenneth Harper
sc John Cresswell, Joan Henry
orig story Joan Henry
cast Diana Dors, Yvonne Mitchell, Michael Craig, Athene Seyler

Young Wives' Tale

1951 79m bw
pc ABPC
d Henry Cass
prod Victor Skutezky
sc Anne Burnaby
orig story Ronald Jeans
cast Joan Greenwood, Helen Cherry, Nigel Patrick, Derek Farr

Index

111, 112–13; and nationality 16; body
36, 38, 107, 108, 109, 111, 113, 114,
115, 122, 129, 130–31, 132, 132;
contemporary British woman's film
155, 157, 160, 162, 165, 168; desiring/
desirable 79, 80–81, 87–91, 101, 115;
English femininity 9–10, 36, 37, 39, 40,
47, 101; female identity 13, 115, 126,
146, 155, 157, 160, 162, 165, 168, 180;
feminine types 96, 98–99, 100, 102, 103,
104, 108; feminist politics 139, 140,
145–46; films *about* women 13–14, 124,
125–26; media 111, 113, 115, 122;
Neagle, Anna 9–10, 39; normative 102,
103, 105, 170; re-feminisation 13, 100,
101, 102, 103, 108, 164; restraint 44, 54,
64, 68, 70, 79, 157, 163; swinging 111,
115; wartime 11–12, 39, 52, 101, 102;
woman-in-prison genre 103, 105, 108,
109; *see also* ageing; Davis, Bette;
female group film; Moseley, Rachel;
Neagle, Anna; sexuality
feminism 1, 14, 70, 72–73, 124, 135, 138;
ageing 170, 179–80, 182; cinema critics
3, 124, 170; female liberation 13, 20,
70, 91, 113–16, 117, 135, 170, 181;
feminist cultural politics 14, 139–40,
153, 161, 163, 164, 168; feminist film
theory 138; films 124, 139; 'girl power'
164, 166; literary and theatrical
adaptations 8; post-feminism 14, 138,
146, 164, 165, 182; Potter, Sally 124,
139, 203; Second Wave 95, 182; Third
Wave 182; *see also* Ashby, Justine;
Harper, Sue; man
film industry 14, 19, 116, 124, 136; 1970s
14, 124, 127, 128–29, 131, 132, 135,
136; British 14, 50–51, 116, 124, 127,
128–29, 131, 132, 135, 136, 138, 143,
150, 153; patriarchal structures 108,
124, 135, 138, 170; *see also* Harper, Sue
First a Girl 126, 191
friendship 12, 15; contemporary British
woman's film 15, 160, 161, 162, 163,
164, 166, 167–68; female group film 12,
94, 99–100, 102, 104, 105–6, 107, 108;
older women 15, 173, 174, 175–76; *see
also* Ashby, Justine; female group film

Gainsborough 13, 127; Calvert, Phyllis
11, 66–70, 71, 74; *Caravan* 4–5, 13,
125; 187; *The Constant Nymph* 23,
188; costume drama 12, 25; *Fanny by
Gaslight* 66–68, 190; *Love Story* 6, 12,

77, 81–87, 198; *Madonna of the Seven
Moons* 5, 12, 64, 68, 199; *The Magic
Bow* 66, 69, 199; *The Man in Grey* 5,
65–66, 199; melodramas 4–5, 8, 10, 12,
54, 66–69; *Millions Like Us* 5, 52, 79,
95, 155, 200; *Miranda* 74, 79–81, 201;
The Root of All Evil 64, 69–70, 74,
207; *Two Thousand Women* 5, 12,
155, 212; *The Wicked Lady* 5, 6, 7,
125, 213; *see also* Calvert, Phyllis;
McFarlane, Brian
gender issues 14, 42; contemporary
British woman's film 14, 79, 154, 157,
158, 161, 165, 168; gender norms 13,
100, 102, 103; gender-neutral politics
14, 145–49, 151; gender politics 13,
94–95, 96, 97, 100, 102, 104, 107, 108;
gender roles 3, 25, 79, 94–95, 100,
102–3, 104, 108, 111, 157, 160, 164;
picturing Cornwall: gender, desire and
the 'prospect view' 81–91; *see also*
femininity; feminism; man; Moseley,
Rachel
The Gentle Sex 12, 52, 95, 191
Girl with Green Eyes 13, 111, 112,
114–15, 191–92; *see also* Landy,
Marcia
Girl's Night 6, 192
Glancy, Mark 10–11, 49–61; British
audience 10–11, 49–61; literary and
theatrical adaptations 11; *see also*
Davis, Bette; Hollywood
Good Time Girl 96, 102–3, 192
Great Day 95, 192
Greatheart 26, 28, 192–93

Harper, Sue 13–14, 65, 124–37; 1970s 14,
127–36, 138–39; actresses 14, 128,
133–35, 136; British Board of Film
Censors 130–31; British film industry
14, 124, 127, 128–29, 131, 132, 135,
136; class and sexuality 126; Collins,
Joan 133, 134, 135; comfort-zones 14,
126; costume film 25; female agency 13,
124; female audience 13, 124–25, 136;
female group film 109; feminism 14,
135, 138; femininity 13–14, 124, 125–26
(female body 129, 130–31, 132); films
about women 13–14, 124, 125–26; films
by women 13, 124; films *for* women 13,
124–25; gauntlet-throwers 14, 126;
Jackson, Glenda 128, 129, 133, 134–35;
limit-texts 13–14, 126; methodology 13,
133; *Miranda* 79; Modernism/